MORE
JUSTICE,
MORE
PEACE

Crevon Terrance, FEMA mediator and former member of the Ohio Supreme Court Dispute Resolution Commission

Angelia Tolbert, president of Absolute Resolution Services, Inc., Little Rock, Arkansas

Maria Volpe, professor of sociology, director of the Dispute Resolution Program at John Jay College of Criminal Justice–City University of New York; director of the CUNY Dispute Resolution Center

Books in the ACR Practitioner's Guide Series are *field guides* for the benefit of practitioners actively engaged as third-party intervenors, scholars, educators, trainers, researchers, and participants in conflict resolution processes. Each book is a practical guide that illuminates thought processes that lead to action—the underlying rationale for practice decisions—rather than simply describing "what to do." Grounded in Reflective Practice principles, the books examine the application of theory and research in relation to practice choices and guide the reader/user in a deeper understanding of why we make particular choices in our work.

Association for Conflict Resolution®
VOICES, CHOICES, SOLUTIONS

About the ACR

The Association for Conflict Resolution (ACR) is a professional organization enhancing the practice and public understanding of conflict resolution. An international professional association for mediators, arbitrators, educators, and other conflict resolution practitioners, ACR works in a wide range of settings throughout the United States and around the world. Our multicultural and multidisciplinary organization offers a broad umbrella under which all forms of dispute resolution practice find a home. Website: www.acrnet.org; Twitter: @ACRgroup.

MORE JUSTICE, MORE PEACE

When Peacemakers Are Advocates

EDITED BY
Susanne Terry

ROWMAN & LITTLEFIELD
Lanham • Boulder • New York • London

Executive Editor: Elizabeth Swayze
Editorial Assistant: Dina Guilak
Senior Marketing Manager: Karin Cholak

Credits and acknowledgments for material borrowed from other sources, and reproduced with permission, appear on the appropriate page within the text.

Published by Rowman & Littlefield
An imprint of The Rowman & Littlefield Publishing Group, Inc.
4501 Forbes Boulevard, Suite 200, Lanham, Maryland 20706
www.rowman.com

6 Tinworth Street, London SE11 5AL, United Kingdom

British Library Cataloguing in Publication Information available

Library of Congress Cataloging-in-Publication Data available
Names: Terry, Susanne, 1937– editor.
Title: More justice, more peace : when peacemakers are advocates / edited by Susanne Terry.
Description: Lanham : Rowman & Littlefield, [2020] | Series: ACR practitioner's guide series | Includes bibliographical references and index. | Summary: "More Justice, More Peace: When Peacemakers Are Advocates is an attempt to broaden the vision of those practitioners with a passion for bringing about necessary change in our society who also work to bring people together to explore issues, solve problems, and overcome differences"— Provided by publisher.
Identifiers: LCCN 2019049144 (print) | LCCN 2019049145 (ebook) | ISBN 9781538132944 (cloth ; alk. paper) | ISBN 9781538132951 (paperback ; alk. paper) | ISBN 9781538132968 (epub)
Subjects: LCSH: Conflict management. | Mediation. | Reconciliation. | Social justice.
Classification: LCC HM1126 .M669 2020 (print) | LCC HM1126 (ebook) | DDC 303.6/9—dc23
LC record available at https://lccn.loc.gov/2019049144
LC ebook record available at https://lccn.loc.gov/2019049145

To Stephen, Sarah, and Lon

Contents

FOREWORD

FOR FOURTEEN YEARS OF MY LIFE, DURING COLLEGE AND FOR TEN years afterward, I was an activist advocating for a variety of social justice and peace issues in the United States and abroad. I felt that advocacy, specifically nonviolent action and the strategies and tactics of Gandhi and King, were the best and possibly the only way to achieve the social justice and peace that were so badly needed during those times.

Over forty years ago, however, I found myself in the middle of a number of serious disputes where parties needed effective ways to talk with each other to resolve their differences and had significant difficulty doing so. At that time, I realized that there was another important role needed to assist people in negotiating for social justice and peace, the role of mediator. (Both Gandhi and King stressed the importance of negotiation both before initiating nonviolent action and later, to consolidate gains, changes, and individual and social transformation.)

Mediators are intermediaries who help bridge the gap between people in conflict. They assist them to establish or improve communications, enhance problem-solving and negotiation procedures, and help reach agreements. They can also help parties, if they so desire, to transform their relationships for the better.

Since becoming a mediator, I've had to find ways to reconcile a range of conflict paradoxes—dilemmas, polarities, contradictions, or dualities that frame how I've viewed conflict, my role in resolving it, the approaches with which I've chosen to respond, and my preferred outcomes.[1] When I became a mediator, I had to grapple with the issue of "how can I be both an impartial conflict resolution practitioner and an advocate for social justice on issues about which I have great passion?"

Susan Terry, the editor and a contributing author of *More Justice, More Peace: When Peacemakers Are Advocates*, is a friend, colleague, and mediator. Susan, too, has grappled with some of the same questions I have and has assembled a group of stellar dispute resolution practitioners who have shared their wisdom about how to reconcile some of the paradoxes between striving for social justice, resolving disputes, peacemaking, and reconciliation.

More Justice, More Peace is a remarkable and insightful read. While initially intended for conflict professionals working to help parties resolve various types of disputes and conflicts, it is equally relevant for any person who wants to create a more just and peaceful society and reconcile serious differences between people and groups. The book provides concrete examples of creative ways advocates for justice and peace have achieved tangible results in handling difficult problems, from interpersonal disputes to violent conflicts that involve multiple parties. It provides great insight into models and procedures, and hope for the future in how such issues can be addressed in more effective and successful ways.

Many of the chapters begin with fascinating personal descriptions of incidents where authors experienced injustice in their lives and developed values that led them to engage in some aspect of advocacy for justice and peacemaking. Their experiences will no doubt result in reflection by readers about how they also have developed their own values about advocacy and peacemaking.

Beyond describing the development of the authors' values, each chapter details how they have dealt with specific issues and the paradoxes and tensions between seeking justice and providing process assistance to resolve conflicts. Some of the key questions addressed include:

- How can tensions be resolved when seeking justice and making peace and reconciliation seem to be at odds?
- What are potential relationships and tensions between advocacy for substantive outcomes and advocacy for fair and just procedures?

- What are possible roles of individuals or groups as advocates for substantive justice and intermediaries who provide "impartial" procedures to resolve conflicts?

- What does it mean to be "multipartial" and committed to helping all parties to satisfy their interests to the greatest extent possible?

- How can advocacy and process assistance be combined during various phases of a dispute or conflict resolution process to produce better results?

- What are the responsibilities of mediators to address significant power imbalances between parties and, if necessary, consider how to actually empower those who have not had a voice?

- How can intermediaries move from resolving multiple disputes with similar causes and dynamics, which are critical to settle for those involved, to addressing and changing the systemic or structural factors that cause them?

How these issues are addressed is illustrated in fascinating case studies of authors' initiatives. Some chapters focus more on interpersonal or small group disputes such as those between elders and members of their families where power differences may be significant and the psychological well-being of all concerned is critically important. Others explore a wide range of conflicts including reconciling refugees and members of host communities in Germany; ways that religious orders resolve disputes; strategies to giving voice to Native American and minority communities; efforts to address the history of racism and white supremacy in Charlottesville; methods to counter violent killings and abuse of women and children in Baltimore; approaches to achieving systemic change to address sexual abuse in churches; and ways of resolving a range of public and natural resource and development disputes in Latin America.

Finally, a group of chapters present methods to promote and achieve reconciliation between parties that have been involved in intractable conflicts and who have experienced significant polarization and trauma.

The authors of chapters in *More Justice, More Peace* have addressed and found creative ways to reconcile the major tensions and paradoxes between advocacy for social justice and peacemaking. Readers of *More Justice, More Peace* will find the experiences and strategies detailed by experienced practitioners both insightful and inspiring. Hopefully, it will inspire them to implement some of them in the future themselves. *Essayons* (Let us try)!

Christopher W. Moore, Ph.D.
Partner, CDR Associates
Author of *The Mediation Process: Practical Strategies for Resolving Conflict* (San Francisco: Jossey-Bass, 4th edition, 2016)
Boulder, Colorado
2019

NOTE

1. Bernard Mayer, *The Conflict Paradox: Seven Dilemmas at the Core of Disputes* (San Francisco: Jossey-Bass, 2015), 2.

ACKNOWLEDGMENTS

THIS BOOK CAME ABOUT, AT LEAST IN PART, IN RESPONSE TO MY sense of despair about the daily terrible news of the world. My field of endeavor is conflict, and yet I felt overwhelmed by my concern for our civilization, our planet, and our children's future. Even as I struggled, I realized that I needed to escape an encroaching sense of paralysis and act in a positive and helpful way. Right away, I saw the possibility of a book that explores the work of a number of practitioners who have stepped out of the strict confines of role description and forged new and exciting practices. I wanted to make it possible for their stories to be told. I am indebted to them for their openness and hard work on this project.

I will always be grateful to Larry Mandell, one of the founders of and longtime president of Woodbury College in Vermont, who hired me to create a mediation program for the school. This thirty-six-year adventure was my opportunity to be both practitioner and teacher. Over the years, my colleagues in that program were among my best teachers and mentors. I am especially grateful to David Specht, Tammy Lenski, Alice Estey, Julian Portilla, Neal Rodar, and Jen Knauer.

Michael Lang has been my steady companion in developing a deeper understanding of reflective practice. This book is an outgrowth of that understanding. I could not ask for a better colleague or friend.

My husband, Stephen Parker, has carefully read my work, given wise advice, and best of all, he has kept me laughing. Both he and our children Sarah and Lon Gowan have provided me with a never-ending supply of vibrant models of living justice and peace. They have inspired both me and participants in my trainings by their examples.

Annette Keach, by some magical power, has kept the office running and helped me locate long-squirreled-away documents that I buried in the depths of my bizarre filing system. I am grateful for her patience, generosity, and good humor. My friend Bonnie Dasher-Andersen has been a source of encouragement, tech savvy, and sage advice. Just when I felt overwhelmed by this project, Bonnie would appear and say "What do you need?" When my computer hardware fails or baffles me, my friend Sigurd Andersen, with a smile and no complaint, appears at my office and says, "Okay then, let's see what we can do."

Cheryl Jamison has championed this book from the time the idea first formed, and our late-night calls gave me a better lens through which to shape and guide this project. The Editorial Board for the Rowman & Littlefield Reflective Practitioner Series has been a steady source of support through their thoughtful questions, good advice, and enthusiasm. Elizabeth Swayze at Rowman & Littlefield has been my patient teacher as I faced the challenges of an edited volume. She both kept me grounded in the practicalities of publishing and set all of us involved in the project free to tell the stories of the work we do.

Thanks to Nancy Welsh for reflections and guidance on my chapter and to Frank Dukes for thoughtfully and good-naturedly responding to every single one of my questions or requests for advice.

Bernie Mayer's pioneering book *Beyond Neutrality* began to put into words what had already begun to be my practice and what I taught my students. I am grateful not only for *Beyond Neutrality* but for all of his work and for his leadership in the field.

The contributors to *More Justice, More Peace* are appreciative of colleagues and other individuals and institutions that have shared in and been supportive of the good work it has been our privilege to do.

It has been a joy working with this group of contributors who have given us an intimate look at their experience of justice and how it came to shape the work that they love.

Chapter 1

And Justice for All

A sense of justice has always motivated me; that indigenous people were the original peoples, and yet, often, we're not present at the table or our voices are not heard. And the other thing that motivates me utterly is the need for healing.
—Joy Harjo, Muscogee Creek Nation
23rd Poet Laureate of the United States
First Native American poet
to hold this position

Susanne Terry

The Pledge of Allegiance says "liberty and justice for all." Which part of "all" don't you understand?
—Pat Schroeder
US House of Representatives 1973–1997

A Small Incident; a Powerful Consequence

I was thirteen years old and in the ninth grade. My English class was with a teacher whom I had come to respect a great deal even though she was extremely strict and had a formidable personality. She and my mother, also a teacher, were friends, and

I knew they consulted about my progress in school. I had received a grade on a paper that was a few points lower than I had expected. It was a good paper, and the corrections that she had marked were minor. I noticed one, though, that concerned one of my punctuation marks; it puzzled me. It had to do with a comma that should have been a semicolon, and her marking of it was the difference of three points on my paper, moving me from an A to a B. I clearly remembered putting a semicolon there, and when I picked up the paper and looked more carefully, there it was—a faint dot above the comma. At a point in the class when people were turning their attention to small group discussions, I went up to the teacher's desk. She was standing, and I stood beside her, sharing the paper and explaining her mistake. She made small murmuring sounds as her head bobbed up and down. She then took her pencil and lowered it directly onto the punctuation mark in question. She began to explain the purpose of the semicolon and why it should have been used in that instance, all the while using her soft lead pencil to make meaningless scribbling marks completely covering my work. I looked down at the paper in disbelief. My correct punctuation was now completely obscured by her scribbling. Any vindicating evidence of my correctness was eradicated. She never missed a beat, saying, "It was a good paper. Next time, though, don't make that same mistake."

I walked back to my desk, my face flaming, experiencing something I had never felt before. My paper had been correct. I believed that she knew it was correct. I believed that at worst, her marking the paper was a deliberate attempt to disguise her error, and at best, an indifference to a student's evidence. I believed that she knew that I could see through what she was doing. I had been in the right, but she had the power of the teacher's lead pencil. In addition, she was in a position to make it seem not only as if I had made a foolish mistake but also that she had to patiently explain it to me. Her tone had implied that perhaps I was even making a deliberate false claim to correctness. At that moment, I realized that one of us had to pretend that what both she and I knew to be true and real did not exist. Only one of us had our story prevail. Only one of us set the rules. Only one of us got to say, "Here's what was *really* happening—now we all agree on that, don't we?" She got to be the benevolent teacher who could now encourage me to do better in my next steps. The rule of the game was that this was how it was and it was my job to accept it. It seemed so very minor in her eyes and was a small part of her otherwise busy day. But for me, I was galvanized into a new awareness of who has power and who doesn't. In light of the gross injustices of the world, it was a tiny event, but it was one that set me on a lifelong path.

GUIDANCE FROM PAST EXPERIENCE

From that time on I began to notice interactions between individuals and in groups, and I eventually devoured articles and stories about local, national, and world events to see if there were familiar patterns that matched my own growing awareness of social injustice. I learned to ask questions:

- Who sets the rules?
- Who interprets the rules?
- Who enforces the rules?
- Who says when the discussion or debate is over?
- Who determines if there is a consequence for attempting to continue the debate?
- What is the mechanism for recourse?
- What happens when a person or group attempts to reclaim hidden truth in the story of what happened?
- Who stands to benefit from the status quo?
- Who stands to be further subjugated by the status quo?
- Who gets to talk about what is happening as if it is normal?
- What tools are used to keep the status quo?
- What is the collective story that is told by those who benefit that helps keep this in place?
- What is the collective story that is told by those who do not benefit? Does it tend to perpetuate the situation or change it?

- What is the role of those who are somewhat removed yet still a part of what is happening?

These questions and others became part of my tool belt and travel with me wherever I go. In any situation in which I am working, I am attempting, to the best of my ability, to find and understand the answers to those questions.

> *Until the lion learns how to write, every story will glorify the hunter.*
>
> —AFRICAN PROVERB

In my early years, I had more than enough raw source material with which to study these questions. Every day was an opportunity to look at what was happening to others and to try to figure out my role in the situation. I quickly learned to be the naïve and well-meaning advocate for those being treated unjustly. I wanted to side with the right people. My enthusiastic wish to participate and do the right thing occasionally was helpful, but I suspect that it often had a dangerous consequence for those who were being treated unjustly. My attempts, I suspect, added insult to injury. I later learned about strategic thinking and the design of strategies that could make the difference. Into my mid-adult years, I then learned about conflict resolution practices and the power of the tools of listening, understanding, and problem-solving. I later began to understand the dangers of these tools when used in situations where they could and would perpetuate the status quo.

JUSTICE AND THE CONFLICT PRACTITIONER

To weep in trouble is human nature, but taking trouble to wipe someone's tears is humanity.

ABHIJIT NASKAR

The Merriam-Webster dictionary chose "justice" as the 2018 word of the year. Peter Sokolowski, Merriam-Webster's editor at large, told the Associated Press that searches for "justice" throughout the year, compared to 2017, were up 74 percent on the site that has more than a hundred million page views a month and nearly half a million entries. "People seemed more often to use it 'as a kind of a cry,' Sokolowski said, referring to the demand that the system work and fairness prevail. "*Justice* implies a bureaucracy of fairness," Sokolowski said, "an expectation of having your side of the story listened to."

I am a conflict engagement practitioner. I am a social justice advocate. I have no intention of ceding one to the other. For years I, like others in my field, made the decision that in some arenas I would work as a neutral or impartial "third party" to help resolve conflict and in other arenas I would work for justice. When facilitating an impartial process in which I believed that the parties could come to a conclusion that they experienced as just, I did not think that what I believed or understood about justice had a role in the process. Today, in a world of disarray and with deep divisions, I can no longer compartmentalize my work or my life in quite that same way. Our conflicts occur within structural and belief systems that are designed to be self-sustaining. Those systems will not yield to the voice of any person or group if they cannot even get into the heart of the conversation, much less gain enough leverage to end the injustice being suffered. To the extent that I can understand the disadvantage that a group of people are experiencing, I have the responsibility and opportunity to use that understanding in some responsible professional manner. Exactly how that plays out remains somewhat unclear in many instances.

In my professional community, there has been significant and important work done in this area, but we are far from being knowledgeable enough or proficient enough to practice what we are beginning to see as inevitable—carrying out our work guided by a fundamental underlying bias for justice.

Within the alternative dispute resolution and peacemaking communities, there has been a growing disquiet about whether some of our well-intentioned processes are counterproductive to efforts for justice for subjugated peoples. The subject has been raised time and again, with the fairly consistent response that processes of mediation, negotiation, and facilitation are all helpful in bringing about a peaceful resolution. We have often failed to grasp that often our processes in themselves, well-intentioned though they are, can do violence to the most disenfranchised persons involved.

WHEN PROCESS IS A TOOL OF DISEMPOWERMENT

A few years ago, a local community was dealing with the issue of the use of Native American images and names as mascots. The town was overwhelmingly opposed to changing the name of the sports teams from "Indians" to anything else. There was eventually a town meeting called and an outside facilitator brought in. People were called on to speak in order of their signing up. Each person was given three minutes to speak, and when the time was up, the facilitator courteously asked them to finish their thought and conclude.

Early on in the meeting, a young woman in the community was called on. She had grown up in a household with intimate knowledge of local Native cultural practices. As she rose, she said that she was now offering her time to a highly respected Native elder and representative to the Abenaki council. The elder rose to speak. The facilitator interrupted, saying that people would speak in the time for which they had signed up. There would be no substitutions. The elder, embarrassed, sat down. Later, her name was called from the sign-up list. She began by first speaking about the history of her people in this geographic area, and then she spoke about the importance of connection to tribe and its history. She began to tell us about the struggles of Native peoples to retain their autonomy and tell their own history. At three minutes, the facilitator let her know that she needed to bring her remarks to a close. She spoke on. The facilitator, seeing that she was making no sign of wrapping up or even "getting to the point," let her know, politely but firmly, that her time was up. She looked confused, but the facilitator insisted. The chair of the town's governing body, the select board, stood and spoke to the moderator. "I'm sure that we can find a way to be flexible here. It sounds as if there is important information that needs to be shared and we can bend the rules a bit." The facilitator thanked him and then explained that here in this setting, others needed to be considered also. Everyone would get their fair share and no more. The elder would have to turn over the microphone. We were now in a showdown that illustrated the exact problem with appropriating another culture's names and symbols. The young woman, by offering the elder her place in the speaking lineup, was following the tradition of inviting elders to speak first. The elder, in speaking, was doing so according to her cultural tradition, that of setting context, telling the story, and holding the history out for all to hear. Her people's historical manner of speaking truth was now being prohibited, and worse yet, she was being lectured about the "correct" manner of participation. The town could put a cartoon picture of a Plains Indian on their sports teams' jerseys and call them the "Indians," but would not permit the elder to employ her traditional Native manner of speaking. For those two women, the only tool they had against overwhelming odds was voice, and they were prohibited from using it in the manner familiar to them. Through no bad intention, the deck was stacked against them and would not get unstacked.

Another circumstance of cultural unawareness had occurred years before when I was relatively new to working with religious orders. My partners and I were preparing for a general chapter meeting of a religious congregation, or order, of women. This group of Roman Catholic sisters met every six years to make decisions about the direction of the order and the commitment of resources. There were to be fifty official delegates from eight countries, speaking English, French, Kikongo, Japanese, and Italian. Prior to arriving in Rome for our eight-week stay, we learned that the sisters from Zaire, in all of the years that they had been seated as delegates, had never spoken in the large group. In spite of warm encouragement, they indicated that they were content to listen. Our team arrived a week early to meet various delegate groups and find out about their experience at previous chapter meetings and, most importantly, how their cultural group deals with conflict. When we spoke with the sisters from Zaire, we asked how they handle a situation when they have a different opinion or point of view. "Oh," one sister said. "We listen." We asked if they then expressed their own point of view. "Oh no. We wait three days; then we tell a story that shows that we have understood the point the other person was making." We were curious if then they expressed their opinion. "Oh no, we wait three more days and then tell a story that shows that maybe there may be other

Be careful when speaking. You create the world around you with your words.

DINÉ (NAVAJO)
PROVERB

ways to view the situation." What then? "After three more days, we tell a story that illustrates how another idea we have may be a possibility." It was now clear to us why they had never spoken in the deliberative body. Their cultural norms required that they give full respect to the others' ideas. In the meantime, the group would have long since moved on. We learned that the "three days," while sometimes strictly observed, more commonly meant "a respectful period of time." As a result of this, we asked each group of delegates to speak to the group about how they go about listening, dealing with differing ideas, and dealing with conflict. We designed processes that allowed days between the introduction of topics and first, second, and third considerations of those topics. The Zaire sisters made many valuable contributions and gained voice in their highest deliberative body.

What we don't know can seriously harm others. We have, in the last few years, become aware of needing to be more culturally aware and of needing training for help in understanding differences. We have sought out trainings to "increase awareness"; however, those trainings are often too truncated to be of substantial help, and we move on to other things that we consider to be crucial to our professional preparation and ongoing education. Embarassingly, we often appropriate processes and tools from other cultures and use them in ways that superficially and temporarily manage how discussions take place but do not allow exploration of the roots of the conflict itself. Nor do we fully appreciate the traditions, practices, and values inherent in those tools and processes.

THE MANY FACES OF JUSTICE

Most of us think of justice in the ways that I described it in my story of the teacher and the correct punctuation mark: "Something is not right here." A quick look at the current literature, including items in the bibliography of this book, will show that there are many aspects of justice being studied and compared. The bibliography of *More Justice, More Peace* contains a number of volumes highlighting work being done. The terms are many and include:

- Social justice (a set of moral principles that guide a society and its institutions)
- Retributive justice (response to an offense focusing on punishment of the offender and compensation to the victim)
- Procedural justice (parties' experience of how they are treated when dealing with an issue or dispute)
- Restorative justice (repairing of harm to relationships and community)
- Relational justice (produced by cooperative behavior or dialogue in a post-conflict situation)
- Transitional justice (addressing massive human rights abuses)

For the ordinary person, justice remains difficult to define yet easier to identify when experienced. For most of us, justice has to do with respect, recognition of harm, equal voice and access, equitable share of resources, fairness, and setting things right.

WHAT DO WE DO WITH WHAT WE KNOW?

There is a great deal of excellent research and writing on justice. In the last few years, there has been outstanding work in the field with a justice perspective (e.g., by John Paul Lederach and Leah Wing) and a number of articles articulating a challenge to our previously stated claim to neutrality. We are at a fascinating time in the development of conflict work, with a number of exciting opportunities as well as perils. We are asking ourselves if it is possible to both "work for justice" and also facilitate a process that does not side with one party against the other. In the meantime, we conflict workers are looking to one another asking, "But what do we do? Are we advocates or impartials? How should we be working?" I recently began to think about colleagues of mine and others who are working guided by both the principles of impartiality and justice. Finding examples of practitioners trying to make justice possible while serving all persons involved was not difficult. However, no one I know doing this kind of work thinks they have found all of the answers to how it should be done. All of us have questions about what we do and don't do, and we all want to know how to do it better. But these practitioners didn't wait until they thought they had all of the answers. They moved ahead. Some of these practitioners have contributed chapters for this book. Their stories will describe how they shaped their work not by the rules of what they had been taught that they could or could not do. Rather, they started with the question of "What is the harm here, and how can I best help?" They chose to see the picture whole, not only through the stories or the eyes of the parties but through their own insights about how systems, prejudices, biases, privilege, and injustice work. It informs the questions they ask and the way they choose to work with people. In some instances they find that they need a new role definition and that they must be especially diligent about being transparent and consistent in carrying out that role. For some, it means that at some times they choose to be advocates; at other times they are support persons, sometimes mediators, sometimes facilitators. In this book we will get a glimpse into the path that all of the contributors have traveled.

THE PARTIES DIDN'T CREATE THE PROBLEM

During much of my professional career, a large part of my practice has been working as a facilitator and consultant with women's religious communities within the Roman Catholic Church. Most of that work was pure pleasure; I had the opportunity to facilitate meaningful discussions about how these organizations could leverage their resources to effect social change and alleviate suffering among the poor and disenfranchised. I know the women in these groups to be generous, risk-taking, and savvy.

I have also been called upon to help these same groups deal with their conflicts with the church hierarchy and with injustices and indignities that are still difficult for me to think about. In those instances, my role morphed into that of both a facilitator and a coach. I had a set of skills and experiences I could share, and those sisters, in their wisdom, could take that information and shape it in ways that would give them, if not a seat at the table, at least a place in the room. I didn't know what they should do, but I could offer them some tools I had used in other situations and they could decide what worked best for them. I was seeing over and over that the institution would use every advantage available and suppress voices of dissent. And yet I worked side by side with many good men—priests, brothers, bishops, and a cardinal or two—who chose to support these women in their struggle.

One instance of work that I was privileged to do was to try to be a healing presence to a religious community when one of their own sisters had been alienated from the community. Anne-Marie[1] was a sister in a progressive, modern, justice-oriented order. A controversial public statement had been signed by many women and men in religious life in the United States who were taking an unprecedented, outspoken stand regarding a social issue on which there is strong doctrine to the contrary of their statement. The Vatican acted swiftly and sent a message to the leadership of all of the communities to which these signers belonged that the members must retract their statement or be dismissed from their order. Within a very short time all of the men but none of the women recanted. There was then a long and painful period of time with discussions, demands, and negotiations for each of the orders seeking to protect their sisters yet not place the order itself in danger with the church. Most of the cases settled with some form of agreed-upon statement by the sisters. Anne-Marie left her order before agreement could be reached, and she then issued a public statement that included a charge that her order had failed to support her for following her conscience. In actuality, the leadership of her order had, without equivocation, supported her independent right to speak and had defied a church hierarchy's demand to dismiss her from their order.

None of the women involved were to blame for this situation. The pressure cooker they were in was not of their own making. And yet the result was that they were at odds with one another, women who had called each other sister for many years and had taken a vow to be faithful to one another.

In work that I did in this and numerous other situations like it, part of my job description was to assist those involved in developing an analysis of their situation that confirmed that they had not created the problem. The friction they were experiencing had arisen out of the hierarchy and injustice of the structure of the institution. These women were free to leave both their religious order and the church if they so chose. There were times when I wondered why a woman would choose to remain part of the institution that was so out of step with how she understood the world. Professionally, this was a challenge for me in that while I couldn't understand why a sister wouldn't just leave the church, it was not my role to say or imply that she should. One day I was talking with one of my clients, a leader in her order, who was speaking about the precarious situation in which both she and her order found themselves. I asked her what kept her struggling on. She said that many times she had been asked why she didn't just leave religious life and the church. She said it wasn't a choice. "It is my church—mine and the people's. It doesn't belong to the hierarchy; it belongs to all of us. The church I know and love is one of justice and love. They may eventually throw me out but I won't just walk away." Because the church, the people's church, was precious to these women, I needed to speak and work in a way that respected that to which they had committed their lives.

This work was difficult, and I needed help in charting a path. I called upon friends in religious life as well as other conflict workers to help guide me. Often I was unsure what was right for me to be doing, but I always understood what this was about: to use my skills as a facilitator and my understanding of conflict to assist these women and the men who supported them in helping to bring justice to these unjust situations in their own lives in the church. The justice of "setting things right" took place among the sisters themselves; relationships needed to be healed or kept intact and lines of communication kept open. The importance of strategically remaining in a position to "speak truth to power" was critical to these organizations. They wanted to be able to continue to raise the issues of importance to women in religious life in the United States and some other countries, and they wanted to do it face-to-face with men in authority. Although progress has been infinitesimal in some areas, these women leaders have continued to speak fearlessly, forthrightly, and respectfully to those in high positions of power.

The church is only one institution that has been forced to deal with issues of injustice. A few years ago, I was asked by a director of a state human services office to help facilitate healing among staff members as a result of a terrible situation that occurred two years previously. The prior director of a local office had targeted one of the men in the office, ridiculing him publicly and gossiping about him behind his back. She had spoken about him to other employees in a demeaning manner and implied that they should have nothing to do with him. He was not the only recipient of the abuse, but suffered from it the most. One coworker finally blew the whistle on the behavior. The regional director immediately put the local director on leave, after which her actions were investigated and her employment terminated. At the time, the traumatized office staff didn't want to talk about what had happened; they just wanted to go back to work and give themselves time to recover from the abusive situation. Now, two years later, I came to their office to see how they were. Little by little, each of the fifteen people spoke about how sad they were about what happened and how bad they felt. One woman, the person who had finally reported their boss's behavior, finally looked at her wronged colleague and said, "I watched what happened with you and I did nothing. She [her former boss] would call me into her office and trash you. I didn't know what to do. That is no excuse. I let that happen and I am so ashamed. I feel dirty and I feel like I lost a part of myself that I can never get back." Her injured colleague said, "And it was you who finally put a stop to it. You stood up even though you thought you could lose your job. Thank you." After two and a half hours, everyone, including me, wiped away tears and thanked each of the other people in the room. In one way, nothing had changed; the suffering they experienced for two and a half years couldn't be undone. But in two and a half hours these workers had taken some big risks and transformed their workplace, claiming it back from fear, intimidation, and shame. Although their office had been functioning at a high level of efficiency in the two years since, until that day things had not been addressed and all of the staff had been saddened by what had happened and their role in it. They were now in a place of beginning to rebuild trust. In that session, there was recognition of the harm that had been done as well as acknowledgment of courageous action. Nothing could rewrite the history of injustice, but they could set themselves on a new path that restored relationships.

CHOOSING AND DEFINING MY ROLE

One of the many challenges for me, as for other conflict practitioners today, is to discern whether or not, in spite of a situation being sad or tragic, intervention is likely to perpetuate the injustice. We struggle with a wish to respond to the needs of the individuals yet are aware that systemic injustice becomes stronger with each instance that isn't exposed to the light of day. Sexual abuse cases settled with nondisclosure agreements keep the worst of those tragedies hidden. Unequal access to resources, systematic suppression of workers' rights, employees in hostile workplaces, communities with discriminatory housing practices, and inhumane treatment of immigrants seeking safety and well-being for their families are a few examples of the kinds of conflicts with which societies are faced. Practitioners can become overwhelmed by the extent of societal injustices if we do not remain connected to others who are dealing with the same issues.

In the fight among politicians, the children lost again.

CHARLIE ANGUS

Like many others who have a strong moral sense of justice and a commitment to addressing injustice, I have at times become involved in specific events in which I have no professional role. In those instances, I am a citizen and I have determined that my path is solely to be an advocate and voice for justice, not seeking to be impartial but wishing to be fair. In these situations, I have a stake in the issue and the outcome; yet I cannot set aside my knowledge and skills at addressing conflict. As a result, as an advocate for justice, it is important to me that I act in ways that I consider to be responsible and helpful to the larger issues and constituencies. As a conflict worker, I have skills including conflict analysis, strategy design, and solid communication skills that can be useful to parties in the situation—even as I seek to right a wrong or pursue a just result.

Several years ago, a local library was facing personnel and financial crises and the governing board needed to find a solution to the problem quickly. One Monday, at the end of the workday, all the staff, with no warning, were called in to a meeting with three of the board members and the director. The director handed each staff member a folder containing a letter and a severance plan. Staff were told that the library needed to restructure its operations to "face the challenges of being a 21st century library." Board members explained that there would be a new organizational structure. Everyone's positions under the old structure were terminated, but they were told that board members "hoped they would re-apply for the 'new' positions." Board members said some people might be hired back but others would not. The head librarian was six months away from her previously announced retirement. Another librarian was the sole support of an adult disabled son who required constant care. Several staff members were in tears; all were stunned.

Over the following days and weeks the staff puzzled over why the board would not have included the staff in discussions of how to weather the crisis. As word spread, people in the town, library staffs across the state, and loyal members of the library, as well as some former board members, were outraged at the process and lack of opportunity of the staff to offer alternatives or participate in any meaningful way.

I wrote a letter to the executive director stating that the process violated common decency and would harm the library's reputation. The executive director shared the letter with the board. I requested and received a face-to-face meeting with the executive director, whom I had not previously met but understood to be a decent man who was well-liked by the staff. I let him know that I wanted to speak as fairly and honestly as I could with him. I felt that I, as only one person, could simply share my personal and professional assessment of the situation along with what I believed could be the consequences for him. I wanted to speak respectfully and forthrightly. I also wanted to do my best to provide a perspective of how this action would impact the executive director, the board, the employees who would be let go, and the supporters of the library. I did all this both as a citizen of the community and user of the library and as someone with experience in analyzing and responding to conflict.

I let him know that it was my belief that by his agreeing with the actions of the board, he would no longer be trusted by the staff. He would always be seen as being aligned with a board in a process that was secret and did not allow staff an opportunity for input or to help find a solution to the financial situation. I suggested that it was within his power to ask the board to reconsider its decision and give the staff the opportunity to see what could be done to solve the library's challenges.

Later, I participated in a public protest, supported individual staff members, and spoke with library supporters, including former board members. I don't know how the board came to its original decision, and I don't know whether the director appealed to the board after my meeting with him. Things moved on with a sense of unease and sadness, and within four months the director left to take another position. The beloved library, in spite of the memory of that dark time, is slowly moving forward and continuing to serve the community.

When acting as a private citizen speaking up for justice, it is important to ask myself whether I am acting in a manner that is consistent with the values that are compelling me to engage in the issue and whether I am using my knowledge about conflict in a manner designed to address the conflict situation in the most constructive way possible. In the instance of the library, I felt I had a responsibility as well as an opportunity to see if I could influence the outcome in a positive manner.

LOOKING FORWARD

The highest reward that God gives us for good work is the ability to do better work.

ELBERT HUBBARD

Each of the experiences that I have spoken about here has taken me another step toward a new vision for the work that we do. I believe that we have a new and exciting frontier ahead today, but it will be some time before we have a clearly marked path to it. I am confident that the course will be set by the brilliant and talented young people who are carrying on the good work of assisting families, communities, and nations in dealing with conflict.

The chapters that follow are the personal stories of nineteen conflict workers. Each has their own story of their early awareness of justice and how that influenced the work they have done. Each has their own story of *giving justice a seat at the table*.

This book is an invitation for each reader to consider even more meaningful ways to do the good work of assisting people in bringing about "more justice, more peace."

NOTE

1. Not her real name.

CHAPTER 2

Or It Can Swallow You Whole

ERRICKA BRIDGEFORD

ALL OF THE HARD WORK HAD LED TO THIS BASIC MEDIATION Training. For almost six months the Maryland Office of the Public Defender and Community Mediation Maryland (CMM) had been working together to design a shared neutrals program for public defenders around the state. Now, when someone had conflict at an office in one county, there would be trained mediators available from another county who could mediate, thereby ensuring that mediators wouldn't know the participants. We'd planned how to build strong quality assurance systems, starting with having newly trained mediators be apprenticed by experienced mediators at their local community mediation centers. So many pieces were in place, and this forty-hour Basic Mediation Training was an exciting and necessary part of the program. As CMM's director of training, I was simply giddy about leading this training.

Erricka Bridgeford

We were into day 2 of the five-day training, on January 23, 2007. On day 1, the trainees had done a great job building community with one another, having deep conversations about how their perceptions of conflict impacted their lives, and opening themselves up to what it meant to truly listen to others, without judgment. They were learning the Inclusive Model of mediation, which is designed and taught by CMM, and requires mediators to avoid giving opinions, advice, or suggestions to mediation participants. Given that the trainees had a lot to unlearn, since "listening like a lawyer" would be problematic in the Inclusive Model, I was happy to see how much the group had already opened up. By lunchtime we were all in pretty good moods. When I checked my phone to see if I'd missed any calls, I had no idea that my life would change forever.

I saw that my mom had called twice. She'd called once from her office and once from her cell. As I looked at my phone, my heart sank, and I said out loud, "Oh, that's not good. My mother called." One of the trainees heard me and replied, "That's not bad! It's nice that your mother called you." For a second I thought maybe she was right. My mother worked at the community mediation center in Baltimore City, and we had a very good relationship. She could have been calling me for any good reason, but somehow I knew she wasn't. So I said, "Nope. There's something about her calling that doesn't feel right." I called her office and was told that she wasn't there, and that she'd left with my cousin, Nkenge. My heart had now plunged into my stomach. Why was she with Nkenge in the middle of the workday? While I was panicking in my head, I heard the person on the phone say that they were going to go get the supervisor, who probably had more information. My mother's boss got on the phone and said, "Have you talked to your mother?" "No. I saw that she called me, so I was returning her call," I said. There was a brief silence. "OK. Well, after you talk to your mom, let me know if you need anything."

Now, you would think that this would have made me follow up with a slew of questions. But my soul knew what the supervisor meant—something was very wrong. There was no need to ask her about it. I had to get in touch with my mother. I thanked the supervisor and immediately called my mother's cell phone. When she answered, I had left the training room and was walking down the hall.

"I have to tell you something. But don't scream."

"OK, Mommy. What happened?"

"There is a rumor around the old way that someone who looks like your brother was killed yesterday."

"Who? Corny?"

"Yes."

"That doesn't make any sense. The only people who look like my brother are my other two brothers. So one of my brothers got killed? Is that what you're saying?"

"Yes, baby. That's what I'm saying."

I was on the floor in the hallway by the time she reached the end of her sentence. I couldn't breathe, as I listened to her explaining that someone was coming to take over the training, and she was coming to pick me up.

Somehow I had ended up on the bathroom floor. I called my husband to tell him that I was losing my mind. He saved my life in that moment. What he said to me would help to shape my mindset about my pain for the rest of my life. "E, you are standing on the cliff right now. You are looking over the cliff of your sanity, and you have two choices. You can jump off of the cliff and let yourself lose your mind in the pain. Nobody would blame you. But if you jump, you will not be able to get your mind back. The pain will take you. Or you can choose to be in whatever pain comes and hold on to your mind. If he is alive or dead, you can't change it. But you *can* choose not to lose your mind. Don't jump, baby. Step back from the cliff. Stop looking over the edge."

There is no greater violence than to deny the dreams of our children.

Kailash Satyarthi (2014 Nobel Peace Prize recipient)

On January 22, 2007, my brother David Isaiah Thomas ("Cornbread" aka "Corny") was the twenty-first person murdered in Baltimore that year. I had gotten into mediation work because one of my other brothers, Pop, had been labeled DOA when he was shot in an argument in the spring of 2001. He survived and became a mediator years later. But at the time, my boss had conflict about how often I was going to the hospital to visit him. The local community mediation center came to give our staff conflict management training, and I was hooked. The pain of almost losing a brother to violence had catapulted me into this grassroots peace work. Since justice was not going to come from "the system," peace work—helping others avoid violence—was the only fairness I could find. Now, I'd been doing this work for six years, and it still had not made me exempt from "getting that phone call." Here I was, in the middle of training new mediators, and my brother was being murdered at the same time.

What in the world do you do with something that feels *that* unfair? I thought it would kill me. I thought it would steal my voice, because I felt I had nothing left to say with my brother snatched from this world. I stopped showing up to a lot of trainings. I refused to even read work e-mails. When I did show up for trainings, I showed up late or ended early. Some days I'd be on my way to lead a training, and I'd pass a cemetery on the way there. I would pull over and scream my guts out for the next few hours. After a few months of drowning like this, it was the values of the community mediation movement that saved my job.

Lorig Charkoudian, my supervisor, pulled me up and showed me what walking our talk looked like. She asked me what I needed in order to continue doing my job. I told her that I needed consequences. I was in so much pain that it seemed like I couldn't function. But if I knew there were consequences for not functioning, maybe I could pull myself together. I needed some kind of structure that would help me see how to show up in the world while I was in so much pain. Lorig said, "OK. So you need accountability and CMM needs to protect its reputation. Let's make a plan together that will uphold CMM's reputation and get you the accountability you need in order to do your job." We made a plan together for a three-month probation. It included these agreements:

- I had to show up thirty minutes early for everything.
- I had to call Lorig from a phone in the building when I arrived places.
- I could never leave places before I was scheduled to leave.
- I had to call Lorig from a phone in the building at the time I was scheduled to leave.
- If I broke one of these agreements more than one time, I would be put on a three-month, unpaid suspension.
- During the suspension, CMM would continue paying for health insurance.
- During suspension, I had to be in therapy.

Had I worked *anywhere* else, I would have been fired. It would have been "professional" to fire me because of how my trauma impacted my job, but it wouldn't have been fair. Fortunately, the values of community mediation were all about people having the power to make decisions for themselves and to decide what's best for them. The community mediation movement believes that we each have within us what we need to resolve our own conflicts, and that we just need safe spaces in which to do it. So, once again, any semblance of justice, for me, would come through engaging with this work. Through this planning process with my boss, I learned that I was able to function without my brother in the world. I found out that I still had a voice. Because I was able to keep teaching mediation and conflict management skills, I found that my pain gave me a deeper passion and clearer vision about doing peace work in such a grassroots way. I could clearly see how honoring each person's journey helped in my healing, saved my livelihood, and meant that my brother didn't die in vain, though his murderer wouldn't be brought to justice.

As time went on, I kept losing people to violence. By 2017 I'd been to so many funerals of family and friends, while I was still doing peace work. Sometimes there were two funerals on one day. Yet I was still committed to alternative dispute resolution (ADR). People often asked me, "How do you keep from feeling defeated? How do you keep facing so much violence while teaching peace?" My answer became clearer to me, the more violence I encountered: "Since violence is a public health issue, it has become an epidemic. This means it spreads, and will touch all of us. It touches some of us more than others. Since it keeps coming back to me, I have two choices. I can either let the pain crack me open to keep trying to heal the world or I can let it swallow me whole. There is nothing in between. I choose to let it crack me open. If it swallows me up, it would have the last say. That means all of my people would have died in vain." This is the mind-set that birthed Baltimore Ceasefire 365.

Doing nothing for others is the undoing of ourselves.

HORACE MANN

In May of 2017, my son, Paul, was an AmeriCorps member at the Baltimore Community Mediation Center. We'd both had a long day of grassroots peace work when he told me that the murder rate in Baltimore was the highest that it had ever been. I was, to put it calmly, pissed. I ranted for a while about how "people need to use their street cred and call a ceasefire!!! What is wrong with people?

How can murder be at its highest when we're out here doing all of this work? Why won't they do more??!!!" On and on I ranted, all the way on our ride home. I could feel the pain trying to gulp me up. By the next morning I remembered that I was "they," too. I was only so angry because I thought there must have been more I could be doing. In 2015, a guy named Ogun had told me he wanted my help in calling a citywide ceasefire, and we hadn't made it happen. It was pretty hypocritical of me to be ranting about what other people weren't doing when I hadn't given it my all.

On my ride to work the next day, my thoughts were racing and my head was spinning. I had this vision of there being three days when people all over Baltimore committed to being peaceful and celebrating life. My heart was overwhelmed at the thought of what it could mean for Baltimore to intentionally celebrate life for three days. My chest was tight with anxiety at the thought of getting more than six hundred thousand people to choose peace for three days. This is when the fear almost silenced me. "What if people get killed during the ceasefire?" I thought. "What if people laugh at the idea, and nobody really goes along with it?" These questions made this *the longest* drive to work that I've ever had. This is how it played out in my head:

Question: "What if people laugh at the idea, and nobody really goes along with it?"

Answer: "The question suggests that Baltimoreans don't want life for themselves. Why would people *not* go along with three days of peace and celebrations? Sure, some people may not understand it, or may doubt that it will work. But you are not alone in being tired of murder. People are devastated and traumatized. People think there's nothing they can do about all of this violence. A lot of people will welcome the opportunity to promote commitments to peace. People will definitely plan celebrations, and the city will be filled with cookouts. I believe in Baltimore, and I know Baltimore wants peace for itself."

That conversation with myself was pretty easy to get through. Once I understood that the question was rooted in a belief that people want murder, I knew that it was a lie. I understood that the impacts of oppression and negative narratives about my city made me question even whether people would think this idea was worthwhile. I got a little more inspired when I listened to my heart and heard other hearts calling for peace all over the city. *Everyone* would appreciate a break from so much trauma.

But the next question was a harder conversation.

Question: "What if people get killed during the ceasefire?"

First Answer: "True. So never mind! If I don't mention this to anyone, nobody will know I was thinking it."

This answer made my stomach hurt. Where was the justice in doing nothing about murder in my city? I wanted to pull the car over because of how upset this made me. But why was it upsetting? Suddenly I could hear my murdered loved ones saying, "OK. So you're just going to let us be dead in vain? You know how to say this thing out loud. You're just not going to do it, huh?" My entire essence was being tested. It felt like an earthquake in my body. That's when I realized the *true* answer.

Confirmed Answer: "Maybe people will be out in the streets doing outreach to let people know about the ceasefire, and they will come across someone who is plotting to be violent. The person who is plotting will not be able to unhear this message about peace and celebrating life. They will not be able to unremember this conversation they had about how we can have at least three days of peace if we all agree to it. So, after they walk away from this conversation, they will have a rumbling in their spirit. Even if they follow through with the violence, they will be more aware that people cared enough to want peace for them. Just like this is making my spirit rumble, it is time for the city to have a shared rumbling in our spirits. And if someone is killed, we will have a different community response than usual. We won't just keep going about our day. We will stop and notice that someone was killed, because we were all hoping together that it would not happen. We will show up to the murder location to pour love and light into that community. We will give a monetary love gift to the family. We will all feel the loss. We will create a bit of justice together by telling murder it will not have dominion over Baltimore."

By the time I got to CMM's office, my face looked very serious. Lorig asked me what was going on with me, and I said, "I'm pretty sure we're going to have to call a ceasefire in Baltimore."

Little did I know at the time, my sixteen years of work in ADR had prepared me for this new challenge. Particularly, I would be able to seamlessly use the values of community mediation as the foundation for this new effort. There were things I would naturally incorporate without even knowing that they would seem like unicorn magic to a lot of people. Here are ways community mediation values showed up in the new effort:

I cannot do all the good that the world needs. But the world needs all the good that I can do.

JANA STANFIELD

Collaboration

The first thing I did was to contact Ogun, to hear his idea again. He told me that his vision was to have nearly everyone in Baltimore talking about the upcoming ceasefire. I told him that my vision was to have three days of celebration happening all over the city. Together we decided to:

- Combine both ideas and have three days of no murder and life-affirming events. It would be Friday through Sunday, August 4 to 6. Since it was currently May, this would give us some time to spread the word.

- Not have anyone's name or organization presented as the "sponsor" of the weekend. This is where the value of "inclusion" also showed up. We knew that if people felt that particular organizations were leading the effort, they might not be as inclined to participate if they didn't know or trust those organizations.

- Let people know that this ceasefire was being called by everyone who wanted to have peace in Baltimore.

I called people from the organizations I'd ranted about in that first conversation with my son. It dawned on me that maybe they wanted to use their street credibility to call a ceasefire and just hadn't thought of it. As soon as I started presenting the idea, I was interrupted with, "I am IN. Whatever you need, let's do it! And it can't just be about guns. It has to be about all violence, like domestic violence and child abuse. People need to promise to just be peaceful for three days and see how it feels in our city!" I immediately found out that people were all the way on board. They had so many ideas about how they would do outreach and what kinds of events they would host.

I set up a public meeting, which welcomed anyone who wanted to have a "life over death weekend" in Baltimore. People came to hear information about the idea and to decide together what to officially call it. A group of about fifteen people decided to name it "Baltimore Ceasefire." They agreed that when you hear the word "ceasefire," you know it means "Don't kill anybody." This group also decided that social media pages, an e-mail address, a logo, and posters and flyers should all be made. The group agreed that all the materials should send the message that this belongs to Baltimore. At future public meetings, organizations worked together to plan outreach and events.

Here are the very first logo and flyer:

CRIME SCENE DO NOT CROSS CRIME SCENE DO NOT CROSS CRIME SCENE DO NOT CROSS
BALTIMORE
CEASE
FIRE
"NOBODY KILL ANYBODY"
NO VIOLENCE FOR 72 HOURS.
WE HAVE TO START SOMEWHERE!!!
(AUGUST 4TH 2017 - AUGUST 6TH 2017)
#BALTIMORECEASEFIRE
#BALTIMOREPEACECHALLENGE
FOLLOW TODAY @
FB: BALTIMORECEASEFIRE |
TWITTER: BMORECEASEFIRE |
IG: BALTIMORECEASEFIRE
CRIME SCENE DO NOT CROSS CRIME SCENE DO NOT CROSS CRIME SCENE DO NOT CROSS

CRIME SCENE DO NOT CROSS CRIME SCENE DO NOT CROSS CRIME SCENE
DO NOT CROSS CRIME SCENE DO NOT CROSS CRIME SCENE DO NOT CROSS
BALTIMORE RESIDENTS "PRESENT"
BALTIMORE
CEASE
FIRE
NOBODY KILL ANYBODY
(August 4th 2017 - August 6th 2017)
FOR MORE INFO CONTACT: BMORECEASEFIRE@GMAIL.COM
#baltimoreceasefire #baltimorepeacechallenge
CRIME SCENE DO NOT CROSS CRIME SCENE DO NOT CROSS
CRIME SCENE DO NOT CROSS CRIME SCENE DO NOT CROSS

Inclusion

BCF365 purposely includes everyone who loves Baltimore, whether they live in the city or not. The movement belongs to everyone who is doing anything to address the root causes of violence, the present traumas of violence, and the aftermath of violence. This means that there is nothing too small that a person can do to participate in BCF365.

The movement comprises two parts, the Baltimore Ceasefire and the Baltimore Peace Challenge. The Baltimore Ceasefire calls for a commitment not to kill anyone. However, there are many people who don't think about murder as an option in their lives. This is why the Baltimore Peace Challenge calls for a commitment to be more peaceful. It asks everyone to check their thoughts, words, and actions to ensure that they are as peaceful as possible. By including both the Ceasefire and Peace Challenge, this movement invites everyone to help create the Baltimore they want to see.

Public meetings became a standard part of the movement. Ceasefire weekends happen every February, May, August, and November. In between each Ceasefire weekend, there are public meetings held in all nine sectors of Baltimore. This means that no matter where you live, there is a meeting that is scheduled in your area that is accessible by public transportation.

Self-Determination

The organizers of Baltimore Ceasefire 365 do not approve or deny anyone's participation in the movement. People decide for themselves how to participate, which means that nobody is pressured to make their participation seem "good enough."

The movement maintains that every good thing that anyone does adds positivity to Baltimore, making no effort too small. For example, some people participate by changing their profile pictures on social media to the current BCF365 logo. While this might seem like a small gesture, we believe that unified imagery matters. When many people use the same picture to represent their social media pages to the world, together it sends a strong message about what we all want for Baltimore.

People decide for themselves what "life-affirming event" means to them. They can participate in the movement by planning to finally speak to the sibling they've been ignoring, or they can plan a twenty-four-hour resource fair in their community. Every event matters and adds to the beauty of the weekend. People are often confused about this point, and ask us for permission to do their event. It seems unreal that we are *really* saying that they can do whatever they want to celebrate life. The practice of communities making decisions for themselves feels like unicorn magic to a lot of people.

These values have become the foundation that keep Baltimore Ceasefire 365 strong. There is absolutely a lot of hopelessness around violence and murder. The negative narratives about Baltimore include self-degrading labels like "BodyMore Murdaland" and comments like "Throw the whole city in the trash." In the face of such consistent negativity, we needed a unified positive narrative that could firmly stand up to the hopelessness. The idea of unity has been given legs and arms; people see what it looks like to move with unity, while deciding for themselves how to be involved. I have been blown away by what this has meant for Baltimore. There's no way I could have known that mothers who'd become prisoners in their homes from the grief of losing a child to violence would say that this movement gave them something to do. I could not have known that a "life-affirming event" would look like hundreds of people walking to all the locations in a community where people had been killed, to call each name and pour love into each space. I knew that people would be moved to action, but I didn't know that hundreds of students around the city would one day create an art exhibit that would take up an entire floor of a building, inspired by Baltimore Ceasefire 365. And while I knew Baltimore was very able to go three days without murder, nobody thought a Peace Challenge weekend would start a stretch of eleven and a half days in which nobody would be killed.

How did I come to understand how to merge my ADR values with my activism? It wasn't easy. As someone who is constantly finding ways to keep traumas from swallowing me whole, I have thought a lot about the differences between my responsibilities as an activist and as an ADR practitioner. Had I not grappled with it, I wouldn't have been able to do anything outside of ADR, and the pain would have consumed me.

Never doubt that a small group of thoughtful, committed, citizens can change the world. Indeed, it is the only thing that ever has.

Margaret Mead

As a mediator in the Inclusive Model, it is my job to never let participants know what I think or how I feel about their conflicts. Yet as someone who has seen conflicts end in murder, and as someone who understands how many conflicts are caused by the social injustices that people have to live with every day, I can't only be involved in work where I hold my opinions about what needs to change in our society. Desmond Tutu's quote gave me much to think about: "If you are neutral in situations of injustice, you have chosen the side of the oppressor. If an elephant has its foot on the tail of a mouse and you say that you are neutral, the mouse will not appreciate your neutrality."

After the homicide of Freddie Gray, I *had* to come to a firm conclusion about why my role as a mediator was just as important as my role as an activist, and how one informed the other. Baltimore was in an uprising that had been brewing for hundreds of years. Yet the rise in violence after the Uprising would be blamed on the Uprising . . . as if oppression had not existed in Baltimore before 2015. In that time of turmoil, those of us in the community mediation movement felt horrified and helpless. We asked ourselves, "What can we offer at this time?" We decided that we would offer what we know best. We offered a safe space for people to come, vent, and be heard without judgment. We filled the Baltimore center with mediators who would listen to community members. We planned a Basic Mediation Training just for people who were inspired to be the change they wanted to see in Baltimore because of the Uprising. We brought together police, business owners, youth, residents, and community leaders for a three-month dialogue about what they wanted to see happen. This conversation lasted for two years, and the participants created a diversion program for West Baltimore youth.

What I noticed in this time of turmoil was that we were a bridge. Whether people were on "the side" of the community or the police, community mediation had its doors open and its ears and quality processes ready to facilitate conversations. While we were not telling people what to do, being nonjudgmental did not mean we were doing nothing. In our roles as ADR practitioners, our goal had always been to look at social injustices and pay attention to how relationships mattered in how those injustices impacted people's lives. What we kept finding was that relationships *always* mattered. In 2015, relationships mattered again. There was a huge gulf, and people were standing on each side, yelling at each other across the gulf. They couldn't hear each other's perspectives clearly, and they couldn't see each other's humanity. As mediators and facilitators, we provided a bridge for people to walk across. We understood that we had to be a stable bridge. If we let our opinions weigh down or uphold one side, then the entire bridge would be lopsided, and it would land everyone into the depths of the gulf.

Standing firm on the values of collaboration, inclusion, and self-determination enabled us to offer processes that were strong enough to help people decide what justice looked like after the Uprising. When I thought about what could be strong enough to help me as an activist, it was those same values. In my work as a mediator, I work with people who consider themselves victims and offenders in their conflicts. In my work to address murder, I find myself working with people who are vulnerable to becoming per-petrators and victims of violence. In both scenarios, regardless of my role, people need to be heard, they need to have a voice in how to move through their lives, and they need quality processes that help them find out what power looks like for them. This realization fuels my commitment to continue bringing the values of my ADR work into my activism. It also reminds me that if I choose to do otherwise, there will not be enough bridges in times of injustice, and we will all end up in the depths of the gulf.

CHAPTER 3

Leaning into Justice

E. Franklin Dukes

MY AMERICAN SOLDIER FATHER MET MY LUX-
embourgish mother in Luxembourg City right
after World War II ended. The son of a career
military officer, he had dropped out of college
one month before graduation to join the army.
She and her family had suffered the deep injustices, deprivations, and risks of living five years
in an occupied country during wartime.

Her brother, my uncle, survived the Hinzert

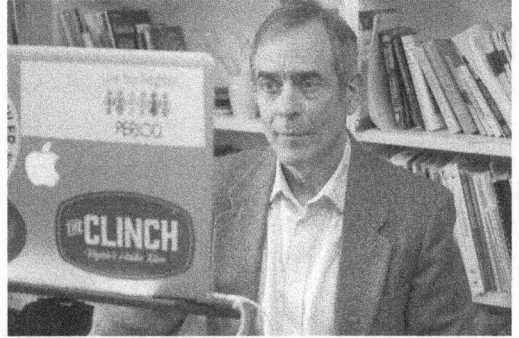

Frank Dukes

concentration camp in Germany, a death sen-
tence for many of his fellow prisoners. In addition to the violence
he was dealt and their agonizing fear over his fate, my mother's
family endured a Gestapo raid in their home, my grandfather's
beating in a Luxembourg street, open as well as anonymous threats,
and many other deprivations. The Nazis kicked my mother out of
two high schools, the first time for throwing gym shorts on Hitler's
photo, her second and last chance for a diploma ending when she
refused to join the Hitler Youth.

My father's story showed me that following your heart is
more important than pursuing a conventional path. My mother's
story ingrained in me an understanding of the deep harm that
hate and violent conflict can bring. Together, my family history
instilled in me the sometimes competing, sometimes comple-

mentary notions that it is necessary to work—and sometimes fight—for both justice and peace.

My career has been a continuing quest, and sometimes a struggle, to integrate those two ideals—the fight for justice and the search for peace. I cannot say that I have found *the* way for everyone to do this; but I have been finding *my* way.

DISCOVERING MEDIATION AND FACILITATION

In part because I grew up with this family history, it was not too difficult for me to accept an offer to attend the US Air Force Academy upon graduation from high school. It was much more difficult to leave the Academy prior to graduation, acting on my own gradual realization that I could not surrender my own moral agency to a government that did not appear to share my own values, much less those of many peoples and nations around the globe, most notably as manifested in the ongoing Vietnam War. Thus my first effort to learn how to deal with conflict—through force—ended after two intense academic years and three summers in Colorado Springs.

Beginnings as a Mediator

Fast-forward several years, time that saw me driving a truck, working in a gas station, and eventually graduating from the University of Virginia (UVA) with a major in music. My motivation for entering the conflict resolution field was prompted by my inability to deal well with conflict. The peak of that realization came while I served as a youth soccer coach, when I was unable to effectively confront a team parent who also was league president. His boorish behavior as we won our games by large margins had led to complaints from other teams. Although I ultimately withdrew as coach and took my son off the team in protest, that was not the outcome I wanted.

I realized that until I could deal well with conflict I would be unable to have the impact I wanted to have, not only with individuals like the league president, but with family members and within the community-at-large. I became driven to find ways to be more effective at handling conflict.

Important Lesson

That search led me in 1984 to join Charlottesville residents developing a new community mediation center. Along with that discovery came a second key experience, with our center's—and my own—very first mediation. A landlord-tenant case had been nearly settled by phone, with our center's director arranging the agreement. With me joining her as co-mediator, we met the parties in person to work out the last details of the agreement. The tenant, an African-American woman, told the leasing company representative, a white woman, that she would bring the payment on Friday evening after she got paid. The company representative replied that there was no need to rush over after work; the tenant could bring the payment the following Monday. We two mediators, also white, applauded the good will of the company representative and wrote up the agreement that way.

It was not until later that week that I began to realize the potential harm of what we mediators had done. The tenant might have had her own reasons for bringing the payment on Friday evenings, but we privileged our own judgment over hers. We did not consider that she might have been unwilling to share her reasons in front of the other party, and that we should have met with her alone. We denied her agency. It was a mistake I was determined never to repeat.

Despite this early misstep, I was delighted to find this newly emerging field, and dove into community and family mediation in Charlottesville, graduate work at George Mason University, and my eventual role as mediator and facilitator at the Institute for Environmental Negotiation (changed in 2019 to Institute for Engagement & Negotiation) at UVA.

COMPETING IDENTITIES: ADVOCATE AND THIRD PARTY

Since then I have witnessed firsthand innumerable examples of couples, families, organizations, and communities benefiting from the services of impartial, independent third parties. I have led and cofacilitated many transformative processes that left participants with outcomes they had not imagined possible. I admire and seek to emulate many of my colleagues who are dedicated, smart, capable, and caring. Outside of my family roles, I most cherish my identity as a third-party facilitator and mediator.

But I also have struggled with that identity, even as I have embraced it. While I do believe that any society needs the third-party role that my colleagues and I provide, I have come to believe that there is a parallel obligation to fundamental matters of human rights, social justice, and equity.[1] Limiting myself to traditional conceptions of a third-party role can cause me to ignore—and can even interfere with—attention to those issues both in my community as well as in my work. I believe that unless and until I and my colleagues act on this realization, not only will we miss important opportunities; at times we will be complicit in perpetuating injustice and sustaining inequity.

There may be times when we are powerless to prevent injustice, but there must never be a time when we fail to protest.

Elie Wiesel

It is this realization that has compelled me to expand my conception of what I can do both as a third party and as a responsible community member. In short, I have sought ways as a third-party, independent, and impartial facilitator and mediator to incorporate social justice into my work. At the same time, I have grown my role in my community as a visible public advocate for various forms of social justice.

Challenging the Conception of Neutrality

How did I come to that stance?

During my original training as a community mediator, in 1985, I accepted without question the contemporary Western tenets of neutrality, as defined by our trainers and as described in Western mediation literature. My role was to guide the parties through the mediation process, and the best way to do that was to be neutral, favoring neither party, taking care not to advocate for any particular solution. "Trust the process" was a mantra that seemed to produce extraordinary results.

Although our mediation center had few cases,[2] the community mediation process enthralled me. Even though I could be anxious when facing parties in conflict, I discovered that I had a talent for focusing on their concerns, helping them understand one another's needs, and reaching agreements that they had not thought possible.

At the same time, my studies at George Mason University made me aware of challenges to the field's acceptance of neutrality. In 1987, as I began my last year of the master's program in conflict resolution, Jim Laue arrived on campus. Jim brought with him the Conflict Clinic, a small organization that was mediating public policy cases. I envied the skills of the staff[3] and wanted to learn to be like them.

Jim and Gerald Cormick had authored "The Ethics of Intervention in Community Disputes,"[4] a seminal work challenging neutrality. As a sociologist and observer of the brutality inflicted on civil rights advocates when he worked for the Community Relations Service in the 1960s, Jim brought an understanding of power and a skepticism about neutrality. He knew how power imbalances and inequitable distribution of resources drove community disputes. Laue and Cormick made it clear that mediators working on community issues are not and cannot be neutral: "merely by advocating the negotiation or joint decision-making process as a way of dealing with a conflict, the mediators are advocating . . . positive change rather than repression."[5]

Shortly after that, I came across empirical evidence that a stance of neutrality could be harmful. Among other insights, Sara Cobb and Janet Rifkin's seminal work "Practice and Paradox: Deconstructing Neutrality in Mediation"[6] illustrated how mediators can favor one narrative, and thus one party, over another even while assuming a stance of neutrality.

My Own Stance toward Neutrality

With these and other readings and experiences, I gradually arrived at my own stance toward neutrality. In short, there is nothing in any literature or in my experience that indicates that anyone outside of our field believes that third parties are "neutral." In fact, my experience has been that a claim to neutrality leads to distrust, as the claim is seen as impossible or evasive. This claim may also be viewed as a sign of not caring about the parties and issues, or an unwillingness to acknowledge fundamental power differences among the parties.

While *neutrality* is problematic, I do value *independence* and *impartiality*. Independence can mean many things: being able to say no to work; relying on other sources of funding than that of a single party to a dispute; and not having demands by my own or other institutions that could unfavorably affect my third-party role. Impartiality means an inclination and ability to favor no one party over any other. Impartiality does not mean treating all parties the same, for different parties have different needs that may need to be met in order for them to participate effectively.

Finally, and most importantly for the purposes of this chapter, visible advocacy for social justice does not mean having to forgo a career as a mediator and facilitator. In fact, not only is that possible, a reputation as an advocate for social justice may even help advance that career, as people come to see such a stance as an indicator of integrity and caring.

The hottest places in hell are reserved for those who, in times of great moral crisis, maintain their neutrality.

DANTE ALIGHIERI

COMBINING ADVOCACY WITH THIRD-PARTY WORK ON SOCIAL JUSTICE

How may this integration be done?

What does a third-party practice that includes a strong focus on social justice look like?

What does advocacy look like for someone working as a mediator and facilitator—or for someone who is seeking to join the field and wondering if these two roles may both be pursued?

A Bigger Vision for Third-Party Work: Transforming Community and Governance

In this I have been guided by my dissertation, as I described in my article "Public Conflict Resolution: A Transformative Approach,"[7] and in my later book *Resolving Public Conflict: Transforming Community and Governance*.[8] In these works I worried about whether a field of public conflict resolution that only accepted the concerns and cases of sponsoring agencies served an "ideology of manage-ment." Were we willing to serve as just another instrument in the toolbox of judicial and administrative efficiency? Could we not be instead a movement for social justice and change?

Rejecting an Ideology of Management

This ideology of management, found in law, public administration, planning, and other fields related to governance, assumes a world-view that sees a beleaguered state being battered by obstructionist community members and interest groups. It focuses on neutrality, efficiency, technical concerns, and proficiency. The public is viewed as either an obstacle (angry and capricious) or a burden (requiring wasted time engaging in public participation). The primary driver of work is to serve authorities through the delivery of services that meet those same authorities' needs.

This ideology may not necessarily be accepted intentionally, but results as an easy corollary of the search for paying work. The inev-itable outcome of practice based on this ideology is an affirmation and replication of existing power relations. This is a failure on a number of fronts:

- We are failing to plan for and seek other outcomes that par-ticipants in the processes we convene tell us that they value.
- We are failing to fulfill the considerable potential for learning, recognition, and creativity offered through these processes.
- We are failing to address the deepest challenges, and hence deepest needs, of contemporary democratic society.

A Transformative Vision

We can do better. What I call a *transformative vision* embraces a very different humanity and society than the ideology of manage-ment. It sees our work as a vehicle for transforming the private and public institutions of democratic society. It does so with three primary goals:

Table 3.1.   Comparison of Management and Transformative Approaches

Aspects	Ideology of Management	Transformative Vision
Vision of human nature	Maximize self-interest—the so-called "possessive individual"	Socially constituted Relationship-seeking
Key public problems	Apathetic and obstructionist citizenry Legislative, administrative, and judicial gridlock	Alienation from governance Atrophied public life Fragmentation of community Racial disparities, economic inequality, and environmental injustice
Sources of conflict	Uncivil behavior Obstructionist interest groups Scarcity of resources Miscommunication	Denial of individual and cultural identity, security, and recognition Illegitimate policies and structures of governance and other systems Power disparities
Role of governance	Resolving conflicts of interest by authority accountable to majority rule	Strong democracy of community deeply engaged in self-governance Integration of interests
Accountability	To governing authorities	To community as well as governing authorities To process participants
Professional role	Neutral Managerial Technical Solution-oriented	Independent and impartial Facilitator Consensus builder Process-oriented
Process goals	Legal compliance Containment of controversy Public relations Endorsement of preconceived outcome	Social justice and equity Empowerment Mutual learning Civic engagement Synergistic agreements
Process qualities	One-way communication (announcement, hearing) Bargaining Prescriptive	Equitable collaboration: inclusive, responsive, truth-seeking, deliberative, adaptive, trauma-informed Higher ground Elicitive
Determinant of outcome	Relative power	New power alignment on basis of new participation, new ideas, new relationships, enlarged self-interest

- Inspiring, nurturing, and sustaining a vital communal life: *an engaged community.*

- Invigorating the institutions and practices of governance: *a responsive governance.*

- Enhancing society's ability to solve problems and resolve conflicts: *a capacity for collaborative problem solving and conflict resolution.*

Mediation and Facilitation on Behalf of Social Justice

In my third-party work, which is primarily through the Institute for Engagement & Negotiation (IEN) at UVA, this vision is enacted in the ways that I practice as well as in the types of work I pursue.

My work is framed around what we call *equitable collaboration.*[9] Equitable collaboration may be developed in a variety of processes, from one-time community meetings to long-term consensus building. Equitable collaboration involves the following principles (fig. 3.1):

Inclusive: If learning and growth is to be enduring, it has to reach all segments of a community.

How may we move from an inclusion that says "this is a public meeting; all may attend" to an inclusion that seeks out, welcomes, and honors diverse participation? How may we foster an inclusion that acknowledges racial, ethnic, gender, class, neural divergence, and other dynamics in ways that provide for a wide spectrum of participation? How may we foster cultural humility—openness to learning about our differences on each other's terms—while recognizing and embracing those differences?

Responsive: Too many communities view their governing authorities as uncaring and believe that their views do not matter, even when those authorities may intend otherwise.

How can we create processes that acknowledge and respond to participant questions, needs, concerns, and ideas in timely and meaningful ways?

Truth-seeking: Public conflicts invariably involve competing claims. How may we invite honest, more complete learning, even when such learning may be painful to hear and understand? What parties have the knowledge and credibility to help support this search for truths?

Deliberative: Effective community deliberation begins with the premise that people can and will learn from one another. It fully explores issues before seeking solutions. It fosters *brave spaces*[10]—processes where participants honestly and openly confront their past and present. It enhances shared civic thinking, not by a false civility that privileges order over candor but by acknowledgment that we all can learn and grow, and that institutions and communities need to do so together.

Adaptive: Determining the most appropriate process for the situation and adapting it throughout according to participant needs is not only a question of effectiveness; it is a way of respecting people's time. Is there a clear, widely recognized purpose and set of goals for this effort? Are there sufficient resources available to conduct this process well?

Trauma-informed: Undergirding each of these elements is *trauma-informed facilitation*.[11] Trauma-informed facilitation acknowledges that many issues evoke harmful emotions in individuals and groups. The processes by which decisions get made may themselves provoke additional trauma, even with careful attention to process design. What traumas are there associated with a particular set of issues? How may we undertake preparations and actions that prevent, minimize, or prepare and support people facing renewed trauma?

Taken together, these principles foster equitable collaboration, with the learning, understanding, creativity, and growth necessary to produce wise, widely legitimate, and robust outcomes.

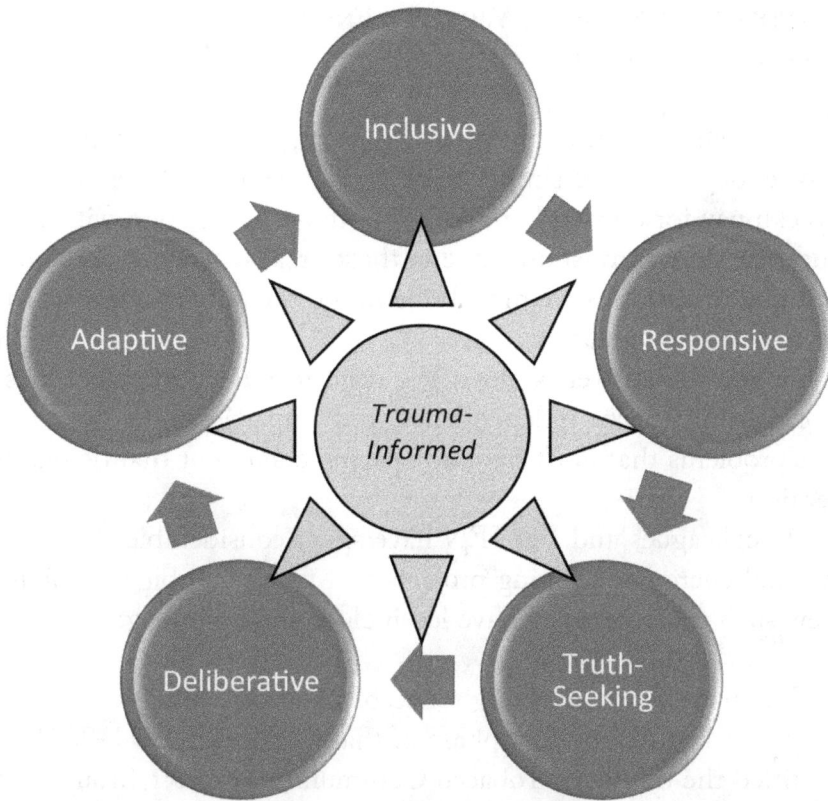

Figure 3.1.   The key elements of equitable collaboration

I recognize that the explicit expression of values such as equity and inclusion may be difficult for those steeped in the language of neutrality to accept. If I might quote myself from *ACResolutions* of a couple of years ago:

> This does not mean that we give up the essential independence and impartiality of our role in favor of advocacy for any one party. Rather, we give up the myth that objectivity and neutrality mean ignoring the environment in which we operate and the varying needs of different parties. We do need to adopt lenses that let us see clearly how problems of race, ethnicity, class, gender, and sexual orientation harm people and whole communities by practices that divide our communities along those lines. We need to consistently raise questions of justice and equity with the sponsors of our work.[12]

Expanding the Scope of Work to Encompass Issues of Justice and Equity

As important as work sponsored by paying clients may be, that is not enough. Do we simply react to the needs of those entities who can pay for our work, hoping that those needs align with our values? Or do we invest our time in those areas where our communities and institutions are most broken, and the potential impact of our work may be greatest?

For me the answer is clear: We need to pursue opportunities to bring third-party independence and impartiality to bear on those problems that don't have any paying client, but that demand attention.

My colleagues and I at IEN have spent considerable thought, time, and energy developing projects that fulfill that bigger vision. A few such projects that I have led include the following:

- Extensive work involving tobacco, tobacco farming, and public health. The first phase of that work from 1994–2001, titled the Southern Tobacco Communities Project, brought together farmers, health advocates, researchers, and community development advocates finding ways to improve economic and community health in farm communities suffering devastating cuts in production. In Virginia, these discussions produced an unprecedented alliance that secured nearly $2 billion for farmer payments and investments in tobacco farming communities as well as programs to limit youth access to tobacco products.[13] Later work has included facilitating strategic planning for tobacco control coalitions and, most recently, a series of dialogues focusing on harm reduction and electronic nicotine delivery systems.[14]

- The Clinch River Valley Initiative (CRVI) began with my concerns about harms to Appalachian communities as the coal economy declined and as mountaintop mining transformed treasured landscapes. It took nearly eighteen months of listening to environmental advocates, economic development staff, local and state government officials, educators, and other residents before determining that the work that we do—bringing together people with different, often conflicting views, to see whether they might be able to do together what neither can do separately—would be welcomed in the coalfields of southwest Virginia. CRVI has become a powerful coalition building local economies while protecting and enhancing natural resources, focusing on the Clinch River—one of the most biodiverse river systems in North America.[15]

- Transforming Community Spaces (TCS) began in 2015 in recognition of the need to help communities and institutions facing conflicts over monuments, memorials, building names, and other sites identified with histories of harm such as violence, slavery, colonialism, and environmental disaster. The TCS pilot, Charlottesville Acts for Racial Equity (CARE), began in 2018 and is leading development of a Truth Commission to address central Virginia's history and legacy of slavery, segregation, and discrimination and to repair ongoing racial disparities.

Each of these projects required an unpaid investment in time and energy before securing foundation and other financial support. Each required listening to multiple parties to ascertain whether and how this could add value to communities addressing challenging circumstances, and a willingness to walk away if it did not. Each required organizing and fund-raising even before applying facilitation and consensus-building practices. Each also required a leap of faith on my part (and often that of my colleagues) that this investment of effort would bring about positive outcomes even as such outcomes may not have been imaginable at the outset.

BEYOND THE PROFESSIONAL ROLE: BRINGING OUR SKILLS AS A COMMUNITY ADVOCATE FOR SOCIAL JUSTICE

An expanded conception of the third-party role is not enough to fulfill my responsibility to social justice. Because I reside in Charlottesville, my advocacy has focused primarily on race. I live in a community that has enduring, destructive racial disparities affecting education, income, housing and neighborhoods, health, safety and criminal justice, and more. While we each will have our own calling based on our own values, capacities, and circumstances, in recent years this advocacy role has included:

- Creating a project with shared community-university leadership that has challenged UVA to address its own racial disparities. The University and Community Action for Racial Equity (UCARE) serves as a powerful voice for racial equity within UVA as well as in the community.
- Leading petition drives:
  - to support Muslim colleagues at UVA and their families, friends, and others in the community.
  - against naming a federal courthouse after Justice Antonin Scalia in a location that was formally an African-American neighborhood destroyed by "urban renewal."
  - for local jurisdictions to issue condemnations of Confederate flags.
- Serving on the Charlottesville Blue Ribbon Commission on Race, Memorials and Public Spaces to reveal and challenge the long-hidden impacts of white supremacy in my own community.
- Speaking out against white supremacy and for racial equity in public meetings, classrooms, faith communities, television, radio, and print.
- Showing up as a community member at public and private demonstrations.
- Joining an advocacy group, SURJ (Showing Up for Racial Justice).
- Supporting our local Black Lives Matter chapter when asked to do so.

NONVIOLENCE AS THE FOUNDATION FOR ADVOCACY

My third-party and advocacy roles are not entirely separate. My commitment to each is deeply informed by the principles of nonviolence. Nonviolent action is strategic, active resistance to oppression while not denying the humanity of the oppressors. Nonviolence is the essential cornerstone of sustainable change; it is so for moral, strategic, and tactical reasons.

Strategically, any effort to support or sanction violence except in cases of authentic self-defense diminishes the impact of moral arguments for social justice. *Tactically*, violence nearly always favors those who are better armed, better trained, and with the most resources and power. Furthermore, the victims of violence are often the most vulnerable and the least able to defend themselves.

This support for nonviolence is not always welcome among others working for social justice. There have been a number of widely shared commentaries decrying the "fetishization of nonviolence"[16] as acts of overt white supremacy increase. But blanket arguments against nonviolence are often disingenuous (as though the only possible responses to threats are to fight them or to ignore them), or provide a willful distortion of nonviolence. This is more than irresponsible; this is dangerous.

There are legitimate arguments involving nonviolence, of course, and there is an argument to be made against what I would call the co-optation of the language of nonviolence.

When people ignore deadly violence against people of color, immigrants, members of the LBGTQIA community, and others, but condemn the uprisings in Baltimore, St. Louis, Cleveland, Charlottesville, and other places, *that is co-optation of the language of nonviolence.*

When people deplore violence, but don't show up themselves for nonviolent actions, *that is co-optation of the language of nonviolence.*

When people proclaim a moral equivalency between groups whose basis is to deny others their humanity, whose leadership threatens harm, and who celebrate their command of physical force, with those whose nonviolent actions may be accompanied by disorder and confrontation, *that is co-optation of the language of nonviolence.*

In our every deliberation, we must consider the impact of our decisions on the next seven generations.

IROQUOIS
CONFEDERACY
MAXIM

Peace has to be created, in order to be maintained. It is the product of Faith, Strength, Energy, Will, Sympathy, Justice, Imagination, and the triumph of principle. It will never be achieved by passivity and quietism.

DOROTHY THOMPSON

When people ignore the very real physical and psychic harm done by racism and other forms of structural violence, such as higher rates of infant mortality and lower life expectancy, to name just two egregious forms, while decrying the disorder of confrontation and protest, *that is co-optation of the language of nonviolence.*

Conclusion

Were I myself just entering this field, here are some thoughts about what I would want to hear:

Be clear about what values you are serving by doing this work. When both ethical and practical dilemmas arise, as they will, those values guide you in making the best decisions.

Never stop learning. By no means does every practitioner need to have a degree in conflict transformation. But every practitioner should be familiar with the literature in their field. My work has been deeply enriched by the writings of colleagues and by my regular participation in professional conferences.

Get a solid grounding in the cultural and historical context in which you work. If you are practicing in the United States, that means understanding how racial dynamics, including the persistent influence of white supremacy, have shaped our communities, our landscapes, and our narratives about who we are.

Be bold. Many of my most challenging projects have also been the most rewarding.

Finally, our society urgently needs people who value social justice and who are also deeply committed to peacebuilding. As the United States has seen a rise in hate crimes, mass shootings, and overt white supremacist activity, many people who were content to ignore politics and issues of social justice or whose level of advocacy had been minimal find themselves wanting more—much more. In addition, many who had already been active in politics and issues of social justice, whether at local, state, or national levels, have found themselves questioning whether they are capable of meeting newer challenges.

The positive side of this change has been palpable in many ways—new awareness and learning about deep problems and challenges, new relationships and coalitions, and new energy and commitment to action.

But there has been a downside as well. As the numbers of new activist groups have increased, as opportunities for protest grow, as media outlets offer day-to-day and even hour-to-hour reports of the latest outrage or the newest call to action, many become overwhelmed at the sheer numbers of demands, opportunities, appeals, choices, and responsibilities. What do I do? Is it ever enough? Whom should I be accountable to? Am I making a difference?

I developed figure 3.2 to help me think about what my priorities should be and to remind myself of the need for self- and other-care and for continued learning and growth. I include it here with the hope that people doing something like this for themselves may help others, including those who may be feeling isolated, uncertain, or overwhelmed. Creating a diagram of this sort

Personal Social Justice & Peacebuilding Pyramid

Emphasis varies depending on identity, circumstances, community needs, and capabilities

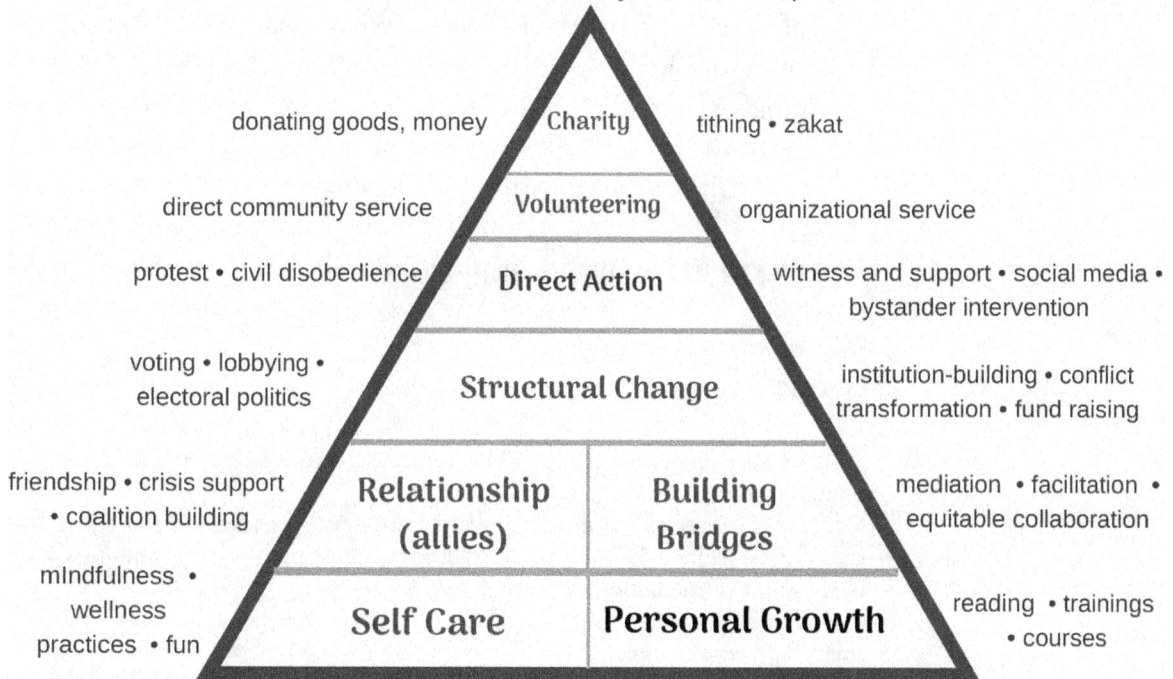

donating goods, money	Charity	tithing • zakat
direct community service	Volunteering	organizational service
protest • civil disobedience	Direct Action	witness and support • social media • bystander intervention
voting • lobbying • electoral politics	Structural Change	institution-building • conflict transformation • fund raising
friendship • crisis support • coalition building	Relationship (allies) / Building Bridges	mediation • facilitation • equitable collaboration
mIndfulness • wellness practices • fun	Self Care / Personal Growth	reading • trainings • courses

Figure 3.2.

may help you to find your own path—to ascertain what your own strengths and needs may be and how they may match your own community's needs and resources.

Some more context will be helpful. I am white, male, highly educated, financially stable, mostly abled, cisgendered. At a personal level, the system has privileged me much more than most people reading this. Furthermore, my strengths and deficits will be different than yours. What I need to work on may not be what you need to work on; what I am good at doing may not be what you are good at doing. So the arrangement that I show represents what I think needs to be my own options, *not* yours. And as your circumstances change, so should the elements that you prioritize shift as well.

My career has been a persistently challenging, intensely rewarding, sometimes painful, and as-yet incomplete journey. I do not always meet my goals. But I take solace in the words of Archbishop Desmond Tutu:

> Forgiving and being reconciled to our enemies or our loved ones are not about pretending that things are other than they are. . . . True reconciliation exposes the awfulness, the abuse, the hurt, the truth. It could even sometimes make things worse. It is a risky undertaking but in the end it is worthwhile, because in the end only an honest confrontation with reality can bring real healing.[17]

I invite you to join me in shaping those "honest confrontations."

Notes

1. For convenience' sake the phrase "social justice" will be used to refer to human rights, social justice, and equity.

2. Those cases could be challenging in ways that the texts did not teach. My second case began when a landlord handed a subpoena to the tenant—hardly in the spirit of mediation.

3. Frank Blechman, Marci DuPraw, and Bill Potapchuk, all young, very smart, and very capable.

4. James Laue and Gerald R. Cormick, "The Ethics of Intervention in Community Disputes," in *The Ethics of Social Intervention*, edited by Gordon

Bermant, Herbert C. Kelman, and Donald P. Warwick (New York: Halsted Press, 1978), 205–232.

5. Ibid., 216.

6. Sara Cobb and Janet Rifkin, "Practice and Paradox: Deconstructing Neutrality in Mediation," *Law & Social Inquiry* 16(1), Winter 1991, 35–62.

7. Frank Dukes, "Public Conflict Resolution: A Transformative Approach," *Negotiation Journal* 9(1), January 1993, 45–57.

8. E. Franklin Dukes, *Resolving Public Conflict: Transforming Community and Governance* (Manchester, UK: Manchester University Press, 1996).

9. IEN Associate Director Kristina Nell Weaver coined the term.

10. Brian Arao and Kristi Clemens. "From Safe Spaces to Brave Spaces: A New Way to Frame Dialogue around Diversity and Social Justice," in *The Art of Effective Facilitation: Reflections from Social Justice Educators*, edited by Lisa M. Landreman (Sterling, VA: Stylus, 2013), 135–150.

11. There is an extensive and growing literature on trauma and conflict and facilitation. See, for example, Elsa Falkenburger, Olivia Arena, and Jessica Wolin, *Trauma-Informed Community Building and Engagement* (Washington: Urban Institute, April 2018).

12. E. Franklin Dukes, "Righting Unrightable Wrongs," *ACResolutions* 7(4), 2008, 15.

13. Frank Dukes, "From Enemies, to Higher Ground, to Allies: The Unlikely Partnership between the Tobacco Farm and Public Health Communities," in *Participatory Governance: Planning, Conflict Mediation and Public Decision-Making in Civil Society*, edited by W. Robert Lovan, Michael Murray, and Ron Shaffer (Farnham, UK: Ashgate Press, 2004).

14. For a description of those dialogues, see http://www.virginia.edu/ien/tobacco/.

15. See Chapter 5 in Susan F. Hirsch and E. Franklin Dukes, *Mountaintop Mining in Appalachia: Understanding Stakeholders and Change in Environmental Conflict* (Athens: Ohio University Press, 2014).

16. An online search will find numerous references to the phrase "fetishization of nonviolence."

17. Desmond Tutu, "Truth and Reconciliation," *Greater Good Magazine*, September 1, 2004.

CHAPTER 4

Working from the Heart

HELEN WINTER

I REMEMBER SITTING WITH MY GRANDPARENTS IN OUR LIVING room when they were still alive. I must have been about eleven years old, and they told me about a conflict they had in their building with other tenants. I do not remember exactly what the conflict was about (maybe it was about shoveling snow in the wintertime), but I do remember that I tried to advise them as best as I could—always instinctively keeping in mind that it mattered most that they came out of the situation getting along with the people they shared a house with.

Helen Winter

After a long time of listening and advising, they made me so proud when they said: "Helen, we are so glad to discuss this with you; you are a great listener and counselor and already show a very grown-up approach at your young age." When they said this to me, I knew there was something I would have to pursue, something that moved me that I needed to put my finger on and examine. Back then I could only identify it as a gut feeling.

Today, I am a conflict resolution professional and intercultural mediator among refugees and locals in Germany. I was led to this work by a strong sense of relational justice that was shaped in me early on.

Relational justice seeks to establish or restore the relationships of individuals through dialogue. I believe that a conversation must take place in order for the actors to create a relationship that will

allow trust to form and build a bond strong enough to solve a conflict or difference. Deceptively straightforward in theory, forming a relationship with a stranger or even a perceived opponent is difficult and rare in practice. It is far too easy to avoid attempts at real conversation with people we don't know or even fear.

Because I believe in the power of restoring relationships, studying the complexities of law was not fun for me. I studied law in Heidelberg, the oldest university in Germany, where classes were abstract and logical and did not suit my empathetic nature. In my view, law had been created for the people and society, but the law I encountered at university did not account for people's feelings. I did not see the people behind the facts; in the practice cases there was no regard for relationships—let alone restoring them. It was all about claims and positions and nothing else. Back then I often wondered, "What about the *why*? What about justice? Why do I study law? What ultimate purpose does law serve?" However, the philosophy of law was not part of the curriculum, and none of my professors offered a satisfying answer.

I first encountered conflict resolution studies academically in my third year of studies in an elective seminar on negotiation and mediation, where I gave a presentation on "moral and subjective values influencing the outcome of negotiations illustrated by the movie *Twelve Angry Men*." In my analysis, I recognized how differences in social background, power, and personal moral values influence each actor and ultimately the outcome of any negotiation. Many potential disadvantages originating from power imbalances or different social and moral backgrounds can be circumvented by means of effectively employing the skills used in many forms of conflict engagement/resolution, as in the case of the characters in *Twelve Angry Men*, in which a constructive dialogue saved a boy's life. This seminar became my first revelation as it opened my eyes to the power of negotiation and conflict resolution to overcome such differences and imbalances, making them the strongest weapon of the weak.

At Pepperdine University, during a class called "International Identity Based Conflict and Dispute Resolution," taught by Professor Marco Turk, I had the opportunity to learn about the Cyprus problem. We looked at ways to mediate among a divided population so that the conversations might lead to a reunification of the country. During one of our role-plays, where we put ourselves in the positions of North and South Cypriots, an unfamiliar classmate, Judy,[1] and I were discussing the issue of the missing in Cyprus. The role-play went uneasily. After a while, we figured that we could not really negotiate nor settle on anything with one another. We had no "feel" for each other. I was surprised, because all other role-plays a friend and I had done had gone more easily. At one point my classmate and I paused the role-play and stepped out of character. We began to talk with one another as Judy and Helen: why we wanted to study dispute resolution, where we came from, and how we liked this class. After that, we restarted the role-play. This time it went extremely well. We were able to negotiate and talk to one another about difficult situations and issues. This little incident proved to me that even we, actors in a role-play, need to develop a relationship with the other first in order to be more open to discussing relevant issues. We find it is easier to work toward a solution when we have a relationship with our partner in the discussion. What must it be like for North and South Cypriots? If there is no prior relationship, we have a harder time discussing the issue at hand and aiming at a solution, because we tend to refrain from opening up to one another when we do not feel like we can "feel the other person." This experience showed me how important it is to build a relationship between Turkish and Greek Cypriots first so that they can get to know each other before they talk about political and identity-related matters.

At the age of twenty-six, when I was in California and far away from my home country, a number of things happened to me that eventually led to an identity crisis of my own. When I had left home to pursue my LL.M. degree in California, my father had been fighting a serious disease for the past four years. His health conditions were constantly changing, making it almost predictable that good news was eventually followed by bad news in turn. My father wanted me to live life to the fullest and to follow my goals—even if that meant being far from home for a long time and him being unable to visit me since flying would further damage his health. I struggled between wanting to be there for my family and at the same time trying to become independent and understand what I wanted from life. This was extremely hard—especially when hearing yet again that another treatment had failed or another symptom had emerged. To this day, I sometimes regret having gone abroad for a year and a half because my father passed away only seven months after my return to Germany.

My father had a unique gift of supporting those around him as much as he could and always putting the happiness of his family and friends first. While being a strong leader in the field of public health, he also directed his kindness toward anyone he met regardless of their background or experiences. To most who knew him, it stood out that he created an enormous amount of value for other people throughout his entire life. Because of the example of my father's life, I am committed to serving others, particularly those who are disadvantaged.

Be the change that you wish to see in the world.

MAHATMA GANDHI

As my father approached the end of his life, the so-called refugee crisis arose. In 2015 and 2016, 1.2 million refugees arrived in Germany alone, from Syria, Afghanistan, the Balkans, and other countries, escaping from war, violence, and persecution. Since then, Germany has become ninth in countries hosting the most refugees. This surge has led to increasing conflict within Germany as refugees and locals struggle with accepting one another.

The first time I felt that everyone living in Germany—including myself—was affected by conflicts resulting from migration was during an incident in Cologne on New Year's Eve 2016, when twelve hundred women were sexually assaulted by at least two thousand men. The victims were described to have been mostly of Arab or North African appearance. After this, it became inevitable to ignore the challenges caused by mass migration that Germany was facing. This incident was a turning point in the German refugee crisis, both for the public discussion as well as for me personally. Although I was still studying in California at the time, I began to identify strongly with my home country and its challenges. In turn, I focused most of my academic papers on the conflicts that emerged among refugees, Germans, political parties, the media, and the government. I wondered how to apply my knowledge of dispute resolution to these conflicts and how to be of help despite being so far away from home. I was asking myself, "How can I give back to society?"

As a result of my very own identity crisis, the threat of losing everything I love actually gave me new strength in finding out who I wanted to become and what value I wanted to create for others. Life had revealed its finitude to me, and I recognized that my comfortable way of living was unstable and threatened. I could lose people I loved and they would not come back. Reliable peace had to come from within me. That is why, at a time when I was in great pain, I became more determined in my life and vowed to make more conscious choices.

It was not easy. There were times when finding sleep was my biggest challenge. I made plenty of mistakes then, and I continue making them, but I will learn from them. I struggled, fell down, and had to stand up again and again and again. But what I understood was that I was happiest when I made others happy and helped them solve their disputes. I wanted to become a peacemaker, and I was going to.

In my studies and work, I had investigated various systemic ways to mitigate increasing conflict among refugee populations and intercultural communities. Most of my research had focused on how mechanisms of alternative dispute resolution can help improve refugee lives. My idea for founding R3SOLUTE was originally conceived during a discussion with a colleague at the United Nations after my graduation from Straus Institute for Dispute Resolution at Pepperdine School of Law. The colleague and I started working on the vision to establish peer mediation mechanisms in refugee communities, and soon the idea became a project and the project turned into an organization.

Intercultural Dialogue among Refugees and Germans

Today, R3SOLUTE enables refugees and locals to manage and prevent conflicts in their communities and neighborhoods through story-sharing, conflict management, peer mediation, and mental health awareness workshops. I work as the CEO of a team of ten experts in the field; as well as a trainer for story-sharing forums, conflict resolution, and mediation workshops; and an intercultural mediator. Our work is currently focused on Berlin, where more than eighty thousand refugees have settled since 2015. We collaborate with refugee shelters, language cafés, local citizens, social workers, nonprofit organizations, and other institutions. To this end, we offer interactive workshops that have four aims: First, strengthen mutual understanding by means of dialogue work. Second, build competencies in conflict management. Third, sensitize participants to trauma-related issues. Fourth, train refugees as peer mediators to engage in conflict as third-party neutrals.

When designing the workshop curriculum according to the participants' needs, we, along with refugee colleagues, created role-plays according to real-life conflicts in refugee communities. Our colleagues used their experiences of typical conflicts in their communities and neighborhoods to create relatable simulations. Our most requested seminars are dialogue workshops among refugees and local residents led by trained refugee and nonrefugee cofacilitators. Dialogue work or "story-sharing" has proven to promote understanding of each side, reduce prejudice, and resolve conflict. Due to the diversity of our workshop participants, who include refugees from many different backgrounds as well as locals, we are required to have translators for Arabic, Farsi, and English to ensure that everyone can follow our workshops, which are held in German.

Multiple factors need to be taken into account when refugees settle into their new home country and begin their new lives. Here

Workshop participants warming up for the day

are some examples of the reality of displaced people and some of the resulting unmet needs, which I have encountered over the course of my work with R3SOLUTE[2]:

- Most refugees have already had traumatic experiences involving violence, warfare, and detention; therefore, services need to be trauma-informed.[3]

- Contact between German citizens and refugees is highly limited because refugee shelters are mostly located in the far outskirts of cities or the countryside, where isolation and despair breed anger.

- Racially biased incidents take place on a regular basis.

- Refugees typically live in overcrowded shelters, which lack space and privacy. Conflict inevitably arises within and around refugee communities.

- Socioeconomic isolation within society as a whole (as a result of limited resources and chronic unemployment) causes further psychological harm. Refugees often are powerless.

- Refugees need space and resources to process painful memories. This includes medical treatment, ways to gain comfort in an unfamiliar environment, and skills for responding to unfair treatment.

Above all, I have witnessed that people need to be heard, understood, and respected by their community. However, only a few structured forums exist that are designed according to participants' needs and allow refugees and community members to engage with one another on difficult topics such as discrimination, racism, cultural misunderstandings, and lack of perspectives. Most importantly, story-sharing workshops allow for the creation of a relationship and a safe space.

QUALITIES OF A FACILITATOR OF INTERCULTURAL DIALOGUE

Everyone attending our story-sharing forum for the first time is frightened and does not know what to expect. It is our task as facilitators to deal with the story-sharing forum as a people's process; we address the parties' uncertainty by clearly stating how we will conduct the workshop and ask for people's expectations. Only if we clearly reveal why it is that we are here will the participants come to trust us and the process of dialogue work. As peacemakers, we create an environment where participants feel more comfortable in order to experience less pain. When we, as facilitators, open up and show who we truly are, the participants are more likely to follow our example and do the same. When we are able to say why we personally are there and what motivates us to do this type of work, the participants are then more likely to open up to us and everyone else there.

The parties might experience dialogue work as an extremely new and uncomfortable process, so it is our duty to navigate the participants through productive dialogue and thereby allow them to collaborate effectively. It is less about exploring the facts of a dispute or who did what, and more about mastering the dynamics of communication, tolerance, and respect. As the participants require time to elaborate on their conflict, our goal as facilitators is to actively listen and help the participants feel understood. We are not there to provide judgment, but to assist the people in getting to know each other and in overcoming their prejudices.

In one of our story-sharings, an elderly German lady named Anne admitted her feelings of hatred when teaching German to a woman wearing a niqab, a veil that covers the face except for the eyes. Whenever she would speak to that woman, Anne would feel an inner aggression toward her, because she could not fathom that this woman was veiled voluntarily. Given the atmosphere of trust that we had cultivated—instead of being judgmental of her—I decided to do some assumption testing and explored her frustrations with her. I began asking how she felt when the woman took off her niqab when only women were around. She said then her feelings of hatred would immediately disappear. Eventually, after further exploring her thoughts, Anne concluded: "I guess I am mostly angry at myself for having biases against her. I think this is mostly why I feel so aggressive toward her. Because actually my aggressions are directed against myself."

Authenticity is the key to a successful story-sharing forum. Facilitators need to be more than problem solvers with a script

Those who cannot change their minds cannot change anything.
GEORGE BERNARD SHAW

running through their minds if we want to be successful. Why is it so important to be genuine? When people approach "the other side" of a conflict or share their stories, they are frightened and uncomfortable. Therefore, it is our job as facilitators to make the participants feel comfortable by being ourselves and showing them our respect. Trust is triggered by authenticity, and nobody trusts a person who appears to be fake or trying too hard. The initial point of contact with the participants takes place on a personal level. We are personable, present, and observant when we design the process of the story-sharing we are conducting. We seek to find joy in what we do without having to constantly question our styles. Author Brené Brown has conducted influential research on social work and has concluded that personal connections are the key reason for our actions. She found that hiding our feelings out of shame and fear unravels connection, but that in order for connection to happen, we have to allow us to be seen (excruciating vulnerability).

At one of my workshops, participants were mourning the loss of their loved ones. One of them, a young man from Afghanistan named Jawid, got up in front of the group and told of a recent bomb attack in which his entire family had died while he was in Germany. In the blink of an eye, he had lost all of his family. Hearing this story brought tears to the eyes of all of us in the room, because we were reminded of our own loss of someone we loved. At this point, I had to choose. Should I bring up the recent loss of my father or should I remain professional? After a deep breath, I spoke about losing my father and my own personal story. As difficult as it was for me, it motivated more people to share about their losses because I had shown them vulnerability and therefore became more trustworthy.

Brené Brown[4] has also found in her research that people who have a strong sense of love and belonging conversely believe they are worthy of love and belonging. They have the courage to be sincere and to embrace vulnerability, as they believe that what makes them vulnerable makes them beautiful. What keeps us out of connection is our fear that we are not worthy of connection. In Brown's words: "We numb vulnerability. When we numb vulnerability we numb joy, we numb everything."[5] Therefore, she claims, vulnerability leads to connectivity. From my own experience, this is true. Especially in

Workshop participants doing an interactive exercise

story-sharings of a delicate nature, we as peacemakers must show compassion, even if we show parts of our soul that usually remain unseen. My advice to any facilitator would, therefore, be to not fight vulnerability, because it makes you more authentic and creates better discussions. As facilitators of intercultural dialogue, we have to deal with other people's extremes that are often displayed in situations of conflict. It is not a rare phenomenon that people start crying when talking about their horrifying past. In these situations, we cannot be afraid of their, nor our, emotions. Rather, we have to embrace them. Every tear shed, every word listened to, will give people new strength to reinvent their lives.

CHALLENGES OF BEING A FACILITATOR OF INTERCULTURAL DIALOGUE

One of my biggest personal challenges is to endure the suffering and pain of others even after the story-sharing or mediation is over.

It is hard not to become emotionally involved when I witness this much pain on a constant basis. Even seeing the living conditions of refugees in overcrowded shelters can be quite depressing. It is difficult not to want to become involved in politics when I see the turnover of management and attachment figures in refugee shelters, leaving inhabitants with new rules and destroying past relationships and partially reestablished freedom. I see many people who cannot cope with the situation turn to drugs or alcohol abuse. Often children suffer the most.

Many people try to help, and the situation could be much worse; however, the administration is slow and it takes a long time for projects to be integrated into the system of rules. Even collaborations among different nongovernmental organizations (NGOs) and other organizations can be a challenge because other projects are regarded as competition for funding. Networks are difficult to build, and almost no one knows who is responsible for which domain. Oftentimes, when I had finally found the responsible person in the bureaucratic jungle, I needed to convince people with whom I had never previously interacted of the benefits of our work. They had never even heard of conflict resolution and dialogue work. These people were ministers, managers of a shelter, politicians, or representatives of institutions. That's why it is important as a seeker for social justice to know your "why"—because in these situations you will need to convince people from the bottom of your heart to make them truly listen to you and buy into your idea.

Another challenge is getting everyone at one table in the story-sharing. This includes those who will not come because they are isolating themselves, refrain from social interactions, or dislike "the other side" too much. Reaching those who would most benefit from a dialogue can be quite an experience. For these reasons, it will sometimes feel like change is going to take forever. In these situations your worst enemy is frustration. Do not buy in. Change is possible in small steps, and you will feel it within every person whom your work has impacted.

To avoid criticism, do nothing, say nothing, and be nothing.

ELBERT HUBBARD

When facing personal or practical challenges, remember the rewards of your work. The biggest reward for me has been to give people a voice and make them feel heard in a safe environment. Once we brought together refugees and Germans who had fled the former German Democratic Republic. The GDR was a socialist and communist dictatorship that existed from 1949 to 1990, when the eastern portion of Germany was part of the Eastern Bloc during the Cold War. Once both sides shared their experiences of fleeing their home and how it had affected their lives, they realized that, after all, "the other side" was not so different from them as they had expected.

What touched me the most in another workshop was to learn that a young refugee had converted to Christianity and could not return to his home country because the death penalty would await him. When his father passed away, his family kept it secret from him so as to avoid making his exile more painful, with the result that one day he learned the news on Facebook from people offering their condolences. Hearing this story was shocking for all of us as it showed not only the effects of being unable to return home but also the associated pain such as having to find out about a loved one's death on social media.

In our story-sharing sessions, people are free to ask anything they want, especially questions that are normally regarded as impolite or too direct: "Why do you sit away from me on the bus?" "Why do you guys talk so loudly in Arabic on the phone? Do you know what that sounds like?" "Are all German songs Nazi songs?" "Why do you think we are terrorists?"

Facilitated dialogue becomes art when people are allowed to ask and say anything they want, within certain rules like not interrupting each other, speaking non-accusatorily, and treating each other respectfully. But delicate questions must be asked to invite deep discussions. Participants find that story-sharing of this kind challenges all of us to really listen, respect, and appreciate people for who they are. In the same room, with the right level of support and vulnerability, it is hard for people to ignore the call to understand one another. Moreover, sharing stories makes the storyteller realize how much their voice matters. Seeing others care about our experiences gives us a sense of validity and dignity. This is incredibly empowering, as we realize that we are not helpless and alone. We appreciate the amount of impact this work can have in people's lives, and how they will go about their daily lives with a different mind-set and new insights on "the other side" than before.

Lessons Learned

From my work I have seen that it is possible to take the knowledge I have obtained to become a conflict resolution professional and apply it to a context where it is needed the most. We should not look away when we see injustice, prejudice, or hatred. In fact, I would argue that it is our responsibility, if not our job, to become justice seekers—not just in the workplace, but in those homes that are at the edge of cities, where neighbors and nations are divided. Dialogue is the only hope we have left in a world that is becoming ever more polarized.

In a time of destruction, create something.

Maxine Hong Kingston

I have learned a great deal about curriculum design and procedures of dialogue work. Of course, it is impossible to create the most ideal story-sharing forum from scratch. It was important to simply do it and fail and then do it better the next time. We are still in the phase of trying what works well and what does not. It is a constant learning experience. For example, we discovered that it is beneficial to include in our workshops the social workers in the shelters, to show that everyone is equally having a learning experience, although there were times when staff members would leave the workshop punctually at six p.m. because their shift was over—discouraging everyone else. However, there were also times when members of the state office for refugee affairs dropped in for a routine visit to one of the shelters and joyfully joined our workshop. Communicating at eye level is key to successful dialogue work. Therefore, we co-train with refugee and nonrefugee facilitators. This has proven to establish profound rapport and initial credibility because our refugee trainers have lived in a similar shelter before and know what conflicts to expect.

I have also learned a lot about managing an organization, which I had never done before. And even in this respect, trust is an essential element. Letting go of trying to control colleagues and trusting that they will manage their tasks to their best capacity is a fundamental skill of mediation but also of leadership. When leading an organization, there will be many times when you doubt your mission: remember your "why" and keep going. At the end of the day, it is the experience and goodwill that counts. You will never fully understand everything about promoting conflict resolution and dialogue work in areas where it is needed the most. There will always be questions and answers that yet have to be discovered. Just to name a few that I am still trying to uncover beyond my story-sharing work: Can all cultural barriers be resolved—are they all reconcilable? Do female and male refugees need different mediation methods? To what extent can peer mediation work in the long run?

To an aspiring lawyer, mediator, and social entrepreneur, I would say this. The work is not easy, but it is rewarding and it is an adventure. You will never be bored, as you can never fully know what to expect. Remember your "why." Do not be afraid to fail. It is always more fulfilling to try making peace than to close your eyes before injustice. Caring is a choice.

As conflict resolution professionals, we all have in common that we want to make peace. That means we need to ask ourselves: "Where am I needed the most, and what can I do to contribute to change?" To quote Abraham Lincoln, "As a peacemaker the lawyer has a superior opportunity of being a good man. There will still be business enough." If you can identify that *opportunity* and niche for yourself, you will create a bigger purpose for your own life by adding more value and purpose to the lives of many others.

NOTES

1. Judy and all other participants' names in this chapter have been changed.
2. Helen Winter, "Sharing What Divides Us," Harvard Negotiation & Mediation Clinical Program, March 27, 2019, http://hnmcp.law.harvard.edu/hnmcp/blog/sharing-what-divides-us/.
3. Alison Abbott, "The Mental-Health Crisis among Migrants," *Nature*, October 10, 2016, https://www.nature.com/news/the-mental-health-crisis-among-migrants-1.20767.
4. Brené Brown is a research professor at the University of Houston and the author of five number-one *New York Times* bestsellers.
5. Brené Brown, "The Power of Vulnerability," TED Talk, July 8, 2019, https://www.ted.com/talks/brene_brown_on_vulnerability.

CHAPTER 5

Productive Confrontation

Challenging Privilege, Power, and Access

Mary Dumas and Marina Piscolish

Step into a group's culture—their hierarchies, power struggles, policies, norms, and practices—and you enter a river of long-flowing history. As facilitators and mediators, we understand that these features have been in place long before we arrived. Our ability to assist clients with meaningful change is defined by our effectiveness in helping them discern and constructively confront often unseen, undiscussable, and unsustainable aspects of their environment.

Conflict and change practitioners can responsibly employ conflict intervention roles and skills while supporting others to confront persistent injustices that bind people, organizations, and communities to painful practices and unjust pasts, impeding access to a healthier future.

How did we come to work this way? Our shared commitment to culturally responsive and socially responsible ways of working evolved for each of us as an independent and often solitary process over our thirty-plus-year careers. Our approach might be described as "diving deep in a shallow pool," given that clients often understate the complexity of issues at play in their situation. This tendency to minimize the work sometimes occurs because people don't realize the complexity of their situation. Other times,

Mary Dumas

Marina Piscolish

it is because, as we all know, the truth can be quite disruptive before it sets you free.

Power and justice issues are often best dealt with directly, explicitly, and transparently, asking conflict practitioners to lift heavy conversations. At other times, we can reimagine our field's best practices to deftly introduce and address systemic injustice during facilitated processes, indirectly and experientially.

For example, in work with both Hawaiian-focused and non-Hawaiian-focused groups, distinct cultural contexts were revealed when moving in and out of these settings. Noteworthy differences in "normal" meeting routines arose, with Hawaiian gatherings most often beginning with mindful preparations before ever turning to an actual agenda: prayer, ample food, honoring ancestors, expressions of gratitude for the land and gathering place, robust personal introductions . . . and only then, the agenda. In typical non-Hawaiian organizations, far less attention to context-setting and personal connection happened. Agenda review follows the welcome and introductions, each treated efficiently. Ground rules, if addressed, often feel hurried. Agendas reveal cultural values and inevitably privilege certain people, leaving some right at home and others quite far from home.

These reflections led to a practice innovation to begin any gathering. Create space for people to enter not just intellectually, but emotionally and spiritually as well. Design secular, culturally accessible ways to be connected from the start. Elevate passion, purpose, and the power of relationships. Encourage creativity, humility, perspective, and a sense of serving a cause greater than ourselves. All can benefit from this practice, and some actually need it to be fully present. With responsive and responsible design, "just an agenda" can become an agenda for justice.

Unattended persistent friction in groups, organizations, and communities creates social and cultural crosscurrents, stirs up tensions, and brings institutional imperfections to the surface. To address these forces, we ask hard questions in assessments and use a trauma-informed approach. We first take the group's pulse, assess their collective courage for hard conversations, and then let them lead the way. People in complex settings benefit from incremental reflections, allowing time to listen and learn. Reflections intentionally, and sometimes unintentionally, activate issues that some would prefer stay buried or at least left outside the room.

Our careers have been spent translating the twin aspirations of "culturally responsive" and "socially responsible" into powerful process designs and group experiences with transformative potential. We have found practical tools for these tough conversations and powerful rules for responsible engagement, no matter the issue, or where you sit at the table.

NAVIGATING THE ORIGINS OF CHANGE

We met well into our conflict resolution careers while attending a conference. Happy coincidence or destiny, who knows? Minutes into our conversation, we knew we were kindred souls. We'd found another "facilitation nerd"! A shared niche in intercultural, deliberative, healing practices; reputations for productive confrontation of justice-related issues with clients and colleagues; and a change management orientation were revealed. A common thread—interest in and applied study of whole systems and complex change— emerged from our distinctly different paths to this work, products of early lives and formal education. Regardless, we arrived at a very similar place, as nonaffiliated private conflict engagement practitioners, innovating practice and taking risks born of deeply held beliefs and value-based intentions.

MARINA'S ORIGIN STORY

My commitment to engaging conflict grew out of my interest in justice. It explains why I don't separate good facilitation from advocacy. Born in the '60s, I came of age in the 1970s. Enough said, right? Sure, I am a product of my times. But my passions were shaped by where and how I was raised, not just when.

Sunday Mass, extended family, and traditional food and music made Nonna's house feel more like Italy than a coal-mining village in western Pennsylvania. My grandparents immigrated in the early 1900s. I was born to fairly old parents, aged forty and forty-eight.

Both lived through the Great Depression and experienced early-twentieth-century anti-immigrant prejudice. My grandfathers, uncles, and my own father also knew the risks of trying to unionize the coal miners. These stories of struggle, told and retold, were lessons in empathy, cultural identity, and assimilation. We walked with "double consciousness" before it was a thing. I grew up in a home where justice mattered; so said my family, my faith, and my country. It defined me.

At sixteen, I flew to Cali, Colombia, as an exchange student. Like most travel, it offered contrasts in sameness and difference. Dramatic differences were my struggles to speak and be understood; a live-in maid, confined to a tiny room near the kitchen, who saw her children one afternoon each week; country club membership; and a beautiful home where every evening we shooed away beggars, their babies in arms, saying, "We have nothing!" I felt the weight of the world's unjust social systems, and for the first time, I felt complicit. It changed me.

I became a social studies teacher, passionate about empowering children to change this world. During my first year, a single conversation drove me to find my truer calling. One afternoon I dropped by the principal's office to share my plans for a powerful, fun learning experience involving three teachers and our combined classes. I shared this as a courtesy (OK, maybe as a humble brag), only to hear, "Permission denied!" Dumbfounded, I asked what aspect of the project he found disagreeable. As I persisted for an explanation, he sputtered, "We've never done that before! If you do something never done before, other people will want to do things we've never done. I can't have that!" I departed speechless, my students' needs unmet. Shaking, I knew in that moment that I needed skills and courage to challenge the status quo when power is centralized and change is unwelcome. I realized the inevitability of conflict.

A forty-hour mediation course crystallized my purpose: to proselytize that conflict is an opportunity for positive change. Eventually I pursued a Ph.D., studying (1) conflict, (2) complex organizations, and (3) change. Professional conflict and collaboration services would be a Trojan Horse, inviting democracy to hierarchy à la Dewey,[1] shifting organizations' cultures from places of "power over" to places of "power with."[2] My formative work in school systems expanded to other complex systems, including the environment, health care, higher education, government, nonprofits, and cross-sector efforts.

Only later did my understanding of trauma-informed approaches develop, after I relocated to Hawaii. I arrived in Hawaii in the 1990s, a decade marking the hundredth anniversary of the illegal overthrow of the Hawaiian Kingdom, an inflection point in identity consciousness and civil rights activism. My long-standing concern for power and justice expanded to address legacy harms. I learned how to work where the past is always present.[3] Historic, intergenerational trauma and its resulting institutionalized systemic harms became the backdrop for my work in the Pacific. It challenged me.

My primary tools for understanding injustice and trauma were empathy; intellect; and political, philosophic, and moral reasoning. Not until I encountered trauma firsthand, embodied and direct, would I more fully appreciate the struggle required to reclaim life, regain a sense of personal safety, and trust in resilience. Life would soon afford me several such growth opportunities. Deaths, public betrayals, private abandonment, natural disasters, being a victim of crime, and knowing the shame of being scammed each made a dramatic appearance in my life. All occurred over a short time, leaving me with a clinically treatable case of post-traumatic stress disorder (PTSD). This was the education I was missing. The post-traumatic growth challenge became clear: how to remain open and capable of authentic connection while discerning danger and responding to risk. Now I bring this awareness to each engagement. With gratitude, I recognize that what didn't kill me truly made me stronger . . . and, I believe, a better practitioner.

We must accept finite disappointment, but never lose infinite hope.
MARTIN LUTHER KING JR.

MARY'S ORIGIN STORY

I arrived in this world with the attentiveness of a middle child, an observer, and thinker. Our family of seven's version of 1960s Americana took place in Wisconsin amidst the aura of Lombardi's Green Bay Packers football. Slogans like "The measure of who we are is what we do with what we have" and echoes of Catholic Latin Mass rang in my head. I was drawn toward the mystery of humans, holiness, and groups aspiring to create something wholesome together.

Early observation of the dissonance between stated, collective goals and actual impacts was fueled by study of the Holy Wars in grade four and a changing world around me:

- Nixon's presidency and Watergate echoed in the background of dinner for what seemed like an eternity—we need transparency and good people to govern right.
- Feminists cheered on Billie Jean King as she shut Bobby Riggs up once and for all—how is female competence *still* a question?
- Sister Rita, my eighty-plus-year-old Latin teacher, introduced me to the Four Noble Truths of Buddhism—so many just and kind paths to peace in this world.

Early questions of equity arose from direct experiences, as my family did not talk about race or class. Family trips to Texas, back when youngsters could fly free, were timed with lambing season at our maternal grandparents' home. The creek out back had poisonous snakes to tame our troop of Midwesterners. Yet we passed black children playing there on our way to the "whites only" swimming pool on the other side. Our grandparents' black housekeeper, who'd accompany us to the ice-cream parlor but not inside, did not answer questions, nor did my parents.

I was a girl athlete before Title IX came into law, experiencing firsthand the impacts of federal policy. As a secondhand observer of abusive priests and the church's ineffectual systems for dealing with them, I was aware far too young of the misogyny bred by entitled males and double standards of conduct, ethics, and consequences. A childhood steeped in practices of solitude, moral review, and reading saved me from a far more cynical state. Weekly bike pilgrimages across the Fox River Bridge provided a journey through predictable seasons of the natural world and a lifetime library habit.

Early study of contemplative practices continued as I completed community college and watched Howard Gardner's theory of multiple intelligences[4] emerge as I worked as a hired caregiver of infant twins and toddlers. Tibetan Buddhist teachers provided instruction in mental development practices. Shamatha, a concentration meditation, came first, shortly after the death of my first child. My life had emptied rather quickly of fantasies, false hopes, friends, and even family as it tumbled through the aftermath of sudden infant death. Instruction in being with emptiness along with daily practice supported the deep morphology of change my family experienced. So began a lifetime of learning how to stabilize a nonjudgmental awareness and a brave, kind view that faces confusion and suffering rather than turns away.

Procedural justice centered my continuing study as a young, working mother. My undergraduate degree in psychology integrated: (1) human development, (2) trauma and its impacts across the life span, and (3) intercultural peacemaking practices. Multiparty cases came into focus when I served as chair of a volunteer group leading a small library expansion. Over two years we negotiated with the small city, a countywide library system, and the library users, including hippies from the hills, multicultural students, and small-town founding fathers. When all was said and done, the city planner tapped me on the shoulder asking for my card; I took the hint. Decades of volunteer service in domestic abuse shelters and criminal courts quickly expanded my mediation practice into public safety and health collaboration initiatives, first as a professional facilitator and later as a county-appointed domestic violence commissioner. Multiparty initiatives, trauma-informed organizational change, and collaborative leadership training remain the core of my private practice thirty years later.

I stay inspired by working with other creative navigators of power to identify just alternatives to the status quo. As a lifelong learner, I am motivated by the call for a universal language of trauma-informed group work. Our current callout culture needs a new vocabulary to caution people on the limits of "power over" models of change and inspire pathways as co-learners. We all have the means to inspire shifts toward using "power with" principles and strategies at home, work, and community.

Reflective Practices That Guide Our Way of Working

*Anyone can become angry—that is easy, but to be angry
with the right person at the right time, and for the right
purpose and in the right way—that is not easy.*
—Aristotle

Mindful conflict is being aware of and attentive to parallel processes of recognizing exposed systemic social justice issues, i.e., the "ghosts at the table,"[5] and discerning possible responses given the group's tasks, purpose, and agency. Although this can be scary, there are powerful and effective ways to make room for "ghosts" through assessment, preparation, and ongoing awareness. A relaxed focus and willingness to speak up are required when productive confrontation of critical issues is called for. Intervention can be designed to open up brave moments for client agency and choice.

In writing this chapter, we independently reflected on our best practices based on wide-ranging experiences with public, private, nonprofit, research, and interjurisdictional and interdisciplinary collaboration efforts. Incredibly, we discovered several shared defining practices:

- Engage client from inspiration through implementation and build capacity using a developmental approach.
- Consider impacts of complexity and power dynamics within a whole-system orientation.
- Assert the value of a solid assessment.
- Be willing to take risks on matters of justice, equity, and access.
- Apply a trauma-informed, mindful conflict approach.

These practices function as mental floss when a system's complexity, history, current fears, or pain swamp the group's ability to think about alternatives. Matters of justice, equity, fairness, and access are approached directly, explicitly, as part of the substantive deliberations. Or they can be approached indirectly and experientially, through design and modeling of ethical or "just processes" that afford participants an experience in procedural fairness, equalizing power and access. Both explicit and experiential approaches have their place in a conflict resolution practice.

Practice 1. Engage Clients from Inspiration through Implementation and Build Capacity Using a Developmental Approach

Start with the end in mind to understand the group's aspirations and intended impact. Clients are asked to imagine their future after the facilitated process is concluded in order to anticipate the conditions in which the change will live after we're gone. Our developmental approach meets leaders where they are and supports evolution from cautious, to hopeful, to courageous.

It's not unpatriotic to denounce an injustice committed on our behalf, perhaps it's the most patriotic thing we can do.

E.A. BUCCHIANERI

Commitment to working in a socially responsible way means looking out for long-term success and ways to increase their ROI (return on investment). Systems change over time; people who learn and reflect together grow together. A developmental capacity-building approach supports systemic change by preparing people for new roles, responsibilities, and relationships. Clients often contract with us for a combination of synergistic interventions to address issues upstream and downstream from the immediate focus, including (1) facilitated problem-solving; (2) mediation of discrete conflicts; (3) capacity building to enable collaboration and constructive confrontation of conflict; and (4) institutionalization of structural changes in collaboration, conflict management, or stakeholder engagement practices.

"Stewardship planning" models responsible change management and creates a viable landing place for the ongoing work. The importance of institutionalizing an agreement, innovation, or change cannot be overlooked. A conversation about who will steward this effort as it moves forward beyond the participants' tenure, and how that stewardship will actually occur, ideally leads to a concrete plan outlining shared leadership and accountability systems. A practical, "big picture" approach is aspirational because sometimes a client relationship will span years, election cycles, and retirements of participants.

Marina's Illustration

A community college anticipated turnover of top-tier leaders. A facilitated retreat was held to address their concerns. It resulted in a shared commitment to attract, recruit, and retain next-generation leaders. Executive leaders invited emerging leaders to a two-day skills training session called "Constructive Confrontation, Collaboration, Consensus Building and Conflict Resolution." Immediately following, they practiced consensus-building on a high-stakes issue, a campus-wide reorganization. Along the way, related conflicts had to be mediated.

To build a "deep bench" of capable leaders committed to a healthy campus and campus culture, time and sustained effort are required; thus institutionalization. They redesigned leadership meetings to incorporate a collaborative style and a new permanent program to support emerging leaders. A continued executive coaching and expanded skills training all contributed to a culture shift.

A comprehensive, phased approach allows momentum and energy for the work to build from within the organization. Organized into discrete tasks as several small, outcome-oriented contracts, these iterative conversations promote consciousness about accomplishments and, most importantly, renew commitment. If groups are going to dive deep, we feel best when they choose it little by little, again and again.

Practice 2. Consider Impacts of Complexity and Power Dynamics with a Whole-System Orientation

People are often uncomfortable with complex projects that require sustained cooperation, much less consensus. Be forewarned: When practitioners work in large organizational systems or across multiple jurisdictions, people talk about power—the power they have, the power others have, and the power they want others to use on their behalf. *This is not whining.* It reflects scouting for assistance, mustering courage, and agency.

A whole-system approach[6] puts power and politics in clear view for all, early and often. The facts regarding a group's collective power, and its limits, help name tensions that may not be fully understood or appreciated by all. Cooperative teams within and across organizations can productively grapple with frustrations on their way to break through strategies *if* they recognize and use their shared power and its limits, with collective interests and goals in mind.

Mary's Illustration

A patient-centered health care project was designed to help hospitals and community partners prepare for upcoming financial changes under the Affordable Care Act. Specifically, reimbursements for "unnecessary" patient readmissions, within thirty days of hospital discharge, would be reduced or eliminated. This critical stage of recovery involved many parties making misunderstandings and complications costly, medically speaking and financially. A facilitated process to define "unnecessary readmissions" and then reduce their occurrence across departments brought together multiple providers.

The leadership team worked with clinical experts and mixed departmental teams to invent, conduct, and analyze "real tests of change" in sixty- to ninety-day cycles. It was essential to understand and appreciate the performance limits of each part of the system. Unsustainable ideas had to be tossed. Staff needed to speak up quickly to those in power to ensure viable interventions. Over an eighteen-month period departmental teams identified trends and the business office analyzed cost patterns. The leadership team tested strategies of care across institutions. Sharable metrics defined new norms for a seamless, thirty-day intervention delivered following discharge, no matter the setting.

Most people enter into collaborative endeavors to align their resources and goals with others and leverage success. When we're lucky, it's a creative, growth-enhancing experience for all. A whole-system approach requires a sustainable mechanism to share knowledge and support peer-to-peer learning, especially in the early years.

Practice 3. Assert the Value of a Solid Assessment

It can be tough to speak up about organizational issues or invite help with a complex change. The act of seeking outside support is courageous because it involves risk. It also takes considerable trust to invite another to help navigate an important juncture or difficult transition. Let's face it, if we do our job right as mediators and facilitators, no matter what exactly the job is, we "stir the pot." We open spaces for new conversations and give people permission to speak their truth.

Our ability to reason has not given us special status, only a greater responsibility.

JOSEPH M. MARSHALL III

If there is a singular, special thing that explains why clients engage as deeply as they do, it is likely our use of assessments to understand the context and situation before recommending work to be done or committing our involvement. Without adequate assessment, we risk failing to understand the need. Our clients risk treating the problem's symptoms rather than the problem's root cause.

An assessment helps us understand the depth of the pool into which we are considering diving, without having to rely on the client's account, sometimes fraught with subjectivity, delusion, or even deception. The assessment activates honesty about their condition and imagination about the consequence of both action and inaction. Clients consider contradictions, confusion, conflations, and concerns. Initial resistance to an assessment is understandable given fear of costs, both material and psychological. We find ways of working with that resistance, meeting clients where they are, taking them to where the answers might lie . . . in an assessment.

Assessments are needed whether the client is asking for mediation, facilitation, coaching, or training; it is an ethical duty. It's our best assurance that we are being culturally responsive and socially responsible: not wasting their time or money; building rather than eroding trust or adding to ill will between the parties. Past processes conducted poorly can produce cynical individuals and organizational sagas. We don't want to repeat such harms.

Mary's Illustration

After a decade of service to a human resources department, including all-staff trainings in stress management and negotiation, a "next-level" conversation was requested—facilitated help to improve processes and put new communication skills to the test. Private interviews were conducted to identify any "ghosts" and how best to introduce them to the table. Participants created diagrams of power they had (both perceived and actual); these pre-assessments were conducted with union and unrepresented staff, supervisors, managers, and department heads. In the session, we created a timeline naming impactful events and changes. Curiosity was piqued; discussions deepened as tensions eased. This frank, collective "retelling" of recognized myths and mastery emerged from unattributed sticky notes organized by participants into themes, in real time. Twenty years later, the department director marveled about its lasting impact on repairing trust in staff relationships across their complex system.

Individual memories are fractals of a group's full experience. Small shimmers can shake loose new ways of seeing old situations. Once the intergenerational truths of their organizational life are told in common language, the assessment, a group can recollect its past and forecast the decade ahead with accountability to the shared legacy they intend.

Practice 4. Be Willing to Take Risks on Matters of Justice, Equity, Access, and Fairness

> By creating practices and structures that allow for diversity of voices, we promote the engagement of those who are often left out or marginalized in decision making processes, and in so doing, we contribute to social change.
> —BERNIE MAYER[7]

Generally speaking, if we see something, smell something, or hear something important to the work, we feel compelled to say something. That's often the start of our most important client conversation. With mutual consent and under the right conditions, we help groups recognize issues of power and privilege at play, consider their consequences, explore healthy alternatives to the status quo, and then support implementation of agreed-upon changes. Caution and discernment are key given the risks involved. So, being prepared is critical to seeing and seizing the opportunity. Client reluctance or unwillingness to address issues of consequence will cause us to communicate our concerns. If concerns go unheeded, we rethink our involvement.

Marina's Illustration

Routinely, across the Pacific, stakeholders representing diverse places, cultures, scientific or technical expertise, and government authorities travel great distances and invest considerable time and effort, at significant cost to the convener, and thereby, the American taxpayer. These events are mostly deemed successful if they deliver a tangible outcome, an agreement. But too often, agreements are abandoned before implementation: Plans prove impractical materially, politically, culturally, or technically. This realization raised questions about the ethics of facilitating such work in the future.

Eventually another region-wide meeting was being convened. But this time, before agreeing to being involved, after taking a deep breath, Marina found the courage to express concerns. It was suggested that these processes should deliver a higher ROI. Observations were made that many past plans failed to implement because complex challenges of "the system," the stakeholders' reality, were not addressed. For the most privileged, these challenges were largely unrecognized. For the least privileged, they were undiscussable. Unaddressed, inauthentic conversations delivered unrealistic outcomes. If more lasting impacts were desired, things should be done differently.

Pushback was anticipated. The funder asked, "How would you propose we do it differently?" Our alternative: help people "experience" empathy about their differences; better appreciate systemic challenges and structural injustices; and strengthen shared group commitment to a level playing field. This appreciative accounting of community values, natural resources, leadership, and traditional cultural knowledge and practices would prepare the group for braver conversations, to include talk of present-day oppressive practices, and the "ghosts." As a result of this more culturally responsive and socially responsible design, more viable solutions would emerge.

The advice was heeded; viable solutions emerged. The "disruptive design" produced this telling participant comment: "We do indeed have access to resources now. I have a great sense of inclusiveness, trust and gratitude; a certainty that we will succeed." This Pacific-wide effort survives today, fourteen years later.

Practice 5. Apply a Trauma-Informed and Mindful Conflict Approach

> *Organizational trauma and traumatization may result from a single devastating event, several deleterious events over time, or from the cumulative impact arising from the nature of the organization's work.*
> —PAT VIVIAN AND SHANA HORMANN[8]

Trauma occurs at multiple scales and can be experienced individually and collectively. Perceived failures and actual injustices are tangled together. Ignorance and apathy place painful insights in the dark. Over time, silence incubates perceptions, and the stories we tell to put our minds at rest can create cultures of "strengths and shadows" in organizations[9] and communities.

Even with the most thorough assessment and preengagement discussions, uncomfortable truths, real harms, and missed opportunities remain. People and organizations grapple with new laws, new policies, and changing norms. Impatience and skepticism about change can signify delayed, impeded justice or unresolved trauma. Figure 5.1 (p. 86) outlines a trauma-informed framework to conceptualize the group's network of rules, relationships, and prior harms. Highly charged issues, unwelcome by some, require facilitators to pause and challenge rigid status quo or oversimplified thinking and model deep listening to concerns, new and old. The examples in steps 1 to 5 describe a series of scientific information projects to improve freshwater resource data and models[10] implemented by two Native American tribes, state and local governments, public agencies, advisory groups, water purveyors, agriculture watershed improvement districts, and citizen-scientists long at the water negotiating table in Washington state. This type of hyper-structured, government-to-government project spans jurisdictions and professional disciplines. Accessible, usable information was needed by each entity in order to chart a self-determined course of action and contribute to meaningful cooperation on watershed improvements.

- *Step 1:* Get participants more comfortable with being co-learners and leaders. Early on, participants led watershed tours and exchanged information on endangered species, policies, and best practices. Introductory face-to-face encounters and surveys improved cooperation on future step 4 data collection and modeling efforts.

- *Step 2:* Clarify complexity to reduce the heat. Create a single text document that summarizes the legal local, state, federal, and tribal context of the issues. The "State of the Watershed Report" featured historical conditions, traditional practices, and explained in common language how changes in law and policies impact land management, water use, and current conditions.

- *Step 3:* Provide briefings on constraining mandates and flexibilities. Regulatory pain is a common concern. Small courtesies go a long way. Agencies on both sides of the international border invited comment on changing water regulations. Meeting schedules honored planting and fishing cycles, and opportunities for technical review and comment created familiarity with each other's concerns and constraints.

- *Step 4:* Data don't make decisions; people do. Parties considered collective long-term, practical information needs and addressed current pressures with small, tactical data improvements. Surveys allow for quiet, private time to consider new information needs. Shared knowledge was gathered, analyzed, and applied in demonstration projects. Improved understanding and shared effort contributed toward negotiated agreements on limited issues in smaller geographic areas.

- *Step 5:* Name the ghosts at the table and set a place for them. We all have a past, including prior project failures. Our stress responses, mental thoughts, and behaviors can become habituated through early training (upbringing and professional) and fall into patterned roles and conduct. Unstructured time preceding and following meetings, workshops, and private sessions provided parties the chance to name harms and apply new information to illustrate concerns. Assumptions, tested in smaller basin-by-basin interventions, contributed to the co-creation of improved scientific understanding, and ongoing deliberations.

Trauma, like conflict, can occur along scales and transcend generations. Traumatic events can leave legacy impacts in bodies, minds, group systems, and geographic places that perpetuate after the original harm occurred. Facilitators can create openings for the hubris of denial to stop via acknowledgments, however small or grand. Trauma, like conflict, must be accounted for when conducting conflict assessments, designing collaborative engagement processes. Be sure to account for trauma before creating space to call justice issues into focus.

IT'S ABOUT JUSTICE, AND IT'S ABOUT TIME

Conflict and collaboration practitioners are in the privileged position to help facilitate learning and reflection, and, where appropriate, to allow parties recurring opportunities to choose a new path, as they learn and discern, together. Social responsibility requires us to acknowledge differing status, unequal power or access, corrosive norms of privilege, and the effects of trauma, whether contemporary or historic. Cultural responsiveness requires that interventions recognize participants' ways of being and doing things. The longevity of this field requires that conflict resolution practitioners arrive with the skills needed to engage clients in their highest intentions, while addressing injustices that could compromise the quality, impact, and sustainability of their efforts.

While explicit attention to injustices may be called for, much can be accomplished by designing processes that challenge the status quo, experientially. We can temporarily interrupt structural privilege and patterned oppressions when we design and facilitate "just processes" modeling best practices that address fairness, access, and procedural justice. Participants experience a new normal (however brief) where habituated privilege and oppression dynamics are altered. These reasonably safe, discreet, direct experiences, supported with guided reflection, can create shift. Courage and conviction often follow awareness and insight.

Equally important in this work is the art of crafting useful, durable agreements that embed lasting improvements in structures and systems. These written products capture the collective will and way forward, allowing the group to implement change while managing conflict with increased confidence and competence.

Because awareness comes in waves, collectively value those tiny shifts in perspective, emerging insights, and near agreements. Recognize information gaps and unfinished business as openings for future engagement. Honor output from prior discussions so they are not lost or buried. Our processes mark the ways traveled. When the conditions are ripe, the people are ready, and the data arrives, we see groups reengage over shared causes and needed improvements. At the time of our engagement's closure, we trust clients are more conscious and capable of sustaining their important work.

Justice and injustice indeed begins and ends with the self.

Syed Muhammad Naquib al-Attas

START HERE ➡

STEP 1 Name purpose of collaboration.

Develop regional water resource plan update

What changes, challenges and opportunities could be/will be investigated, implemented and/or evaluated?

Identify motivators for changing status quo (e.g., environmental threshold, update, human, fiscal resource change (+/-).

STEP 5 Name the ghosts at the table and invite them.
Identify efforts to raise attention to the issue, prior change initiatives, unresolved truth, justice and reconciliations.
Those impacted and their surviving descendant.

STEP 2. Identify legal precedents and appeals.

Clarify defined mandates, standards or thresholds.

List transparently all duties of care related to today's collaboration opportunities.

Setting the table for sustained collaboration on complex issues

STEP 4. Identify relevant, available data appropriate for the outcome.

Identify what is "knowable" about the issue. Data don't make decisions, people do!

Assess current conditions, known constraints, and prior efforts to learn and/or improve the system.

STEP 3. Identify regulations, mandates (codes, policies) and existing contracts.

Identify related local, state, national, tribal regulation(s) related to the issue, geographic place or service area and intended changes to status quo.

FMI on trauma-informed approaches to sustained engagement contact

Mary Dumas
democracy@
dumas-assoc.com

Figure 5.1. Trauma-informed facilitation: setting the table for sustained engagement on complex issues

These are scary, exciting, and fast-changing times. Our field is being called to engage societies' most serious challenges. Social justice is no longer a near-taboo topic among conflict resolvers at respectable professional gatherings. This is a welcome shift that we enthusiastically support. Hopefully, we all find the courage, conviction, and creative imagination needed to create braver spaces where people work together to right wrongs, challenge the status quo, and build a better, brighter, more just future, for all.

NOTES

1. John Dewey, "Democracy and Educational Administration," in *John Dewey: The Later Works 1925–1953*, Vol. 11: 1935–1937, edited by Jo Ann Boydston (Carbondale: Southern Illinois University Press, 1987), 217–225.

2. Seth Kreisberg, *Transforming Power: Domination, Empowerment and Education* (Albany: State University of New York Press, 1992).

3. Marina Piscolish et al., "Righting Un-rightable Wrongs: Finding the Courage of Our Convictions," presented at the annual meeting for the Association for Conflict Resolution, Denver, Colorado, June 12, 2005.

4. Howard Gardner, *Frames of Mind: The Theory of Multiple Intelligences* (New York: Basic Books, 2011).

5. Mary Dumas, *Toolz for Tough Conversations Instructors' Manual* (Everson, WA: Dumas & Associates, Inc., 2018), Fig. 1, "Trauma-informed facilitation: setting the table for sustained engagement on complex issues."

6. Stafford Beer, *Brain of the Firm*, 2nd ed. (New York: Herder and Herder, 1981); Susan Carpenter and W.J. Kennedy, *Managing Public Disputes: A Practical Guide for Government, Business, and Citizen Groups* (New York: John Wiley & Sons, 2001); Louise Diamond and Ambassador John McDonald, *Multi-Track Diplomacy: A Systems Approach to Peace* (New York: Kumarian Press, 1996); A.M. Turk and J. Ungerleider, "Experiential Activities in Mediation-Based Training: Cyprus, 1997–2013," *Conflict Resolution Quarterly* 34(3), 281–300.

7. Bernard S. Mayer, *Beyond Neutrality: Confronting the Crisis in Conflict Resolution* (San Francisco: Jossey Bass Publishing, 2004), 168.

8. Pat Vivian and Shana Hormann, *Organizational Trauma and Healing* (North Charleston, SC: CreateSpace, 2013).

9. Ibid, 128.

10. C. Bandaragoda et al., "Lower Nooksack Water Budget (LNWB)," 2019, HydroShare under Creative Commons License, http://www.hydroshare.org/resource/d15b9934f34e4c57913b3cb53966d5c7.

CHAPTER 6

Blazing Trails for Justice in Politics and Governance

RACHEL BARBOUR

I WAS ONLY SIX YEARS OLD, BUT I CAN STILL RECALL THE DRYNESS of the dirt, the overcast sky, and the heat of the day. It was 1974 and we lived in Starkville, Mississippi. That day at school, on the playground, I heard a teacher use the N-word. It disturbed me. My parents had modeled social justice and fairness, even though I cannot recall any conversations about race and injustice. So, on that day in Starkville, I knew in my heart what I heard was terribly wrong, and on some level, I was aware of the injustice around me. As a kid, I always rooted for the underdog, and as an adult, I work to stand up for those who are marginalized and those who face daily indignities based on their identities.

Rachel Barbour

After two years in the south, I spent the rest of my childhood in a largely white, conservative, military community in Ohio. We subscribed to two newspapers a day, and I started watching the nightly news with my dad when I was nine. It was "our thing," and my parents encouraged debate and discussion regarding what we watched and read. Living in such a conservative community, my political activism blossomed and I developed a reputation over the years with my teachers as the "token liberal" who would speak out. In high school, my government teacher often called on me so the class could hear "the other side" of whatever current event we were discussing.

I spent the summer before my senior year at Mount Holyoke College in a rural village in Kenya, documenting oral history for a local cultural center. I interviewed elders about traditional crafts that were being lost because of the impact of missionaries and urbanization. I lived without electricity and running water, and saw a level of poverty I had not seen before. I also learned a bit what it felt like to be in the minority. While I did not experience culture shock when I arrived in Kenya, I felt it profoundly when I came home. I was overwhelmed by the materialism and superficiality of our culture and became angry at friends who were not interested or curious about the world around them. While the term "white privilege" was not used back then, I was angry and frustrated by the lack of awareness of how good so many people's lives were. Some friendships shifted, some ended, and I became far more personally invested in social and political conflict. It was a very difficult time personally.

I spent my senior year working with new friends to force the college administration to terminate its contract with Coca-Cola, as they were still economically involved in apartheid South Africa. We disrupted a meeting of the college trustees so they would understand the depth of our commitment, we protested vocally on campus to gain media attention, and our student government association reached out to student groups at other colleges. Our efforts brought Coca-Cola executives to our campus in an effort to stop the spread of our boycott. I learned the power of strategy and coalition-building, as the boycotts did spread to other campuses, causing Coke to fully withdraw from South Africa. It was my first experience with successful grassroots organizing.

Six years later, I entered the master's program at the Institute for Conflict Analysis and Resolution (ICAR) at George Mason University. My coursework was deeply influenced by the legacy of moral activism of James Laue, whose civil rights work was legendary, and the community work of my advisor Wallace Warfield. I learned to analyze systems, structures, needs, power, and culture and to understand how each shapes conflict and guides intervention. Classmates and I debated neutrality, and I concluded that it is largely a myth. No one can divorce themselves from their backgrounds, values, experiences, or biases. As practitioners, we need to remain vigilant about how each may influence our practice, but we cannot remove them from our analysis of conflict. Further, the concept of neutrality does not address the dynamics of power and power imbalances, except to reinforce the status quo.

My fieldwork, under the guidance of Professor Warfield, also showed me the importance of *multipartiality*:

> Multipartiality, in contrast to being neutral, refers to being clear on one's own affiliations and understandings of the conflict at stake. Even more, it calls for making sure that all sides are equally heard and taken along. This is particularly demanding in asymmetric conflicts, where one side usually would dominate the discourse, expecting the other side to buy into a deal over negotiated concessions. Yet, the needs of other stakeholders might involve a broader view on the root causes and implications of the conflict and therefore a more fundamental process for conflict transformation. Here, the role of a facilitator or mediator is not to take sides or solely to become the advocate of those marginalised and disadvantaged. It is rather to help parties change perspective by pointing at the long-term vision of a negotiated settlement and the need for an inclusive process to accommodate all sides.[1]

Under Professor Warfield's guidance, three other students and I conducted a yearlong assessment of community conflict in South Arlington, Virginia, as it emerged through the use of the county recreation centers. We conducted observations and interviews of all of the parties. Based on our findings, we developed an intervention strategy rooted in multipartiality that accounted for the inherent power imbalances, racial biases, and cultural conflicts embedded in the community. I still believe this type of analysis and intervention strategy is most effective in addressing conflict.

I used to describe my entry into politics as a departure from the field of conflict resolution, but that could not be further from the truth. In reality, my decisions about where and how I work are heavily influenced by my education at George Mason University as well as the values instilled in me as a child. I chose to work at Trailblazers PAC because it requires activism in a cause I believe in; it integrates a multipartiality framework and provides opportunities to promote procedural justice in elections and governance.

One of the penalties for refusing to participate in politics is that you end up being governed by your inferiors.

PLATO

Trailblazers PAC is a national, nonpartisan organization with a mission "to move politics out of the back room and onto the front porch" by challenging leaders of any party to act better than our broken money-in-politics system.[2] While we don't use the terms "procedural justice," "procedural fairness," or "process advocate" in describing our work, that is exactly what we advocate for—making it possible for all citizens, regardless of political views, to meaningfully participate in elections and governance.

We mentor, train, and endorse candidates who run for county-level office and below, who are committed to running on a platform of transparency and clean government. We define transparency as the act of making available anything that is related to government. Clean government is one that acts responsibly and responsively and is accountable and accessible to its citizens. The process of clean government means that leaders share decision-making with other elected officials and voters. Our candidates must embrace these concepts throughout the course of their races and implement them if elected. We decided from the start that Trailblazers PAC must be nonpartisan, as no political party has a monopoly on clean government. The impact of dark money on both elections and governance affects everyone, so ideally, we want all candidates, regardless of party, to meet the Trailblazers PAC standards.

To be considered for endorsement, our candidates must meet five criteria, which represent a significant departure from the traditional model of campaigning. They are:

1. *Have a treasurer and bank account independent from any political party.* We want candidates to have full control over their own money.

2. *Disclose 100 percent of their donations during the course of their campaign.* Even in states with relatively strict disclosure laws, donations below a certain threshold are exempt, enabling local candidates with smaller budgets to legally not disclose most of what they raise.

3. *Fundraise donations from at least 1 percent of all voting households in their district.* Typically, candidates rely on family and

friends for donations who may not live in the district, choose to self-fund, or have their political party pay their expenses. This leaves voters largely out of the equation. However, if candidates raise funds from voters, they are more likely to get more votes. In our experience, a voter who invests any amount is far more likely to turn out on election day. So, while it is more work to get twenty $5 donations than one $100 donation, for example, the candidate who gets all of the $5 donations has the advantage.

4. *Include a commitment to transparency and clean government in their messaging.* Many of our candidates come from communities where their local government is not accessible to citizens, so a message of transparency and clean government resonates across the political spectrum.

5. *Run in a contested race.* We believe voters deserve a choice in who represents them, so we do not endorse in uncontested races.

Through May 2019, we have trained well over twelve hundred candidates and candidate supporters and more than two hundred sixty people have entered our one-on-one mentorship program. We've endorsed forty-one candidates, with 55 percent winning their races. Not surprisingly, voter turnout increases whenever Trailblazers run.

Our nonpartisan status does not mean that we are neutral in politics. It means that we will support candidates regardless of political affiliation who both meet our criteria and align with our clean government values. Being nonpartisan makes our work more effective, as we are able to leverage these values to reach across partisan lines to find common ground in order to advance our cause.

Nonpartisanship appeals to me because it reflects my values regarding multipartiality and procedural justice. Trailblazers promote these issues as nonpartisan because they *are* nonpartisan—no one party has a monopoly on clean government—and we believe everyone should participate in elections and governance, regardless of their political beliefs. As a PAC, this is reflected in our goal to have a 50 percent win rate. Ideally, we would like to endorse candidates on both sides of any race. If every candidate shared our values and followed our criteria, voters would be in a far better position to decide on the substance of the issues, without wondering what special interests might be influencing the candidates.

As a lifelong Democrat and advocate for Democratic causes, I never imagined I would work with, let alone mentor, a Republican candidate. I thought it would be difficult to step away from a partisan perspective, but it was not as hard as I thought. I found my first Republican candidate to be engaging, open, and already running on a clean government platform in a conservative, Republican-controlled county mired in dysfunction. Our conversations were thought-provoking, and I found that he cares deeply for his community and for the rights of voters to regain their role in governing. Voters knew what they were getting when they talked with him. I was impressed by his commitment to being an honest, forthright legislator, and we look forward to seeing him grow.

Being nonpartisan also enables us to play the role of cross-partisan convener. For example, we recently held a workshop cosponsored by Republican and Democratic organizations. Participants from both parties came from urban and rural New York communities. The participants agreed on the central principles of clean government and the value of contested elections. In rural, upstate New York, Republicans dominate and races often are uncontested, while the same is true in New York City for Democrats. At the workshop, once the ice broke, the participants engaged in free-flowing conversations about a range of issues upon which they agreed. This agreement included the belief that one-party domination is bad for everyone; that it can lead to entrenchment, complacency, and corruption; and that voters deserve to have a choice of who represents them. Workshops like this lay the groundwork for more cross-partisan cooperation.

My advocacy for transparency and clean government is primarily done through candidate mentoring, which means I regularly talk with my assigned candidates throughout the course of their campaigns. While these conversations often revolve around the nuts and bolts of how to organize, fundraise, and other issues, I always circle back to strategies on voter engagement, and how they can integrate transparency and clean government into their messaging. Our mentoring program is a high-touch process, tailored

Man's capacity for justice makes democracy possible, but man's inclination to injustice makes democracy necessary.

REINHOLD NIEBUHR

to meet the individual needs of each candidate, but the message to every candidate is the same regarding transparency, clean government, and making voters the centerpiece of their campaign.

The traditional model of campaigning disengages citizens from participating in elections and in governance. Discouraged, unengaged voters don't vote, and turnout is abysmal across the country, particularly at the local level. This means that the majority of citizens are not involved in selecting their leaders. This also means that across the country, local seats may go unfilled or incumbents serve for decades without ever facing a contested election. Lack of citizen engagement is an enormous problem and fuels ignorance and mistrust of our government. It also sends a message to elected officials that no one is watching. Our voter-centered model represents an enormous shift from the current electoral system.

The decision in *Citizens United v. Federal Election Commission* struck an enormous blow to procedural justice, and its impact continues to push voters away and degrade our elections and governments. *Citizens United* allowed unprecedented amounts of money from unknown sources to influence both our elections and the legislative process. Dark money groups are most often associated with federal races, but dark money groups are very active and influential at the local level. Even in states with relatively strong campaign finance laws, there are enough loopholes to allow these groups to manipulate the process. This is why 100 percent disclosure is an essential step to restore integrity in the elections process. Campaign finance is, as the 2018 documentary *Dark Money* discusses, "the gateway issue" that affects every single substantive issue in politics.[3]

The most rewarding part of my work is seeing how our elected Trailblazers become procedural justice advocates, pushing for citizen engagement with their local governments. They pivoted easily from the process of running transparent, honest campaigns to implementing clean, responsive, and accountable government. These elected officials possess an ongoing commitment to engaging constituents, which is translating into better public processes, more citizen engagement and input, and higher citizen satisfaction. Their accomplishments after only one term represent our mission and philosophy in action.

Ask not what your country can do for you; ask what you can do for your country.

JOHN F. KENNEDY

Some of their accomplishments include:

- Making town budgets easily accessible when historically they were not.
- Scheduling town board meetings at times when people are actually available to attend.
- Restructuring meetings so citizens can ask questions during a meeting rather than limiting the time at the end.
- Streaming official meetings online and allowing those online to actively participate.
- Overhauling government websites so that information is clear and up-to-date.
- Forcing on-the-record discussions and votes with county leaders on transparency measures.
- Adding critical information to government websites about the work of all committees, with names of those serving.
- Holding informal "coffee hours" to meet with residents.
- Actively reaching out to educate and involve citizens about county or town budgets.
- Surveying residents about their views regarding the direction of their community.

The personal stories of many of our Trailblazers are also compelling. One candidate, an African-American man and immigrant, overwhelmingly won a seat on the town board of his affluent, white community. He chose to enter the race after racist flyers were distributed throughout his community stating that African Americans needed to leave the area. He won, despite being told he could not because he was black. His governance is deeply influenced by his values of social justice, equity, and inclusion. In his first two years of holding office, one of his many achievements is developing an inclusive process and plan for badly needed mixed-income housing.

Another candidate ran for mayor in his town of six thousand when his party decided not to challenge the incumbent because her husband was the largest employer in the area. He ran because he and others could not access the town budget, nor could they find out when the budget meetings were being held. He also felt the incumbent's priorities did not accurately reflect the needs of the town. As mayor, he has implemented an unprecedented number of avenues for active citizen input and involvement, ranging from streaming meetings online to placing surveys on the back page of water bills.

Lastly, another newly elected mayor immediately acted to open channels of communication with residents of her town by redoing the town website, making it more user-friendly and uploading relevant content. She also is creating more opportunities for citizens to interact with her and her staff. She believes that when people participate, they feel connected and confident in how their government serves the community.

One of the many lessons I learned from my classes and fieldwork at ICAR is how essential it is to build positive relationships in order to reach one's goals, whether advancing a process or a cause. For my work with Trailblazers PAC, I play the role of "utility infielder." I work across the PAC and build relationships with a wide range of individuals and organizations for potential partnering or information sharing, and I create opportunities for our own candidates to connect and learn from each other. Early on, I suggested that we hold conference calls with the candidates in our mentoring pipeline, so now we hold monthly calls on a range of topics, including petitioning, fundraising, messaging, use of social media, and so on. We encourage our candidates to share stories and ask questions so they can learn from each other.

We also hold an annual meeting of all of our endorsed candidates after the election. This provides a wonderful opportunity for them to get to know each other and share pertinent information about lessons from their campaigns as well as how they are addressing corruption in their governments. At our last meeting, a town board member met the incoming mayor of a town in a different area and learned that they are facing similar environmental challenges related to landfills. They now share information about how they each are planning to address these problems. These opportunities to talk on conference calls and meet in person are creating connections that otherwise would not exist and hold great potential to benefit their communities.

We are not aware of any other PAC that encourages this kind of networking and relationship-building.

I embrace this work because I see how it fits into the broader context of global efforts to stop corruption and improve governmental transparency. Last year, I reached out to one of the founders of Transparency International, a global anti-corruption nongovernmental organization (NGO) based in Europe. He invited us to join another group he founded, the Anti-Corruption Advocacy Network (ACAN), a D.C.-based network of anti-corruption organizations. While our work is quite different from that of the other members, there is great value in having a seat at the table. We provide a perspective regarding the influence of dark money at the local level that did not exist before within the ACAN, and it gives us a broader platform to promote our work. The relationships we are building through the ACAN and other organizations are helping to take our work to the next level.

However, political work is not without its challenges. An area for further exploration is to continue examining the barriers that keep citizens from engaging with electoral politics and local government. In our first two years, we've held several workshops designed to identify and explore these barriers and how to overcome them.

Many participants came from poor, rural white communities and poor, urban minority communities. The barriers poor people face, especially people of color, are complex and require further exploration with people and organizations from within those communities. We hope to develop more diverse relationships so that we can refine or develop new models that will allow significant engagement with populations who are left out under the current system.

There are many entry points for practitioners interested in getting involved in politics. My first recommendation is to volunteer on an issue-oriented or political campaign or explore the possibility of running for local office. In addition, the civic engagement arena is rapidly growing with a substantial funding base, and is a natural fit for those with conflict resolution skills. There are also great organizations that run advocacy campaigns, voter engagement programs, and national conferences related to a wide range of civic-oriented topics that would greatly benefit from the involvement of conflict

I believe our sorrow can make us a better country. I believe our righteous anger can be transformed into more justice and more peace.

Barack Obama
(2009 Nobel Peace Prize recipient)

resolution professionals. Big Tent Nation, Bridge Alliance, Living Room Conversations, Unrig, and the National Conference on Citizenship are great places to explore and start networking. There are also statewide membership organizations, networks, and conferences for political parties and for local elected officials that could also greatly benefit from consultants with conflict resolution skills. Dark money is everywhere, so no matter where one chooses to get involved, I hope that questions regarding transparency and sources of funding will always be raised.

More than once, I've wished that practitioners could see how possible it is to bridge conflict resolution work and electoral politics. The urgency to do this is palpable and on display every day in the news. Indeed, in today's toxic political climate, the phrase "common ground" is now associated with compromising our principles and values. This phrase has been hijacked by more than a few congressional partisans in swing districts so they will be perceived as moderates while they actually have little or no interest in the views of others. As a field, we must assert ourselves, take back our language, and get involved. As Shamil Idriss, CEO of Search for Common Ground wrote in an article on Medium after the 2018 midterms:

> There is virtue in pursuing common ground because common ground is not middle ground. It is often new ground. It is not just static, lying below the surface waiting to be discovered. It is also dynamic, waiting to be created. For as we do the hard work of scratching below the surface to understand an opponent's hopes, fears, and values—not just their most visible stances—and to cooperate together in those areas where we can agree, we not only build trust between us. We also ignite an unpredictable, creative, and sometimes transformational process that can give rise to new, previously unimaginable opportunities. And it is that process, patiently and tirelessly pursued, that paves the path to real redemption for even the most divided communities.[4]

No matter what part of the field one works in, we must identify and promote new ways to counter the damage done by the rise of polarization and extremism today. We possess the skills and abilities to seek common ground, and it is essential for our field as a whole and for individual practitioners to stand up and engage in the US political sphere.

One of the many lessons I learned throughout my life is that we must act upon our values of social justice, equity, and inclusion if we want to see change happen. At a time when political leaders promote every issue as partisan, we must reframe and promote issues that actually rise above divisive politics. We also need to look beyond the next election cycle and take a longer view of how and when change can occur. Winning elections is important, but virtually every issue I care about will still exist even if my chosen candidates win. While 2016 was an awakening for some, the reality is that our social and political woes have existed for decades and it will probably take decades more to fully address them.

My hope is that conflict resolution practitioners and leaders of the field will recognize the enormous potential for our involvement in electoral politics. Can you imagine if conflict resolvers regularly appeared on news shows analyzing and reframing today's current events? Or if practitioners regularly published commentaries in the national press? We desperately need leadership driving organized and visible engagement so that we can participate more fully and vocally in the issues driving so much division and hatred today. It's past time for us, as both citizens and practitioners, to stake out our role in rebuilding and protecting our civil society. By getting involved in civic engagement and politics, conflict resolution practitioners can help take back our government and restore voters as the rightful owners of democracy.

NOTES

1. Berghof Foundation, "Multipartiality," https://www.berghof-foundation.org/en/featured-topics/multipartiality/.
2. For more information, see www.TraiblazersPAC.com.
3. See https://www.darkmoneyfilm.com/.
4. Shamil Idriss, "Why Should I Seek Common Ground with My Fellow Americans?" Medium, November 7, 2018, https://medium.com/@SFCG_/why-should-i-seek-common-ground-with-my-fellow-americans-d1430fd6dfa5.

CHAPTER 7

Everyone Belongs

LUCY MOORE

WHO I AM AND WHY I DO WHAT I DO

LOOKING BACK, ONE EXPERIENCE STANDS ABOVE ALL OTHERS IN the formation of my values around justice, equity, and fairness. When I was ten years old, my parents applied to adopt a child. I was an only child and was delighted that I could be more like my friends who loved to complain about a little brother or a big sister. I heard a quality of love in those diatribes that I envied. I wanted to feel that, too. By the time I was eleven, Ronnie had come to live with us. It was a conditional adoption for one year, but as far as I was concerned, I now had a seven-year-old brother. I was thrilled. We walked to school. I held his smaller hand in mine and delivered him to his second-grade classroom every day. After school we walked home, exchanging adventures of the day. My friends were surprised. Suddenly Lucy had a brother.

"Is that your brother?" asked my neighbor Billy as he saw us on our way to school.

"Yup," I answered.

"I didn't know you had a brother," replied a curious Billy.

"Well, I do," I said matter-of-factly, and I squeezed Ronnie's hand.

But this rosy picture was not shared by my mother. She clashed with Ronnie over many things, and indeed, Ronnie was probably

Lucy Moore

not an easy child, having spent his first seven years in an orphanage. His table manners and eating habits had suffered in that atmosphere. His insecurity and anxiety were evident in ways I didn't see or understand. My mother and father had decided that this would not work for our family. I was not consulted, in order, they explained later, to spare me any sense of guilt in participating in the decision. That may have been considerate, but it certainly did not work. After eleven months, one month away from the adoption being final, Miss Wilson, the social worker, came to take Ronnie away. I can remember the sound of her car door shutting. It was heavy and awful and final.

I was devastated, and frozen with fear and guilt. How could someone who was part of our family—for almost a year—be sent away, kicked out, flunked? What if that happened to me? What would I have to do, or be, to become ineligible to belong to this family? And finally, why hadn't I done something to stop Miss Wilson from slamming that awful door and taking Ronnie away?

Sometimes in my life or in my work that moment from long ago comes to the surface. When I am aware that there is a marginalized voice that needs to be heard, that there is someone on the outside who deserves to be on the inside, that someone has suffered an expulsion from where they belonged, those old instincts kick in. I have a deep and hard-earned drive to defend those marginalized voices, make sure that everyone is included who wants or needs to be, that no one is excluded for whatever reason. I am hypersensitive to concepts of "not good enough," "dispensable," "unworthy," "unimportant," "less than." I want to know what it means to "belong." Are there inherent rights to belong? Who decides who does or doesn't belong and why?

After college, I worked for a wonderful man, Dr. Robert Coles, child psychiatrist and author, transcribing and editing his series *Children of Crisis*. These were studies of children and families in the South who took part in the integration of schools in the early 1960s. He was interested in why some children were able to deal with the stress, even trauma, of the experience and others were not, crumbling in the face of the hostility coming from white adults and children. The stories were powerful, but what impressed me was Coles's use of those voices. He quoted the children, their parents, and others, letting them speak for themselves, as the experts they were on that experience. I saw that intermediaries and interpreters often got in the way, resulting in the disempowerment of those who needed most to be empowered. As I typed (on a state-of-the-art IBM Selectric!) those eloquent passages, I felt the power in those stories, told in those voices. I have carried this commitment to allow space and time for participants in my processes to tell their own stories, with particular attention to those often marginalized and "spoken on behalf of" by well-meaning others.

In my twenties and early thirties, I lived and worked in Navajo country. As a college graduate in the late 1960s, I arrived full of ideals about justice and human rights, and with no idea how to be useful. I learned to listen, to observe, to take my time and not rush in with my own ideas about what justice would look like. I also experienced being a minority in another culture. As 1 percent of the population, we non-Navajos were definite outsiders. I was painfully aware of my differentness and went through a period of self-loathing, wishing I were dark-skinned, black-haired, fluent in Navajo, able to make fry bread and weave a rug, like all the Navajo women surrounding me. Surely if I tried hard enough, I would become "almost Navajo." Surely I didn't have to be an Anglo like other less enlightened Anglos. With the help of Navajo friends, I came to realize that it was just fine to be an Anglo on the reservation and that in fact I had much to offer. The last thing my friends wanted was a member of the "wannabe" tribe, pretending to be Indian, denying my real identity. I learned the importance of authenticity and honesty in myself and others.

I was deeply affected by the facts of life on an Indian reservation in the 1970s. I saw people struggling to find a comfortable place between two worlds: the traditional Navajo and the modern American. The trading post economy persisted, where Navajos were forever in debt and chronically short on food. They pawned valuable jewelry and rugs—staples of their cultural identity—to survive, often losing those items because they never had the cash with which to redeem them. Churches and missions abounded, offering help that was welcome, like dealing with death and holiday food distribution, and help that was not so welcome, like pressure (among some, but not all) to convert and give up the old beliefs and customs. I saw grocery carts full of Wonder Bread, Coca-Cola, and cans of Spam, and mourned the demise of the traditional diet of mutton, potatoes, corn, melons, and squash that had supported a healthy population for many generations. I saw Navajos struggling to live the modern way, in reservation towns, but without reliable utilities, functional houses, adequate health care, or a decent education sensitive to their history and culture. It was only a few years earlier that children had been forced into government boarding schools, given new names and new haircuts, and forbidden to speak their native language. The reality of the painful and impossible choices facing my Navajo friends was inescapable. My belief in justice, equality, respect, and empowerment was deepened by my years in Navajoland.

TWO PRINCIPLES I HOLD DEAR:

The trials of my childhood and my early experiences with disempowered people gave me principles that have guided my practice as a facilitator and mediator. Their roots in my very evolution into adulthood make them deeply personal and meaningful to me.

Honor and Include Outside Voices

From the beginning to the end of a project, I am committed to ensuring that all voices are heard, respected, and have weight in the process. Although parties may be represented at the table by lawyers and other experts, I always make room for the group to hear from those whose lives are impacted by the issue, in their own voices. Those voices, often silenced in the process, deserve a place at the table alongside others who may have more education, more resources, and a more mainstream point of view. I have learned that hearing that story, that passion, unfiltered, is a gift to everyone and often an inspiration for others to dig deep to a more authentic and honest level as they move forward to resolve the conflict.

Facilitate the Capacity to Participate

It is almost always the case that there are those at the table with less capacity—money, knowledge, influence, skills—to participate. And so I am careful to do what I can to make them more effective negotiators for their own interests. These words, so innocent, can be sacrilegious in some mediation circles. I was taught that mediators are neutral, never take sides, and defend the process against all bias, including their own. Social justice is for activists, they say, not for the process person. If we have all the interests in the room and the process is fair, then the outcome (assuming consensus) will be equitable for all. I subscribed to this, in hopes that it was true, but experience showed me that it is not always so. And so I confess that my moral compass, set decades ago when Ronnie left and fine-tuned by living in Navajoland, nudges me to champion the underdog, the outsider, to make sure that no one is excluded from the conversation, that everyone belongs.

I offer a process that is equitable for all at the table. Am I coming dangerously close to abusing standards of impartiality with my attention to those less empowered, with my efforts to balance the power? Am I pretending to be "equitable" when I am really trying to redistribute power? I am uncomfortable with these questions and force myself to ask them because I know, in the eyes of some of colleagues, I am on shaky ground. But if I am modeling authenticity—which is what I ask of those in my processes—I must admit that this is who I am. And I have come to believe that the most valuable thing I bring to a process is myself. Who we are, where we've been, what we've seen, all this life experience is relevant in the room for me as well as everyone else.

So, yes, I see myself as a fighter for justice. I do not lobby for a particular outcome, but I do enable those traditionally disempowered to find their voices, to become effective communicators and negotiators at the table.

Keep up the good work, if only for a while, if only for the twinkling of a tiny galaxy.

Wislawa
Szymborska

Cases That Helped Shape My Practice

Here are examples of cases that were formative for me and where these principles shine through.

A River with a Right

Early in my career, I facilitated a discussion in northern New Mexico about water needs of rural communities, both Hispanic and Indian. Lawyers, agency staff, engineers, and hydrologists had spoken academically and technically about water law, supply and demand, and the challenges of water management. When I probed the group about legitimate uses for water, the conversation became more personal. For farmers, irrigation was a top priority. City managers argued that providing urban water benefited a larger number of people. Business, environmental, and recreational interests all defended their uses. I looked for a tribal voice and saw Gerald Nailor, governor of Picuris Pueblo, in the back row. He raised his hand and said he had a suggestion for a new "beneficial use," the term used in the state water law. Heads turned. What other use could there be?

He said the state law should be changed to give a river the right to exist. An environmentalist asked, "Do you mean instream flow for fish and wildlife?" "No." From a whitewater rafter: "Do you mean for recreation?" "No." With each negative response came another effort to link the river to human needs. "Do you mean you want to hear it running?" Finally, in frustration, the governor said, "It doesn't matter if I never see, hear, smell, or touch it. It has a right to *be* there. It has nothing to do with human beings." He was speaking for the river, as a user with its own rights. It was a beautiful, important moment, and one that taught me never to draw boundaries around a topic, but to look to my participants for that.

A Voice for the Visitors

Many years ago, I facilitated a public meeting of three hundred people for the Forest Service about the proposed development of an open-pit copper mine in the beautiful mountains of northern Arizona. I called on audience members, all angry and opposed, and heard every imaginable objection on economic, health, aesthetic, environmental, and recreational grounds. It was nearing midnight, and I was sure I had heard every possible concern when a hand went up in the front row. A diminutive grandmother stood up and in a quiet voice declared, "I don't think an ugly pit will be very nice for the visitors." I asked if she meant tourists. "No." Perhaps family visiting from out of town? "No." And then I saw her finger pointing upward and realized she meant visitors from outer space. She was serious, the crowd was catching on, and I was frozen. And then my deep need to honor every voice kicked in. She had come to the meeting; she cared about the issue; she had a right to speak, to be heard and understood, and to have her issue listed alongside the others on my flip chart sheets, equally and with respect.

I said that I thought I understood her. She was worried about visitors from ... I hesitated ... outer space. I was very aware that some in the audience were on the verge of laughing. I could feel their fascination with how I would handle this. She nodded and elaborated. She didn't want them to look down on our beautiful, blue-green planet and see that big scar. I affirmed that indeed this was a concern that we had not heard, and asked if I could summarize it as "interplanetary concerns, the viewscape for interterrestrial travelers." She smiled and said that would be fine. I turned to write on the flip chart. The audience was silent. I had defended her right to be treated with respect, to have her worry addressed, just like all the others who had come that night. My hope was that everyone in the auditorium went home a little more thoughtful, a little more open, a little more willing to accept the outsider, the one who is different, as a worthy member of the community. Like Gerald Nailor, above, she had also taken us outside the boundaries of the topic, giving us the broadest possible view of what we were talking about.

Different Ways of Knowing

High in the southern Colorado mountains sits the Summitville site, a gold mine, opened in 1984 and abandoned in 1992. The runoff from the site caused serious contamination of the Alamosa River, the lifeblood for generations of Hispanic farmers and ranchers struggling to make a living and protect their rural lifestyle in the beautiful San Luis Valley. The fish died, irrigating systems turned into metal lacework, and property values and economic survival trembled.

The site was declared a Superfund site in 1994, and because the company had fled to Canada, the Environmental Protection Agency (EPA) and the state of Colorado were responsible for the cleanup. As required by Superfund, a technical advisory group

I do not see a delegation for the four-footed. I see no seat for the eagles. We forget and we consider ourselves superior.

 OREN LYONS

(TAG) was formed to serve as liaison between the community and the state and EPA, interpreting data to the community and relaying concerns to the agencies. The community representatives on the TAG were committed to seeing that the river was restored to a standard that would support all their pre-mining uses—irrigation, recreation, and enjoyment of a clean river. The agencies were hoping for a less expensive standard that would be legally defensible and acceptable to residents. As relations deteriorated, the EPA looked to me for mediation help.

The community felt powerless, and in fact they were. The decision-making was in the hands of the two agencies, and of the state water quality control commission that would be setting the standards. The TAG was advisory, but demands for attention and answers had resulted in a mediated forum. Fully aware that my job was not to advocate for any one side, I knew that it was important to build relationships across that divide if any agreement was to be reached. And I knew that within the relationship, power could be shared. That was my goal, within the limits of the legal and bureaucratic structures.

There were two turning points where relationships were deepened and power shifted between the frustrated parties.

The first was a field trip the length of the river. TAG members had pushed to show the agencies what they were living with. The EPA and state reps were reluctant, arguing for efficiency and their need to catch a flight home to Denver the same day. I helped them see the value of a field trip both in understanding the landscape and in showing respect. The community designed and hosted the trip. There were healthy debates among technical experts along the way, and different mixes of passengers rode together in vans from one stop to the next. The field trip helped clarify important differences. For community people, their livelihoods, their recreation, and in some cases their spirituality were rooted in that landscape. For them, the deathly green reservoir evoked a personal fear for the health of families and wildlife downstream. Watching and listening to them, the agency reps, for whom the cleanup was a job, could not miss the point. The change in setting, the informality, the beauty of the day, the picnic lunch, all contributed to a different dynamic among the parties. The atmosphere was relaxed; there was less tension and more humanity; there were laughs along the way. The trip ended with margaritas at a TAG member's house on the banks of the river, and group pictures of smiling people in combinations never before dreamed of.

Another battleground involved the legitimacy of data. For the EPA and the state, science was technical, numerical, formulaic, provable on paper or in the lab, and good decisions were based on good science. For the community, science was a hands-on experience: observations of weather, vegetation, and wildlife sometimes over hundreds of years. Science was noticing trends and making predictions based on cues taken from the environment. Using comparables and models was no way to understand or make predictions about the Alamosa.

The technical and the anecdotal systems clashed over the quality of the water in the river prior to mining. Community members insisted that fish had existed in a certain segment of the river. The agencies maintained that their models and formulae said this was impossible. Ignacio, a many-generation Hispanic farmer, exploded. There had always been fish above the reservoir. His family went on picnics there and caught fish. "Without fish, there would have been no picnic," he shouted. "We had no money to buy a hot dog!" The agencies remained silent, unable to give up their academic, technical conclusions. At a later meeting, Ignacio brought black-and-white snapshots of those picnics, including one of him holding a fat fish. That was *his* scientific evidence—those pictures, his memories, the stories of his community.

Silence is the Mother of Truth, for the silent man was ever to be trusted, while the man ever ready with speech was never taken seriously.

LUTHER STANDING BEAR

We discussed the dilemma of two contradictory "ways of knowing," and eventually came to an agreement. The agencies enlarged their definitions of data and evidence to go beyond the academic and technical. They accepted this local documentation (albeit not in scientific formats) that captured the reality on the ground and the long historical view. The final recommendations from the agencies to the state water quality commission incorporated Ignacio's data (including the photos) and twenty-three other reports from community members who wrote down their memories of pre-mine activities along the river. It was extremely important to the community that their "fish stories," as those reports were known, be included in the body of the state's report, not as an appendix. This was a balancing of power, a demonstration that both ways of knowing were valid evidence supporting the recommendations.

Most significantly, the state gave credibility to the community data by withdrawing its request to downgrade that segment where most of the fish stories were set.

BUILDING ALLIANCES ACROSS CULTURAL DIVIDES:

Most of my practice as a mediator for the past thirty-five years has involved working across cultures. My experience in, and affinity for, Indian country has given me opportunities to work with tribal governments and communities throughout the country. I have also worked extensively with Hispanic communities in the Southwest. And of course, every party at the mediation table brings cultural norms and assumptions, whether it is a tribe, an environmental organization, or a federal agency. In all these cases, and in work-shop settings, I help those in conflict understand the role that culture is playing and perhaps find ways of building alliances across cultural barriers.

In many parts of this country, white advocates and activists are struggling to build partnerships and coalitions across cultural and racial divides. Why is it so hard, they ask, to join forces to fight for a cause that will benefit us both? In most cases, it is the white organization trying to recruit the local land-based community (often Hispanic or Native American) to support their initiative. The initiative may even relate directly to the issues facing the community—a toxic waste dump contaminating a poor neighborhood, the undocumented immigrants' need for safety and support, proposed fracking near an indigenous sacred site. But a common cause is not enough to bring potential allies together when there is a history of colonization, exploitation, and discrimination that deepens the divide.

I have joined with Hispanic and Native American colleagues to help those in conflict understand these cultural barriers that seem to keep even the most committed and well-intentioned activists from success, while triggering and even perpetuating a legacy of deep distrust among the traditional communities in the Southwest. Working in twos or threes and representing different cultures and genders, we are able to create a safe space for difficult conversations among would-be allies.

Faced with the choice between changing one's mind and proving that there is no need to do so, almost everyone gets busy on the proof.

JOHN KENNETH GALBRAITH

Here are two examples.

- An environmental coalition found itself face-to-face with a local land-based community desperate for summer pasture for their sheep. While these two groups have much in common—a love for the natural beauty of the area and opposition to destructive development—the white environmentalists were intent on protecting natural areas from grazing. This campaign opened old wounds in the Hispanic community, still suffering from exploitation by lawyers and real estate operators who separated the community from communal grazing land through often shady dealings in the late 1800s and early 1900s. Then came federal agencies, capturing large traditional tracts to create national forests and parks, damming rivers and flooding fertile grazing and farming lands. To these multigenerational residents, the environmentalists were just the next wave of colonists.

  In an effort to resolve the conflict over grazing land, we brought together environmental leadership and community leaders in a retreat to learn more about each other and explore the potential for working together. The environmentalists learned that the villagers' connection to the land was deep and cultural. They realized that their interest in those beautiful natural resources was by comparison superficial. They cared for the land and were dedicating their work life to preserving it, but they were recent arrivals and did not have those historical, cultural roots or the knowledge gained from living on the land. "You will move on," said a community member. "We are here to stay." And another: "Where is *your* land? Why don't you take care of your own land and leave ours alone?"

  This is a refrain often heard from Native American communities as well. They see wave after wave of mostly Anglo outsiders flowing through with the latest idea, theory, or practice to "make things better" in one way or another. The outsiders ignore traditional ways that are alive and well and leave in their wake resentment and mistrust. In this case, our team was able to bring the two sides to the point where they could appreciate each other's needs and perspectives and agree on joint studies to demonstrate the compatibility or lack thereof of wildlife and sheep. The core of our work involved taking the time to help participants build relationships and develop at least a small degree of trust.

- A nonprofit committed to helping immigrants from Mexico and Central America integrate successfully into a school system found that there were divides between the white leadership and the Hispanic and Native staff. In an effort to develop accountability to those communities of color that they were serving, we offered two workshops, "Strengthening Intercultural Organizations." In this setting, the staff spoke of their experiences of disrespect and lack of support from the board and leadership.

  The leadership struggled to understand the roots of these feelings and their role in triggering them. It was difficult to hear that, in spite of all their good intentions, they were causing pain to the very population they were committed to helping. They grappled with issues of white guilt and white fragility; the staff reaffirmed their commitment to the goals of the organization, and in the spirit of teaching offered specific examples of offenses and missteps. With honesty, the white participants explored those dynamics and learned important lessons. In an exchange of life stories, told in pairs, participants experienced both the powerful content of stories and the impact of deep and intimate listening. All who participated saw that listening, understanding, and empathizing were key to building trusting relationships, so necessary if they were to evolve as an effective intercultural organization.

  In the end, leadership agreed to reach out and include voices of the undocumented immigrants they serve in order to be more accountable and more effective. They also committed to adopting principles of intercultural alliance-building and to developing a board and staff more representative of the cultural diversity of the state and the population they serve.

PERSONAL CHALLENGES:

My instinct is to set my own needs aside and give myself fully to the process and the needs of the participants. But I have learned to honor my own reactions in the mediation session and test their validity. If my mind is wandering, if I am irritated with someone or overly drawn in by someone, I may take this as an indication that all is not right in the room. I may ask the group: "Are we on track?" or "It feels as if something is not being said?" Usually there will be nods of acknowledgment and someone will volunteer a critical piece of information—a lawsuit filed, a new technical report—that is central to the conversation and that needed to be surfaced for a more honest discussion.

I am also challenged by bearing witness to painful stories about abuse, discrimination, even slaughter, particularly from Native American participants. Although I invite this kind of deep honesty and am grateful to be able to provide a safe space for emotion, hearing the pain—historical or current—can be overwhelming. Crushed by the reality of injustice—and the limited role I can play—I have often cried in the car after a session as I carry these stories home with me. It is a balancing act for me to empathize with each person at the table while staying in control of the room and performing my role with both equity and sensitivity.

REWARDS

I have given myself a personal challenge that has reaped great rewards. I am doing everything I can to raise the next generation of peacemakers, through mentoring, training, and cheerleading. Most of my mentees are from economic and cultural backgrounds that make access to the profession difficult. I also meet with graduate classes around the country via the Internet to share my experience. These young people, eager to hear stories from the trenches and eager to get into those trenches themselves, give me hope for the future. For me, this is one more step toward a more just and equitable society, where our conflict resolvers will represent the full range of this country's diverse communities.

Finally, a vignette of the magic that can happen when people connect, human to human, and see each other and themselves as vulnerable, valuable people.

I am mediating a complex and highly emotional process to compensate tribes for the loss of culturally sensitive natural resources that were contaminated by toxic and radioactive waste. We have been meeting for years and have more years to go. At the table are four tribes that have suffered irreparable damage, the federal agency responsible for the contamination, and the state. Recently the federal representative at the table was transferred to another position. At his last meeting, we bid him farewell with a cake and good wishes. I treasure the memory of a tribal member giving him a big hug and saying how much he would be missed. There is real affection in that group, and that gives me hope that we may reach by consensus a fair and just settlement. I am so gratified to have had a role in bringing people together in processes like this one where everyone is valued and everyone belongs.

CHAPTER 8

Field Lessons from Latin America

*Can Dialogue Manage the Dynamics of Extreme
Polarization and Contribute to Justice?*

JULIAN PORTILLA AND GASTÓN AÍN

WE HAVE BOTH WORKED IN LATIN AMERICA AND THE CARIBbean (LAC) for many years in mediation and dialogue around various public issues. We'd like to tell you a little bit about ourselves, and discuss the ways in which we see our work connecting to justice and also about the ways in which the increasing social and political polarization in the region threatens the ability to arrive at just outcomes in dialogue processes.[1]

Julian Portilla

JULIAN

When I was a boy growing up in rural northern New York, my schoolmates would ask me what it was like to ride a donkey or wear a sombrero. I never quite understood why they thought someone who was born in one of the largest cities in the world would ride a donkey. If anyone was going to ride donkeys, it was more likely to be them. Likewise, when I was hanging out with friends in Mexico City, they would talk about the gringos' intent to come and finish the job of taking Mexican land and swallowing the rest of the country. It seemed to me that the gringos I knew didn't really know

Gastón Aín

much about Mexico and would be just as happy if it disappeared entirely from the face of the earth.

My parents were divorced soon after I was born. When I was four years old, my American mother and I came to live in the United States, where I quickly learned English and assimilated. I would spend summers in Mexico City with my father and his family. I was very fond of both my parents, and I didn't see them like they saw each other. They were very careful to speak respectfully about each other around me, but every now and then I got to see sparks fly when they would discuss plans for my vacations. They were so good to me that it was hard to understand what it was they couldn't get along about. And yet, if I asked and they told me, it was obvious from each of their vantage points.

These early life experiences shaped my sense of the ways that good, well-intentioned people's perceptions of the same objects and facts could be wildly different. Living in such different worlds allowed me to get to know and like people in extremely different contexts. Alternating between the company of my rural, small-town, American friends and my urban, big-city, Mexican friends, I learned to see things the way each of them did. I was, after all, shaped by and ultimately from both places. My intentions to become a mediator were born of these early experiences. The day I discovered what mediators do, I was hooked for life. Helping to bridge people's different understandings about something and negotiate a common enough meaning that they could agree on something seemed like a suitable profession for me.

I've worked in many places in LAC, mostly in large-group processes related to land and resource distribution. And while most of the work I've done involves bridging different interpretations of the world, my sense is that with each passing year, the social polarization *within* the societies in which I work is only increasing. For the most part, the increasing polarization comes from the sense that the cost of the macroeconomic structural reforms of the 1980s and '90s were borne by the poor and middle classes while the benefits are now going largely to the wealthy. While I have appreciated the chance to help people determine more just ways to distribute the costs and benefits of various issues and impacts, I often wonder whether the short-term problem-solving I have done in my work greases the wheels of an inequitable machine that is driving us into greater polarization.

So am I doing good work? Am I working toward justice? Or am I simply replicating the unjust dynamics of the places I work and driving us further toward polarization? My conclusion is that I may be doing both, and that within the contexts in which I work, I'm doing what's possible. My consolation and the link to justice is that I'm helping to define whose voice is at the table.

Bringing to the table those who have been excluded by decision-making processes has an impact on the power dynamics of any context and is therefore by its nature a political act. Because it's a political act, it calls into question our impartiality in the eyes of those who have traditionally made decisions. Rather than deny that we are political actors (in the sense that we are, at least temporarily, affecting the power dynamics of a given situation), we need to understand and accept the ways in which our actions to bring certain actors to the table are perceived as favoring one voice over another, even while we see it as impartial because our own lens tells us that those who have been affected should be at the table in one form or another. We need to be cognizant of the ways in which our work lends itself to furthering the inequity where we work and get better at identifying opportunities to do deeper systems- and structural-level work to address the dynamics of inequality. Even so, it's a tall order to imagine that we can work to address a presenting problem that demands a solution for those affected while also working on the larger dynamics that led to that situation. If you're mediating in small-claims court, you're probably not working on justice reform that day.

So I've learned to be more clear and honest with myself about what I'm working on and its larger implications for justice. Sometimes you get to work on Justice with a capital "J," but often you don't. But even in the immediate, problem-solving realm, inclusion of those who are affected at the table is a political act that will ruffle feathers but, in my eyes, contributes to justice with a small "j" since it ensures that in the short or medium term, those voices will get to determine, in part, the outcome of the conversation where otherwise they would not have.

Where justice is denied, where poverty is enforced, where ignorance prevails, and where any one class is made to feel that society is an organized conspiracy to oppress, rob and degrade them, neither persons nor property will be safe.

FREDERICK
DOUGLASS

GASTÓN

I was nine years old in 1983 when Argentina started its own democratic spring after the seven-year rule of a military dictatorship responsible for the torture and forced disappearance of thirty thousand people. Three years later, I entered a high school affiliated with the University of Buenos Aires, the largest and one of the most politicized universities in the country, and got involved in the student union, eventually being elected its secretary general in 1990.

In 1991, after a dispute between authorities and hundreds of students accused of damaging the school building after a traditional graduation celebration and who were about to receive sanctions, the union was asked to intervene, and I had to approach the parties. I felt anxious and excited. Things eventually calmed down.

Months after this incident, the union started promoting and supporting the creation of an institutional consultative space with direct representation from students where key decisions pertaining to discipline issues, academic syllabi, and extracurricular activities could be discussed and determined jointly with authorities. It took a couple of years of coming and going, and after a lot of persuasion, protests, and dialogue with authorities, the consultative council was created. I did not realize that my work with the student union might be called dialogue facilitation until years later.

For me to get involved and to take a stand supporting democratization of public institutions, expanding civic space and participating in extracurricular activities to reflect on what had happened during the dictatorship through cultural and other events felt like an immediate contribution toward restoring the rule of law. I was not alone. Thousands of young people embraced the democratic wave taking over Argentina and started participating in politics through different associations, labor unions, universities, and local structures.

In law school, I studied international human rights instruments, including the UN Charter and the American Convention on Human Rights. I could not help but think that these and other documents seemed too abstract and aspirational. After I graduated, I was fortunate to work for Dante Caputo, the former minister of foreign affairs of Argentina's first democratically elected government in 1983 and later president of the United Nations Assembly. In 2006, Mr. Caputo was serving as secretary for political affairs at the Organization of American States. I was sent to Haiti as part of a special mission to support democracy, and two years later I was deployed as part of the good offices missions to reestablish diplomatic relations between Ecuador and Colombia after a major incident in 2008. I also participated in special and electoral observation missions in several countries in Latin America.

Conversations with Mr. Caputo and other colleagues, exposure to experts, field missions, frustrations, more frustrations, and many more defeats than victories in improvised and not-so-improvised mediation and dialogue processes helped me understand the strategic value and potential of the human rights framework developed by the international community, and by LAC in particular. I was still far from understanding how instrumental this framework could become in materializing aspirations for social justice.

Having finished studies in international relations and African affairs, I moved to Rwanda, where I implemented a program aimed at promoting open debate among civil society groups on the need to expand civic space and to create political parties that could contribute to reconciliation and become avenues for participation in a society still recovering from trauma and horror. Political space was razor-thin in Rwanda, and persuading activists and authorities that functioning political parties and competitive elections were a profitable long-term investment was like pulling teeth, and somehow not that rewarding. I traveled throughout the country and crossed into Burundi several times. I read African authors, talked to hundreds of historians and anthropologists, and asked all the questions that had once crossed my mind about nation-building, genocide, and reconciliation. However, what I recall the most from these years are the personal stories of redemption, recovery, and resilience of some of the leaders, women, youth activists, and peasants with whom I had the chance to speak. I also learned that dialogue can coexist with justice, as the Gacaca post-genocide reconciliation efforts proved in Rwanda.

Two years later, I left Rwanda and joined the United Nations family as conflict prevention regional advisor for the United Nations Development Programme (UNDP) in Latin America. In between context assessments and dialogue process design missions, I became more attracted to socioenvironmental conflicts, and in particular human rights violations by private companies, the challenges of prior consultation of indigenous and tribal peoples, as well as access to information, decision-making, and justice on environmental issues. Along with talented practitioners like Julian, who was part of UNDP's roster of experts, I designed and facilitated multistakeholder processes leading to the passing of critical legislation pertaining to internally displaced people in Mexico, public health sector reform in Panama, citizen security in El Salvador, and prior consultation of indigenous communities in Costa Rica and Panama.

GASTÓN AND JULIAN

There are many international instruments that call for access to environmental information and stress the need for efficient remediation and grievance mechanisms. Here is a sample: the UN Global Compact launched in 1999; the UN Guiding Principles on Business and Human Rights adopted unanimously by the UN Human Rights Council in June 2011; ILO Convention 169, adopted by the International Labour Organization to empower indigenous and tribal peoples; and, more recently, the historic Regional Agreement on Access to Information, Public Participation and Justice in Environmental Matters in LAC. Most of these instruments have been either replicated or incorporated into national normative frameworks of LAC countries and are considered by local judiciaries when adjudicating on these matters.

These instruments advocate and uplift the fundamental values and concepts first incorporated into the Universal Declaration of Human Rights, and at the center of most of them is human dignity, along with social justice, moral rightness, and harmony. It is hard to find a more powerful source of inspiration.

However, effective implementation of these and other international instruments is difficult without political will, but also without the critical contribution of an army of mediators and skilled facilitators capable of creating and sustaining multiple spaces where conflicting views on development and other critical issues can be discussed and eventually resolved. No matter how detailed, progressive, and social/human-rights-oriented the normative framework is, it will not be truly effective and operational without a critical mass of conflict and dialogue experts designing, facilitating, and orienting results-based exchanges around solutions to the critical problems in the LAC region, and in the hemisphere. In other words, without mediation and dialogue to apply the high-minded principles of our legal frameworks, in many cases justice cannot be served.

The application of these frameworks and therefore the achievement of justice is threatened by the increasing polarization in the region. In many places and at many levels, governments in the LAC region are relatively weak. They often cannot or will not implement or enforce regulations. In many cases, when they do attempt to implement regulatory changes, they find themselves paralyzed by social protest, often having to back down. In the United States, we have seen notable examples of this in the 2014 and 2016 standoffs over grazing rights in Nevada and Oregon and the Standing Rock protests against the Dakota Access Pipeline, also in 2016. In each of those cases, however, the federal government eventually made a decision and took decisive action, and eventually the normal course of the rule of law took over again (though whether or not justice was served is a different matter). While these are exceptions in the US context, in the LAC region, examples like these abound and are so frequent that they rarely draw international coverage. In Mexico, for example, fishers who dislike a new or changed regulation have been known to block the border crossing with the United States in protest. The government, paralyzed and terrified by the social turmoil and political costs of implementing the law, concedes. This leads to a downward spiral of government legitimacy and its ability to do its job: to make and implement the rules under which we all live. Imagine a world in which a great number of government decisions turn into Bundy-like standoffs.

It is these situations of polarization and paralysis in LAC into which we have been invited to play mediative roles in helping to convene and manage dialogue. We have been invited into these processes by many different actors: the UN, national governments, multilateral banks, private-sector leaders, and nongovernmental organizations (NGOs). Our experiences have taught us many valuable lessons about convening, impartiality, safety and security, and transparency, among other things. While the contexts are specific, the lessons seem general and—we hope—useful to others. While we have contributed different stories for this text, we present them here in one voice.

UNILATERAL VERSUS COLLECTIVE CONVENING

In highly polarized contexts, unilateral convening of dialogue spaces has proven faulty, weak, or counterproductive in bringing key actors to the table. This is because one of the dynamics of polarization is the absence of impartial actors. No single actor appears to have enough credibility to convene all the relevant parties. Following a coup attempt that ended with a divided society and antagonistic relationships, an elected senior official in a Central American country, determined to show willingness and openness to engage the other side, proposed a broad-based dialogue. Unilaterally, through major national media outlets, he called for a national dialogue aimed at reconciliation and power sharing. This was immediately followed by an announcement by labor unions, students, and several NGOs that they would not attend a process at the sole invitation of the government. Even if the individual convening has not been a primary actor in a controversy or conflict, in contexts of acute social polarization and the existence of the "us versus them" dynamic, there are almost no exceptions to the polarizing dynamic, where neither of the poles will be recognized and legitimized by the other. We had previously advised against traditional unilateral convening, and after this started providing technical assistance and models of collective convening methods that included universities, ombudsman offices, the national church, and two international organizations. Critical for all the parties' acceptance was the principle of cross-trust equilibrium. In other words, while some actors might attend a dialogue because of the credibility of certain individuals convening the dialogue, others not enthusiastic about these very same people might decide to attend if invited by different convening figures.

To be wealthy and honored in an unjust society is a disgrace.

CONFUCIUS

In a land dispute in rural Argentina, peasants mobilized by the Catholic Church took over land owned by a municipality. They did this because the municipality had received land from the national government in order to build housing for the poor. However, once it got the land from the national government, the municipality chose instead to use it for political patronage by using it for such things as construction of a rugby club and a retreat space for the municipal workers' union. Angered by the misuse of the land, the peasants occupied it, and in response, the municipality tried to remove the peasants by force and several people were injured. The peasants filed and were granted an injunction from the court, which said the parties needed to resolve the dispute through dialogue. In the meantime, no new settlements were to be made and the town could not forcibly remove anyone. It was a stalemate.

Who would convene the dialogue? We (the mediators) were invited by the municipality to build a dialogue process, but it was very clear to us early on that the peasants would not attend any event convened by the municipality. But it was also clear that as the primary government presence and official titleholder of the land, the municipality had to play some kind of convening role. So we started looking around for who else might convene. We soon found that the town council included members of each of the major political parties of the area and that the local bishop was revered by all of the occupiers. So in the end, the church, the executive branch of the municipality, and the town council co-convened the group. The town council agreed to convene with the understanding that any agreements that came out of the process would be advisory in nature only to the council but also committed to a good-faith effort to integrate the dialogue agreements into their legislative process. In this way, we found conveners, found a way to connect our ad hoc process with a formal space, and managed to leave the town council feeling like their own formal space was left intact and respected.

Looking at these cases side by side is interesting because they are good examples of big versus little "j." The land occupation case was fueled by a sense of injustice, a sense that the government was not using the land for its intended purpose. The larger, systemic problem was the way in which public land was used in general in the province. The local land grab was simply a manifestation of the larger dynamic. Nonetheless, the level at which we were negotiating was little "j." Any agreement we could reach would only affect those directly involved and, to a much lesser extent, the town in general. It would not, however, affect the larger questions of how land was to be used in the province or of rural poverty in general.

Yet to those involved, these were questions of livelihood and participation. To them, it was all about justice and fairness. And it wasn't just about resources and land. A particularly memorable moment occurred after an enormously frustrating town-wide meeting with more than seventy people in the room. One of the peasant land occupiers commented that he had never seen "that" happen. When asked to clarify, he said that no one had ever listened to them like that before.

The Central American case was most certainly a capital "J" case. National, structural reforms were in question, and the very impetus of the dialogue was a political rupture of the highest level. The issues to be negotiated in those conversations were foundational, the kinds of things that define modern states: security, justice reform, education, health, and so forth.

In both of these cases, there was very little room for the traditional mechanisms of governance to operate effectively. The extreme nature of the polarization had disabled the governments completely, to the point that they couldn't even invite affected parties to dialogue without help from other institutions. In both cases, the selection of who would convene and who would participate were decisions that directly challenged the traditional notions of the proper guest list of decision-making circles. In other words, new voices were going to be at the table to try to sway the outcomes of the negotiations. If they could have done it any other way, neither government would have accepted any outside help or the inclusion of those new voices. In short, polarization fueled by a sense of injustice disables governance, which creates threats to the rule of law (and promotes more injustice, since the state regulates the interactions between the weak and the strong) but also creates some opportunity to let in new voices and *maybe* get to a more just place.

Participation and Transparency versus Efficiency

The extreme polarization to which we keep referring can affect our work as mediators and dialogue facilitators in other ways, too. In polarized contexts that affect a large number of people, LAC culture can lend itself to paranoia about what backroom arrangements are being made during a negotiation and to whose benefit. But having everyone in the room is a tall order for getting things done. So the question is: How can you build a small enough group to remain efficient and nimble and yet retain the trust of the larger group?

In a dialogue on complex health reform in South America, we began the process in the usual way: with a thorough stakeholder assessment identifying as many relevant actors as possible. We asked every actor interviewed to provide input on which actors should be invited to participate in the health reform initiative. We wanted to gauge perceptions and relative weights of potential participants to a dialogue process. With the report and all the names that had come out during the assessment, we called for a preparatory session aimed at exploring basic ground rules and a simplified thematic agenda. The session was attended by at least a couple of individuals from each of the sectors that had been mentioned during the assessment. Around fifty people attended, representing medical schools, patients, administrative unions, the pharmaceutical industry, doctors, nurses, anesthesiologists, authorities of public hospitals, the Ministry of Health, private providers of health services, etc. Thirty minutes into the session, we realized it would be impossible to have an agile and technically oriented exchange with this number of people.

We realized that what we really needed was to have a discussion among the technically relevant people that could in short order be vetted and advised by a much larger group of relevant stakeholders. A week later, we set out to ask each sector that attended the initial meeting to identify the critical actors who could not be absent, those who were absolutely essential to the discussion. We were set on finding ways to have everyone participate in some manner, but we wanted to know whose presence was critical in order for the initiative not to fail. As it turned out, the same core group of names came up during this second round of interviews.

Justice is conscience, not a personal conscience but the conscience of the whole of humanity.

Alexander Solzhenitsyn

After analyzing different options, we suggested the constitution of a small group of critical actors who would meet once a week to tackle the core issues of the reform. We imagined this group consulting with other stakeholders through a system of concentric and widening circles. Every other week, a second, larger ring of twenty actors representing other sectors would join the core group to discuss a second set of issues and give feedback to and advise the core group. Finally, once a month, medical schools and patients would join the other two rings to discuss the profiling of prospective health professionals and issues related to customer service in public health facilities. This allowed for the core group to remain efficient while integrating the recommendations of the larger groups, thereby making them feel included and reasonably assured that the process was transparent. This scheme was in place over a year and produced a comprehensive diagnosis for the health sector in the country, and through executive decree, the government eventually made the space a permanent forum for discussion of health-related issues.

In a negotiation over a management plan of a marine protected area in Mexico, the various sectors present could not agree on representatives. The fishing communities sent a dozen people, but the environmentalists had two, the ecotourism operators had six, and the developers had three. We had to find a way to maximize participation and to include as many voices as possible but also wanted to equalize the weight of each sector. We therefore created a system in which all of the representatives mentioned could speak, but when it came to voting, we would accept only two votes per sector. If everyone or most everyone in the sector agreed, both votes would count the same. If there were significant disagreements within a sector, we would split the sector votes one and one. Additionally, the meetings were open to the public so they could witness the participation of their representatives.

During this process, we had been kicked out of the only hotel in the area with air-conditioned meeting rooms. The owner of the hotel was a developer who did not like our process and believed that the negotiation should be limited to discussions with the three or four actors whom he believed to be the real power brokers in the area. Fortunately for the process, the director of the marine protected area had a more inclusive vision for the process. Eventually we found a decent alternative, and in 95-degree weather in a closed space with close to seventy people in attendance (with about thirty people representing the various sectors), we managed to forge an agreement attractive enough for all sectors to sign.

Here again we have contrasting examples of big "J"/little "j" cases of justice. Designing relatively efficient conversations while also finding ways to minimize the perception that any funny business is going on is a delicate balance between efficiency, participation, and transparency, and we think these two examples illustrate creative ways of achieving that balance. They are also prime examples of the power that comes from changing the composition of who is at the table and in the room.

FINDING THE BRIDGE-BUILDERS

In such polarized contexts, finding enough relevant people who can sit together for a constructive conversation can be quite challenging. The inability to sit together can inhibit the generation of agreements and therefore obstruct the creation of positive change in a society, change that might lead to more just and equitable outcomes than the status quo can provide.

For example, mutual objections, cross-caricaturing, and personal vetoes were common practice among leaders and local authorities of a city with twenty thousand inhabitants that was trying to determine whether to build a small infrastructure initiative that would generate electricity. Years had passed since the first deliberation attempts. In the meantime, controversial representations had arisen in favor of and against the project. Cross-accusations of violence, sabotage, and intimidation were widespread, and a climate of emotional exacerbation was present in the city. In our process design, we mapped the main actors in the conflict based on their relative importance and legitimacy, both institutional and local, and proposed a preparatory session to set the prospective agenda. It was a relatively small group, and everybody showed up as expected. However, from the first intervention onward, a multitude of cross-accusations, personal vetoes, insults, and deeply seated grudges from the past polluted the dialogue, making it almost impossible to continue.

After two months of impasse, we set out to carefully identify individuals with a solid reputation who would be more acceptable to the opposing camp, and who despite the emotional exacerbation had been able to maintain themselves on speaking terms with leaders from the other field. We had already done this in the initial round of interviews. However, it became clear over the course of the two months that people had confused leadership with the ability to dialogue. So we did another round of interviews and really emphasized the bridge-builder aspect over the leadership aspect and got a different list of names. With that information, we reconfigured the group to include more constructive individuals even if they hadn't been the ones to create or even lead the various interest groups present.

It took time, but after a while, we collected the names of fifteen people, eleven of whom decided to participate in a strategic reflection exercise, including a scenario-building training, that eventually allowed for a broader discussion and public consultations on the project. Today, some of these leaders continue to gather and exchange on relevant issues pertaining to the city.

MAPPING RISKS OF REPRISALS FOR THOSE PARTICIPATING IN DISPUTE RESOLUTION PROCESSES

In contexts of acute social polarization around development initiatives, infrastructure-related projects, and/or demands for prior consultation to affected communities, it goes without saying that not everyone is in favor of participatory dialogue or exploring creative solutions to emerging challenges. In settings where opposition to inclusive methods of reaching agreement is so strong that there is a risk of resorting to "resolutive violence," assessing and preventing risks of reprisals for individuals and communities participating in dialogue processes becomes both a responsibility and an obligation for practitioners. If risks of reprisals are detected during the assessment stage of a dispute resolution process, practitioners should establish preventive measures to be applied throughout the dialogue and in coordination with the people or groups identified. Preventive measures might include maintaining the confidentiality of personal information or information about the process throughout, using secure communications, not using identifiable photographs or images, avoiding disclosure about the location of certain parties or places where the process will take place, and entering into confidentiality agreements with drivers and interpreters. Keeping the confidentiality of dispute resolution processes has proven very challenging. In several local-level dialogues on controversial issues and where the community was strongly divided, individuals interviewed during the design phase manifested a preference to hold the encounters in a different city or region and asked for extreme discretion for their own protection. Tailored training for the entire dialogue group can also contribute to gaining knowledge on how to behave in a case with risk of reprisals. The establishment of WhatsApp groups where incidents can be reported and early indicators of risks can be flagged seems to have potential as well. Early decisions on interactions with the press or social media guidelines must be made during the validation of ground rules.

The following is an example of one way to do this.

Simple Early-Warning Systems to Avoid Space Contamination

Amid a dialogue process between a large mining company and an Andean indigenous community, a series of simultaneous episodes and actions attributed to the company were creating an uneasy atmosphere among participants in the dialogue. At the beginning of each weekly session, a considerable amount of time was devoted to discussing accusations, doubts, and grievances the community leaders needed to clarify before proceeding with the official agenda. A small, private company offered the dialogue space a very simple early-warning system based on text messaging since most of the leaders did not have smartphones with permanent Internet connections. The system allowed for local dwellers and leaders to send text messages denouncing what they considered irregularities or suspicious company behavior to a widely publicized phone number. The number of the caller would remain confidential for the operators of the system, and the message would immediately

Throughout history, it has been the inaction of those who could have acted, the indifference of those who should have known better, the silence of the voice of justice when it mattered most, that has made it possible for evil to triumph.

HAILE SELASSIE

be received simultaneously by the local social and environmental unit of the company, the mayor, the chief of the local police, and two designated community leaders. The company would have to investigate and provide accurate information to the recipients of the complaint within forty-eight hours. The system's first case was the alleged killing of a dog on a secondary road by a company truck very late at night. The company recognized its responsibility and compensated the dog's owner adequately. Several cases followed, allowing the system to gather data, to rapidly clarify incidents, and to liberate precious dialogue time that could then be allocated to tackle more structural issues related to benefit sharing, environmental and social issues, and permanent monitoring.

This is a case in which there is an even smaller "j" inside a small "j." In other words, small infractions that could have easily led to a degradation of the trust between parties were addressed early on. It was, in effect, a miniature justice system. The case was not itself a case in which major, national policy was to be developed around mining rights or the ways in which local distribution of the benefits of extraction would happen in general, but it was a chance to look at what kinds of compensation the local operation would have in that community and was therefore a small "j" case.

CONCLUSION

The list of dialogue design challenges we've discussed in this essay—convening troubles; competing technical information; concerns about transparency, safety, and efficiency; and others—are certainly not unique to the LAC context. Indeed, in conflict studies graduate programs all around the world, these are the stock topics of conversation and thought of as challenges to be met with creative design. All of them in some manner or another relate to justice. However, all of these dynamics are all the more important and challenging in contexts of extreme polarization. When the basic functions of government break down due to the depth of the mistrust and relational dysfunction of large groups of society, the ability to talk to one another is severely impaired. And since what we do implies inclusion of voices that are often absent, our ability to create just processes is likewise impaired.

It's hard to consider the LAC context without also considering the US one. In American politics, since the 1980s there has been a great deal of political discourse about *government being the problem*. Over the years, the American political system and society in general have become increasingly polarized. Centrist actors have been replaced by more extreme views on either side. There are many causes, and this is not the place to list them. But our experience in LAC makes us wonder if the current course the United States is on will weaken institutions and the capacity to enforce rules and regulations. We hope that our work to bring together different points of view, work that by its very nature seeks to bridge the gaps between polarized points of view, could have implications beyond the specific situations in which we find ourselves and maybe mitigate to some degree the race toward polarization.

Naturally, we can hope to make no more than a small contribution to mitigating the overall wave of polarization in which we are currently living. Polarization seems to arise mostly from various parties' sense of exclusion and inherent unfairness. Our processes are constantly struggling to find legitimacy and fairness in the eyes of the conveners and participants. Our basic practice is predicated on the notion that by having the right people at the table we can come to fair and just solutions, and that if the right people are *not* at the table, we will inevitably and unfairly externalize the costs of our collective decisions. Polarization of the kind we see in Latin America requires us to work twice as hard to fulfill the basic conditions required for constructive dialogue. But we also hope to have demonstrated that adaptations and adjustments are possible.

NOTE

1. Views, thoughts, and opinions expressed in the text belong solely to the authors, and do not represent the point of view of the Inter-American Development Bank (IDB) group nor MICI, the Independent Consultation and Investigation Mechanism of the IDB.

CHAPTER 9

Pursuit of Peace through Mediation

A Pakistani Struggle

VISHAL SHAMSI

GROWING UP IN A MIDDLE-CLASS MUSLIM HOUSEHOLD IN PAKI-stan, I remember spending vacations at my grandmother's house, where during hot summer afternoons under an incredibly fast and loud ceiling fan she would sit me down cross-legged, cut me mangoes, and teach me verses from the Quran or tell me stories of the prophets. She acquainted me with a beautiful verse from Chapter 5 (Surah Ma'idah), which states: "O you who believe, be persistently standing firm for Allah as witnesses in justice, and do not let the hatred of a people prevent you from being just. Be just, for that is nearer to righteousness. Fear Allah, for verily, Allah is aware of what you do."

Vishal Shamsi

Perhaps the seven-year-old Vishal was only excited about the sweet mangoes and stories of how Solomon ruled the world or Moses crossed the Nile, and perhaps she did not understand the wisdom behind the verses she was taught, but the sixteen-year-old Vishal, who decided to choose law and conflict resolution as a career, recognized the significance of the term "justice" and the incredible burden it bears. Even more so, the Vishal who is currently writing this tries to seek inspiration from the divine wisdom to counter everyday issues that raise complex notions of justice and forgiveness, equality and tolerance.

In a country like the Islamic Republic of Pakistan, made in the name of religion, religious values can be crucial in making a difference. On one hand, religion is the umbrella that teaches tolerance and love despite religious and cultural backgrounds; on the other, it is sometimes gravely misused to spread hate and fanaticism, leaving it to the whims of flag-bearers of law and justice to ensure that the former prevails and the latter is avoided at all costs.

Unfortunately, like religion, law in Pakistan has also been a victim of abuse. Perhaps the biggest illustration of such an intricate cruelty would be blasphemy laws, which ironically, whilst enacted to prevent religious violence, have been an added cause of religious violence. Offenses related to religion were first codified in 1860 by the British rulers of the Indian subcontinent, before Pakistan was an independent Islamic republic. The law made it a crime to insult religious beliefs and intentionally destroy or defile a place or an object of worship, amongst other things. These laws then by default became part of Pakistani law after its independence in 1947 and were not discriminatory to any religion. It was not until 1986, during a dictatorial regime, that the death penalty was introduced for certain blasphemy provisions and it became prejudicial to minority religions. Before this death penalty provision was introduced, there were only a handful of reported blasphemy cases; however, since then, a staggering number of more than four thousand cases have been handled.[1] It is also important to note that while numerous allegations have been made throughout the years, there have been no executions, mainly because at the appellate stage it becomes apparent that the allegations made are false and rooted in personal feuds.

Law and justice should go hand and hand, and a law that doesn't serve the ultimate goal of justice, in my opinion, is not a good law. Nonetheless, a law can also be a good law but its wrong interpretation or incorrect application can render it unjust. My inquest is: Can a "resolution" come through and prevent this injustice or misuse of law? In this regard, I have two stories to tell, one that will help explain where conflict, resolution, and justice stand in my country, and another that is part of my personal journey and has a place very close to my heart.

Washing one's hands of the conflict between the powerful and the powerless means to side with the powerful, not to be neutral.

PAULO FREIRE

A Pakistani Christian woman, Asia Bibi, was convicted on blasphemy charges and sentenced to death in 2010 when one afternoon, while picking berries with three other Muslim ladies in the village, she had a quarrel and allegedly uttered derogatory remarks against the Holy Prophet. The matter was narrated by the other women to a Muslim cleric, who called Asia Bibi for a meeting at which she allegedly confessed her guilt; as a result, the cleric lodged a complaint against her. Subsequently she was arrested and then convicted. She pleaded not guilty throughout the proceedings, and the matter was appealed multiple times till it reached Pakistan's highest court of appeal. In October 2018, after spending eight years in prison, she was acquitted in a landmark judgment given by the Supreme Court of Pakistan, a judgment that shall be remembered and reiterated as a precedent for future cases for several years to come.

The presiding judges referred to numerous verses from the Holy Quran including Chapter 2 (Al Baqarah): "And do not mix the truth with falsehood or conceal the truth while you know (it)." The absolute eloquence and wisdom were reflected when the judge stated:

> Blasphemy is a serious offence but the insult of the appellant's (Asia Bibi's) religion and religious sensibilities by the complainant party and then mixing truth with falsehood in the name of the Holy Prophet Muhammad (Peace Be Upon Him) was also not short of being blasphemous. It is ironical that in the Arabic language the appellant's name Asia means "sinful" but in the circumstances of the present case she appears to be a person, in the words of Shakespeare's King Lear, "more sinned against than sinning."

While Asia Bibi's story had a happy ending, one cannot help but wonder if had the cleric involved in the case dealt with the dispute differently, maybe she would have not spent eight years of her life in prison. The judgment of the Supreme Court itself reads:

> A heated argument took place with the exchange of some bitter words between them and as a result of this disagreement, those ladies, in connivance with the complainant, Qari

Justice is an inestimable treasure; but we must guard it against the thief of mercy.

Muhammad Iqbal

Muhammad Salaam (religious cleric), *ignited the situation and wrongly implicated her (Asia Bibi) in this case*. Furthermore, the alleged extra-judicial confession was not voluntary but rather resulted out of coercion and undue pressure as the appellant was forcibly brought before the complainant in presence of a gathering, who were threatening to kill her; as such, it cannot be made the basis of a conviction.

Asia Bibi's case is an example of what happens when individuals misuse the law, but what about those who try to take it into their own hands? Pakistan has witnessed numerous instances of sectarian and religious violence, including several deaths attributed to public lynching by some violent mob or other, and unfortunately, the country continues to do so. A deeper look at any one of these instances would give the same answer—that the origin was in some unrelated civil or political difference that was not resolved on time or dealt with justly.

Before I share the second story, it is important to give a brief background of how working as mediator and trainer in Pakistan got me here, to share this with you. In 2015, the National Centre for Dispute Resolution (NCDR), Pakistan's first mediation center, and Sustainable Peace and Development Organisation (SPADO), both nonprofit and nonpolitical organizations, collaborated on a project called "Strengthening Alternative Dispute Resolution Mechanism in Karachi." The primary objective was to introduce mediation in three conflict-prone communities in Karachi—Korangi, Sultanabad/Hijrat Colony, and Jamhoria Colony—in a one-year program, through capacity-building of local communities, religious leaders, and police officials in mediation and dialogue. It is pertinent to know that these areas harbor the underprivileged and are extremely overpopulated areas of the city, but they are also thoroughly diverse, where individuals belong to different religions and sects, speak different languages, and follow different subcultures. Most of the inhabitants of these areas are immigrants from various remote parts of the country who have come to Karachi, the metropolitan capital also colloquially known as "the City of Lights," in search of a better life.

It was an exciting opportunity for me as a young professional to work on a one-of-a-kind pilot project. After graduating from law school, I was a bit hesitant to pursue an additional certification to become a certified civil and commercial mediator; after all, my aim was to promote the idea of justice, and I had a misconception in my mind that justice cannot be obtained by "compromise." I was wrong, so very wrong. I worked meticulously and cautiously toward this certification and became a mediator, and working with the NCDR was my first job. I was very much looking forward to seeing the application of what we had been trained for, especially in a country like Pakistan. The stakes were high, as never before had community mediation been introduced in such an urban setting in Karachi. Whilst there have been several other unregulated, out-of-court dispute resolution methods available in different rural settings, locally known as *jirga* and *panchayat*, for hundreds of years in the region, they mostly lean toward arbitration. Mediation, in its finished and modern form, was being introduced for the first time.

To organize the trainings, the plan was to gather participants from various groups, including community elders and people with standing in their communities. These included working professionals, small-shop owners and social workers, religious clerics/representatives of mosques and churches, and police officers. The organizations wanted to equip these people with the right knowledge and skills to handle all kinds of disputes in their community/area, with the exception of serious criminal offenses. The project also wanted to aim for both younger and more active community members as well as elderly members who could share their experience.

To recruit police officers for this training, we went through an extensive police training channel whereby the officers posted in these three areas were given official letters from the deputy inspector general and were asked to participate. The police department was very helpful in this regard. For the remaining two groups, we thought the best method to collect these individuals was to leave sign-up sheets in the area for individuals to voluntarily fill out. A team was constituted that went to drop off these sign-up sheets in some "designated areas" such as community centers and popular roadside cafés. Some senior members of SPADO who had worked on similar projects in the northern rural areas of Pakistan were especially asked to join us for on-site activities since they had worked toward conflict resolution in some of the harshest environments, including parts of North Waziristan, with some of the most difficult people, including tribal and feudal lords. The members of the NCDR had worked in more formal and urban settings previously, so the team, which comprised NCDR and SPADO members working for this community mediation project, tried to give the best of both worlds.

The on-site activities went successfully, in our opinion; the individuals who hosted us at the local cafés and allowed us to market for our trainings were welcoming and somewhat optimistic. They understood how diversity attracted us to these particular areas and expected the members of the community to also be enthusiastic about our trainings. To our joy, within a week of leaving the sign-up sheets, more than one hundred fifty individuals had signed up. They understood that they would not be compensated monetarily for taking days off from their everyday jobs and participating in the training, yet they all voluntarily signed up. It was delightful news for us, as we were not expecting such a turnout in such a limited amount of time. It was exciting, and we were thrilled to share with them what we had worked on; however, it was not until we started working on the logistics that it came to our attention that all the participants who had voluntarily signed up were men—none were women.

How can this be? Could it be an error? Are we missing a sheet? These were just some of the initial reactions of the team I was working with. We checked the sheet several times, making sure that we had not implied or expressed anywhere that this program was only open for men. We discussed amongst ourselves whether the team that went on-site had given any impression that prevented women from signing up but later reached the conclusion that the team had effectively delivered the message, so that was not the case. Eventually we decided to go back on-site and find the cause of this alarming situation.

Contrary to the popular belief that Islam oppresses women or considers them to be an inferior gender, the true teachings of the Quran rather focus on the importance of the equality of the two genders, especially when it comes to education. Prophet Muhammad emphasized that education is *fard* (Arabic for "mandatory" or "obligatory") for both men and women. Prophet Muhammad's wife Ayesha and his daughter Fatima were both well versed and were considered two of the most knowledgeable individuals of their society at that time. In fact, Fatima Al Fihriya, an Arab Muslim woman, founded the first degree-awarding institution in the world in Fes, Morocco, in 859 CE.[2]

The training we wished to conduct was not restricted to any gender; in fact, it was imperative for women to join for our project to realistically work. We had determined that a major chunk of the disputes in these communities were related to domestic disagreements, and that these women were more comfortable with opening up to other women when it came to such matters. Therefore, women had to be part of this community mediation project; otherwise there was no project. We were still baffled: How could not a single woman have signed up? After conducting several surveys of the area and talking to various locals, we came to the conclusion that the men of the area did not want any of the women to sign up. The reason was mainly because these trainings were alien to them, and they wanted to see the content and environment for themselves first. This was a cultural concern; the men wanted to "protect" the women, and only after they were sure themselves would they allow the women to be "exposed" to these trainings.

A little disheartened at first, thinking to ourselves that there was perhaps all the more reason to reach out to the women and men of these communities, we internally discussed what strategies to devise to convince the locals. In the end, we decided that the best way to deal with this issue was to familiarize the community members with who we were and what our true intentions were. Perhaps the sign-up sheets were not enough. We then held several talks with the locals on-site and assured them as best we could about the environment. We tried to be sensitive toward their concerns and briefly familiarized them with the members of the team and content of the trainings.

Consequently, one of the local "community elders" bravely stood up in the midst of other men of all ages and agreed to sign up his sister, who had been willing to train. Soon others followed suit. The founding father of Pakistan, Muhammad Ali Jinnah, was a big advocate of promotion of education and the rights of women and minorities in the new nation of Pakistan. On one occasion he said: "There are two powers in the world; one is the sword and the other is the pen. There is a great competition and rivalry between the two. There is a third power stronger than both, that of the women." On another he stated: "No nation can rise to the height of glory unless your women are side by side with you. We are victims of evil customs. It is a crime against humanity that our women are shut up within the four walls of the houses as prisoners. There is no sanction anywhere for the deplorable condition in which our women have to live."[3] Pakistan was built on progressive ideas, but unfortunately, some cultural practices and customs undermine the value women hold in our society.

Most of the women who signed up for our trainings were socially active in the areas we were catering to. The ones who were particularly thrilled to sign up were midwives and door-to-door polio workers who felt that not only the training could teach them additional skills, but due to their existing rapport with the women of the area, they could really make a difference. The women, however, did request to train separately from the men, and we gladly accepted their request. With a little budget management we were able to make a place and time in our training schedule to accommodate women separately, and so the project got back on track with dates finalized and course material printed in both English and the national language, Urdu.

The training of different groups resulted in different experiences. During the training of women, we often ended up having long discussions on women's rights and the problems some of the women faced from those areas. Many women shared stories of domestic violence that they or someone they knew had been a victim of; some shared how they were not given their due inheritance share or were forcefully married against their will. They also discussed how they dealt with those problems, and while we were the trainers, we had a lot to learn from them, too.

During the training of religious clerics, we discussed the rights of minorities and how intolerance was growing in the society, how it was easy for anyone qualified or unqualified to start a sect or a

Injustice anywhere is a threat to justice everywhere.

MARTIN LUTHER KING JR.

cult and equally easy for them to issue a fatwa as a license to kill anyone they did not agree with. The religious clerics, who included Hindu and Christian priests, shared verses from their respective books pertaining to dispute resolution and peacemaking.

The most challenging training group for me was that of community elders. It was the first group we trained. These men were all older than me, and as the first day of training started, I felt that that was going to be a problem. They perhaps viewed me as a young and only female trainer working in a sea of men. Initially they were hesitant to ask me questions and even more hesitant to answer mine. They were all extremely respectful toward me, but there was an immense gap I could feel, which I knew had to be bridged immediately. I started by asking them questions about themselves and relating to them my own experiences, which I felt might make them view me not as someone who was more privileged or alien to their world, or a female with no "street" experience, but as someone who belonged to the same city and faced similar problems. It took a little bit of warming up and communication skills that I had acquired while being trained as a mediator, but sooner than I imagined, they all became comfortable with the idea of me as their trainer. Successful completion of this challenge felt like a small "win." After the success of the initial trainings, we conducted collaborative workshops and brought individuals together from across areas to form networking bonds, so that in case of any disputes in their areas they could contact each other and provide assistance. This was perhaps the main reason to train police officers, as they in their official capacities and with the unique power they enjoy as a result of it can genuinely provide skilled assistance and play a major role in resolution of disputes. After all, the first forum for the majority of the disputes is the local police station. The community elders and religious clerics can take the disputes to the police officers in their "network," and instead of shoving frivolous complaints down the route of hectic litigation, a genuine attempt can be made at solving the problem or resolving the dispute.

Two months after the conclusion of networking workshops, we conducted a follow-up workshop to see the progress of these individual ambassadors of peace, who were doing their best free of charge and working as dispute resolvers in their communities. The first report submitted to us showed a success rate of 70 percent. The participants discussed with us how it was difficult to familiarize locals with the concept of mediation and attract them to it since they considered it to be another form of localized arbitration, but with time, as cases/disputes started coming to them, people understood that there was no dictation of harsh terms, but rather a forum in which to sit and sensibly resolve disputes. The workshop also provided a platform for these individual mediators to come forward and share their success stories.

This is where the second story I promised comes. Amongst the various beautiful success stories shared by our trained mediators, one in particular showed us that what we thought was a mere community mediation could not only resolve minor disputes prevailing in a household but could actually perform a broader function to help prevent violence and extremism.

The dispute narrated to us involved two neighbors, one belonging to the Christian community, the other belonging to the Muslim community residing in one of the areas where we had trained mediators. The neighbors had a dispute over a motorcycle parking spot right outside their houses. The matter escalated quickly, and they both ended up at their local police station making all sorts of accusations against each other, including that of blasphemy.

As discussed above, blasphemy laws in Pakistan are often abused during disputes, especially if one of the parties is a non-Muslim. It is one of the add-ons that people claim when making allegations against another, leading to serious consequences.

Luckily, in the neighborhood dispute, before the matter could take a foul turn, one of the police officers on duty trained by us realized that the dispute was best resolved through community mediation. Police officers have a knack for these sorts of situations, especially here in Pakistan. Since the police are so frequently involved in all kinds of disputes, they can tell the real problem from what the disputants are claiming to have happened. The police officer on duty was also very well aware that he would not be able to handle such a matter by himself since it involved serious religious accusations—the parties were more likely to listen to someone with religious standing. He immediately called the imam of the mosque of the area and a priest of the church of the area, both also trained by us. Luckily the networking workshops had successfully created helpful connection. The parties along with the religious clerics and the police officer sat together for several hours. We were told that beyond the immediate issues, the neighbors had other deep-rooted past issues that also came up in the mediation session. Since the situation had escalated, it took a few hours before the parties were calm and ready to think clearly. Eventually the parking spot dispute and all the other disputes were resolved. No complaints of blasphemy or otherwise were filed, and in fact, the entire process doubled as a therapy session that not only restored their previous relations but also brought them close together.

It has been almost five years since we concluded this community mediation project. The people we trained are still actively participating in mediation sessions of various kinds of disputes. They work voluntarily and take out time from their own jobs; they do this without any remuneration from us or the parties involved in the disputes, which reflects how truly dedicated they are to making our society a better place. Unfortunately, due to insufficient funding, financial support, and necessary approvals, we were unable to continue this project in other areas of the city, but the immense success of this pilot project evidenced that community mediation has a real role in an urban and heavily populated city like Karachi.

What is justice? Giving water to trees. What is injustice? To give water to thorns. Justice consists in bestowing bounty in its proper place, not on every root that will absorb water.

RUMI

I, personally, prior to this experience never understood the gravity of power and responsibility that comes with being a mediator and that despite being a neutral, the same can play an active role in enforcing justice. Sometimes all you need in such instances is someone doing a reality check and putting things in perspective for another. People who are representatives of the community/society or who can be part of the dispute resolution process have an added responsibility to positively take measures and work toward the broader concept of peace and justice. No community/society is free of flaws; it's how we deal with those flaws that reflect how civil that community or society is. While the international media paints an extremely gloomy picture of Pakistan, it's not all true. The country is brilliant and gifted in numerous ways; however, unfortunately, it has a long way to go when it comes to breaking evil customs and ensuring justice and adequate resolution of conflicts. It is difficult to be part of the system, knowing where it's broken and not being able to fix it. Perhaps even worse is being criticized for criticizing it. What I have gathered from the little experience gained in my journey is that mediation as a dispute resolution mechanism has real promise in a country like Pakistan; perhaps it can even be dubbed as the cure the justice system should be looking for.

Today, Vishal works as a litigation lawyer in Karachi, the same "City of Lights" in which she grew up. She is a lecturer of law in a local institution, still conducts mediation and trainings, and still loves eating sweet mangoes on hot afternoons. She also still vividly remembers her grandmother narrating, "The best of people are those that are a source of benefit for the rest of mankind,"[4] words she strives to live by.

NOTES

1. The Nation: Web Desk, "10 Things You Need to Know about Pakistan's Blasphemy Law," October 14, 2016, https://nation.com.pk/14-Oct-2016/10-things-you-need-to-know-about-pakistan-s-blasphemy-law.

2. Jeffery T. Kenney and Ebrahim Moosa (ed.), *Islam in the Modern World* (New York: Routledge, 2014), 128.

3. Pakistan Agricultural Research Council, "Quotes of Quaid-e-Azam," http://www.parc.gov.pk/index.php/en/quotes-of-quaid-e-azam.

4. Abu Eesa Niamatullah, "The Best of the Best," https://sunnahonline.com/library/purification-of-the-soul/194-best-of-the-best-the.

CHAPTER 10

"I Just Want My Family to Get Along!"

Eldercaring Coordination, Pathway to Justice, and a Legacy of Peace

SUE BRONSON AND LINDA FIELDSTONE

INFLUENCES

Sue

I WAS RAISED BY A MOTHER WHO WAS ON THE AUTISM SPECTRUM. She was brilliant, talented, and had no awareness of emotional expression. Why did she cause me suffering with her thoughtless statements? Why couldn't she hear my pain? Why couldn't she soothe me? I never knew about the high-functioning end of the autism spectrum until decades later a colleague brought me a book on Asperger's that she said sounded like my description of my mother. I now knew that my frustrations had a cause, a name; I was not alone. She was the best mom that she could be.

As a result of my relationship with my mom, I have spent my entire life learning about emotions and trying to teach others the importance of being heard and understood. In college I staffed a crisis hotline on Saturdays from midnight to three a.m. As lay people, listening was the key skill we had to offer; it made a difference in people's lives. Now, as a licensed clinical social worker and mediator

Sue Bronson

Linda Fieldstone

with more than thirty-five years of experience, I believe that building a relationship based on listening is still key to transformation.

Linda

I understand how early years have an inevitable influence on our approach to relationships later on. My family was composed of two parents and two children and one dragon. My job in the family was to tame the dragon; the dragon was my mother's illness. We never named the dragon, but it consumed our lives. Whenever something happened that was hurtful or even dangerous, it was the dragon's fault. Even then I realized that relationships are contextual: What happens to one member of the family can affect all of the others. Taming the dragon made life easier for my father and kept him around; and it protected my younger brother, and even my mother, to keep her healthy and safe.

As I got older, I continued my role as "protector." By then I knew it wasn't children's responsibility to take care of their parents. For thirty years in the Florida court system, I shielded children from their parents' conflict. I have witnessed the benefits for everyone when parents learn how to focus jointly on the care of their children rather than their anger toward each other. Working together can help us tame a dragon or two.

Sue

Some dragons we never see coming. My brother's Disney World vacation ended in tragedy on November 29, 1994, when a twelve-wheel loaded dump truck ran a red light, crushed his rental car, and ended his life. My brother was only forty-two years old. His ten-year-old son, the only one alert, was trapped for forty-five minutes with a broken leg in the wreckage of torn metal, twisted seats, and shattered glass. My brother's wife suffered head injuries and multiple fractures. Her brain injuries affect her comprehension and memory to this day, so that she needs twenty-four-hour supervision. Their thirteen-year-old daughter had several fractures as well. Their other two sons, eighteen and nineteen years old, were home at their respective colleges.

The accident changed our entire family's lives. My brother had told his attorney he would sign the newly updated will and power of attorney when he returned from vacation. It was never signed. I got a firsthand education about capacity, decision-making, guardianship, and conservatorship. Would you be surprised if I told you there were family conflicts? And that some last to this day decades later?

My brother's wife attends all of our family gatherings on their father's side, adding her special joy to our events. Her children, now all grown with children of their own, have almost no contact with their mother's side of the family, although their maternal aunt is the guardian of their mom. Their family tree was cut in half. This is one of the many costs of conflict I hope to help others avoid. Despite every effort to nourish the roots, I couldn't keep their family tree intact. Maybe I could help other families.

THE WORK

Linda

"I just want my family to get along" is the greatest wish for both children and our aging loved ones, each at one end of life's continuum, and each vulnerable to the decisions others make for them. In their pleas for peace and stability lie the foundation for their sense of worth and feelings of safety in this world.

I had seen for years the trickle-down effects of conflict surrounding elders touching even the youngest generations in families. Our courts were addressing the needs of families with children, so why were older families excluded from the "family courts"? Where were court services for older families when they struggled with transitions as their parents and grandparents aged? If parenting coordination services could reduce high conflict levels of younger parents, why couldn't there be a similar process to address hostilities between older family members? It saddened me that older families were left out of the "family" equation. A systemic change was needed so that courts would begin to define "family" with all of its generations. Sparked by a feeling of injustice, in 2012 I began by asking others for help to rectify this discrepancy. After all, families do not age out of conflict.

In some families, the older generation is taken care of by the next generation. Everyone agrees to the needs and desires of the older person and appreciates the shared efforts of family and friends. Not every family is so lucky. *Eldercaring coordination was specifically created as a high-conflict dispute resolution option for families regarding the care and safety of an aging person.*[1] Based upon the concept of parenting coordination, elders and their families are court-ordered to address their nonlegal issues with an eldercaring coordinator (EC) for up to two years. That way, they do not have to return to the gavel of a judge as transitions of aging continue to take place. In eldercaring coordination, aha moments can occur when all the voices of family members are heard, but the voice of the elder remains at the center of their conversation.

Family conflict can reveal itself in insidious ways. Midge received a texted photo of her mom looking out of an airplane window. That is how she found out from her sister that her mom, fragile from the progression of Alzheimer's, had been taken out of state. Midge then had no contact with her mom for over two years. Would she ever see her mom again? Would her mom even remember her? How about extended family members—aunts and uncles who shunned Midge based upon her sister's misleading and disparaging comments? To protect Midge's mother from the litigation and ongoing contention, the judge referred the family to eldercaring coordination at the same time the mother was ordered to return. I began working as the EC for the family just in time for the reunion, hearing the joy in Midge's voice when she embraced her mom, with eighty-two candles on the cake she had baked for Mom's birthday. Midge's mom cannot express her feelings about being separated from her daughter for so long, but her eyes sure light up when Midge enters the room. Many of their activities have changed, but the pleasure they felt dancing in each other's arms is just as exuberant. Since then, with help during the process, the family agreed that Midge be designated by the court as guardian, and both sisters now have the same opportunity for contact with their mother and information about her care. The relationship between the sisters is "still": There is not much interaction as the

No one is useless in this world who lightens the burdens of another.

CHARLES DICKENS

"fight" is gone; there is no storm left in the relationship. Extended family relationships are thriving now equally with both sisters. Their mom is safe, and the possibility of harmony between family members no longer feels insurmountable.

Eldercaring coordination provides a setting where everyone is valued, everyone benefits. The autonomy of the elder, like Midge's mom, is protected, to the extent possible, and the dignity and quality of life of the elder is preserved. The greatest resource for our aging loved ones is realized: their family.

It isn't easy to be an EC. Older family members are experts at being angry by the time they are referred to the process. They have had years of past disappointments, feelings of marginalization, and frustrations exacerbated further by the win-lose mentality of the court process, where their "enemy" can be their spouse, brother, or even child. In the name of "justice," they are really seeking punishment. If the hostility between family members feels like a canyon between them, eldercaring coordination is the bridge that can begin to bring them together. Throughout the process the focus is on family strengths, not degradation: They all "win" when they work together. Justice is preserving the dignity of the elder and their relationships with their loved ones, similar to preserving the child's relationship with each parent and the relationship of the co-parents in parenting coordination.

Bringing eldercaring coordination to older families is a course it seems I was meant to travel. Maybe it is a direction I could not have appreciated as much until now, but the values it holds, compassion, respect, and family, have certainly guided my life to this moment.

Sue

It was my grandmother who taught me about compassion and respect. She cared for her parents, who lived next door, and all the grandchildren and great-grandchildren when their parents were not available. Fresh-baked chocolate chip cookies were always available to welcome us. She made everyone feel they were *the* special one. Grandma's compassion was clear. Everyone deserved respect, no matter what they had done or how they were acting in the moment.

I was reminded of my mother when I read a book about mediation by Jay Coogler.[2] I knew immediately that this was what I wanted to do with the rest of my life. I could use the skills I learned from my grandmother and my mother (by omission). I could advocate for people being heard and treated with respect, regardless of their behavior. My first mediation training was family mediation with John Haynes in 1982. After my brother's accident, I took two guardianship mediation trainings. I continued to attend many training courses on aging and older adults, their mental health, and elder law continuing education. Mediation continues to speak to my soul. I believe in solving differences through dialogue, knowledge, and compassion.

Linda and Sue:

In the fall of 2012, Linda invited Sue to work with her on a new vision. Eldercaring coordination was created specifically to address the unique needs of families that turn to the court for decisions regarding the care and safety of aging persons. ECs reduce conflict among family members so they can work together more productively and focus on the aging person's care.

KEY CONCEPTS IN ELDERCARING COORDINATION

Important concepts in eldercaring coordination include the following:

- Family decision-making centers on the aging person.
- Respect for the family is intrinsic to the process.
- Family privacy and the aging person's dignity are preserved.
- Compassion is demonstrated through trauma-informed, person-centered services.
- Collaboration benefits the elder and all generations of the family.
- Need for adversarial court motions decreases as nonlegal issues are addressed by the family.

Eldercaring coordinators:

- Manage high-conflict family dynamics, focusing on solutions and emphasizing strengths rather than blame.

- Support the aging person's self-determination to the extent possible.

- Honor the family's journey and meet them where they are in the process of change.

- Promote safety by monitoring at-risk situations.

- Develop a support system for the aging person and families.

- Save time, money, and resources, as fees are shared instead of individual court expenses being incurred and nonlegal issues are resolved without waiting for court hearings.

Linda

Eldercaring coordination can change multigenerational patterns to foster dignity and respect. Families are encouraged to develop coping strategies that build relationships rather then destroy them. At some point, I began to recognize the similarity in the behaviors of younger families and older families: parents withholding time with children and family members preventing time with a loved one; parents bad-mouthing each other to their children and family members degrading one another to their loved ones; crucial school information about a child concealed and essential medical information hidden from family members; children's money guarded by parents, elders exploited by family members. ECs model how to make decisions and connect the dots for the next generation to follow a new paradigm, instead of repeating the old conflictual patterns that harm grandchildren and great-grandchildren. Dots are also connected as the family members begin to hear each other and understand the unimaginable cost of their adversarial actions on the elder. Emmet's family, agitated and unhappy with one another, raised their voices in an effort to have their own opinions heard. In desperation, Emmet leaned back and then forward, his whole body seeming to peer into all of the eyes around the table in a plea to quiet the storm in the room. "How would you like it if a stranger

We do not learn from experience . . . we learn from reflecting on experience.

JOHN DEWEY

took over your every move?" he asked. "I never did anything wrong . . . didn't lie, didn't cheat, didn't steal. Why am I being punished by someone taking away my freedom? Don't you know you are burying me in the cemetery alive with all your fighting?" The room became still, everyone reflecting on each word, including me. The image of Emmet, one foot in the grave dug by his own family's conflict, has continued to haunt me, as the understanding of the depth of his losses became more clear.

PERSONAL CHALLENGES AND REWARDS IN THE WORK

Sue

The idea of serving families is great; however, the reality of being with family members means I need to face my own dragons. People amaze me. Despite my training, I can have a hard time with people who choose to behave in a mean way. I understand that bullies get their way, yet I don't understand why people want to be bullies. There may be a good purpose in the unwanted behaviors. Sometimes it takes more effort for me to see it. It helps when I open my heart to want to know their story and how they become this way. It is a decision I need to make over and over again to stay open to who is in the room. This takes empathy, realizing and sharing with them the pain of perpetuated behaviors that have brought them to their current situation. The families involved in eldercaring coordination are not new to conflict; they have lived within the confines of conflictual relationships for many years. Helping them see there is another way takes patience, as they may not be ready to let go of the entrenched animosity that has carried them to this current situation. As Carl Jung said, "Everything that irritates us about others can lead us to an understanding of ourselves."[3]

The greatest reward as a practitioner is seeing families reconnecting and better understanding one another, even if just for the moment. It only takes one person to begin changing the process of family interactions . . . maybe inviting another in from the heart, enhancing the quality of today's conversation and reducing the potential for a family crisis later.

Linda

I love Sue's vision of "inviting another in from the heart" and recognition that even small steps can have huge implications for the progress of a family. We hold monthly meetings with judges and administrators of eldercaring coordination programs that have been initiated in jurisdictions throughout the United States and are starting in Canada. It is impacting when we hear a judge say, "Eldercaring coordination saved that man's life." When an adult child says gratefully, "No one has ever asked me about my children," it is reinforcing that we are not leaving people—of any age—out of the family equation. Family photos preserve the memories of their holiday dinner for the first time in years, as well as the shared bedside of their aging loved one. As they have new family stories to pass onward, I do too. We have also heard from ECs during monthly meetings about families that continue their discord in court, but this time the elders are protected, not isolated: They continue to receive time with family members, coordinated care, and transportation to medical appointments. Elders know they are heard, able to stay in place whenever possible rather than shuffled around and hidden. They may not have that trip to Paris they always dreamed of, but they can go to a French restaurant with everyone at the table!

On a personal note, the most extraordinary experience has been working with such extraordinary people: organizations and professionals that have generously contributed hours and hours of time and effort toward the development of eldercaring coordination; researchers working without grant funding; judges and magistrates and court personnel adding more to their already overburdened schedules; ECs working for sliding-scale fees and pro bono; meetings and committees and subcommittees—all voluntary. The commitment of all those involved with the Elder Justice Initiative on Eldercaring Coordination (Eldercaring Coordination Initiative), which provides ongoing support and education about the process, and the partnership with my two cochairs, is a model of the collaboration we endorse.

The degree of my own dedication to this process has also been a powerful recognition. As eldercaring coordination was being

The warrior, for us, is one who sacrifices himself for the good of others. His task is to take care of the elderly, the defenseless, those who cannot provide for themselves, and above all, the children, the future of humanity.

Sitting Bull

developed (by twenty US and Canadian organizations collaborating with twenty Florida organizations), I found out I had cancer. How was I going to see this through? It gave me such relief that my vision had become a shared vision. Feeling so vulnerable, I wondered what would have happened if my own family was in conflict over my care, delaying treatment, and adding to the confusion of an already horrifying experience. This motivated me even more to ensure access to eldercaring coordination. Looking back, I realize that I scheduled every medical appointment, every infusion, and every procedure around our task force calls so that I did not have to miss even one meeting!

Linda and Sue

When we talk with professionals about their high-conflict cases, they immediately describe the tragedies they have seen: elders being "kidnapped" and relocated, isolated from family members and friends; elders mismedicated and missing treatment while family members are exhausted by the demands of legal battles; children kept from aunts, uncles, and cousins they were once close to as alliances have fractured relationships; elders and children left home while caregivers and parents are consumed with litigation tactics, depositions, and court hearings. One of the greatest personal challenges we have experienced is the transition from understanding need, which judges and professionals clearly articulate, to referring more cases for eldercaring coordination. How can it be so easy for professionals to describe their own cases, those they have read about, and even the suffering they have personally experienced, and so difficult to identify more cases, refer more cases, and be motivated to participate professionally in the process? It is difficult to understand why they wouldn't want to be a part of the solution.

True peace is not merely the absence of war, it is the presence of justice.

JANE ADDAMS

We know change can be hard. Eldercaring coordination brings a new perspective to responding to older families. Can we embrace our elders like we do our children? This challenge is intensified by a legal system that is more focused on procedure than process, the status quo rather than relevance. There is an urgency to motivate this change, as demands on the court will continue to rise as baby boomers age. We have seen that time is of the essence for the elders themselves, as several in existing programs have died between the court hearing and a judge's signed order of referral.

LESSONS LEARNED

Sue

Looking backwards can help us to see forward, and predicting the future can create calm; yet often staying in the present moment is most important. The earlier that situations are dealt with, the more options that exist. And of course, if it touches someone's life, they have a right to weigh in on the decision. One of three daughters went to Arizona to spend time with her parents just before her father's operation. The plan was to stay there for three days. It turned out to be three months as Dad had complications and died and Mom needed help with the changes. The daughters wanted their mother back in Chicago to be near them; they were imagining that the worst would happen if they were not close by to protect and care for her. But their mom had wanted to stay in the warm climate in Arizona. She had been used to relocating frequently her entire married life, according to her husband's job promotions, and now finally had the opportunity to decide for herself where to live. The mom said in a not-so-nice tone, "Your fear of me falling is your problem, not mine. Get over it." I reminded the daughters that there is no need to create dependency where none exists. The daughters realized their mother was looking for support, not someone to take over control of her life.

Another lesson is to preserve as many family traditions possible. In one case, the family's weekly spaghetti dinner was at stake. They all lived within two miles of one another. Three of the families lived on the same lane—divisions of the family farm. Dad made the homemade sausage; Mom made "the best rolls ever"; everyone had a specific dish they brought to share at the family gathering. Dad was having health issues; Mom had found a "new best friend" in the youngest child's feisty wife. The young woman freely spoke her mind and was at the center of many disputes. Due to a verbal brawl in the barn about the feisty wife, a physical fight in the yard, and all the harsh words stated afterwards, the animosity had grown so bitter that the family could no longer all be in the same house. Dad's health, the safety of the youngest son and his wife, and many other issues were addressed. An important discussion was how to make it so everyone could be invited to the dinners, even if some chose to come early or come later when others were gone. The dinners were too important of a family tradition to ignore.

Linda

In eldercaring coordination, families are given tools to help them work together productively, and then have an opportunity to apply what they have learned. When families can chart their progress, no matter how small, it can still reinforce hope for the future. Likewise, the Eldercaring Coordination Initiative is dedicated to providing support for programs, while increasing the access to eldercaring coordination for families in need, with both "learning" and "application" in mind. Just like the family members need to work together, we cannot build the Initiative without a strong collaborative component to connect it to those families in need. Asking for help brings people to the table. Everyone has something to offer; helping them feel valued is an important contribution to any work we do. We can all benefit when people work together.

Collaboration has been a theme throughout my professional life. By creating community partnerships, I was able to build a family court services unit that became a model for courts nationally and in other countries. As past president of the Association of Family and Conciliation Courts, I found the importance of interdisciplinary collaboration even more evident. The natural evolution of the Eldercaring Coordination Initiative also builds on the concept that diversity generates creativity, respectful exchanges broaden scope and outcome, and cooperation builds trust and confidence. The Initiative has established collaborations within court systems, between circuits, in communities, and with institutions to enhance the process and increase public awareness and access to eldercaring coordination. Instead of studying the process retroactively, as is typical, eldercaring coordination has been based on research to inform promising practices from its inception. The work of the

Initiative mirrors the work of the families and upholds the values of those we serve: collaboration, respect, cooperation, and trust.

Just the Beginning

Linda and Sue

We are only at the tip of the iceberg in understanding the dynamics of "older" families in conflict and the toll it takes on everyone. We keep our shields up, protecting others from knowing how we are hurt or vulnerable. Our personal journeys of discovery and opening our heart continue. The journey of aging seems to sweep up so many crumbs of sad and unfortunate life circumstances that begin to define an aging person, which in these cases tip life's balance from the joy and purpose they once experienced.

Once we learn more about these tipping points, we may be able to address these family situations earlier and more productively. Doing so will take many deep breaths and a systemic change in the way we view our older family members and prioritize the later years in life. All the limbs of the family tree can grow better from stronger roots. "This was the best Father's Day!" the family members agreed while spending it together for the first time in years. Influences, work, and lessons learned will continue to guide the progress of the Eldercaring Coordination Initiative in providing a pathway to justice for older adults and leading families to a legacy of peace.

Notes

1. Linda Fieldstone, Sue Bronson, and Hon. Michelle Morley, "Association for Conflict Resolution Guidelines for Eldercaring Coordination," *Family Court Review* 53(4), October 2015, 542–561.

2. O.J. Coogler, *Structured Mediation in Divorce Settlement: A Handbook for Marital Mediators* (Lanham, MD: Lexington Books, 1978).

3. C.G. Jung, *Memories, Dreams, Reflections* (New York: Vintage, 1989), 247.

A Story of a Journey— from Resolution beyond Transformation

David Anderson Hooker

Helping Professions?

Suzette,[1] a 25-year-old African-American woman with less than a successful high school education and four children between the ages of two and twelve, came to the St. Louis County Adult Outpatient Psychiatric Clinic seeking help. She and her children were living at that time in a family homeless shelter. This living arrangement came about because, after being in a physically, sexually, and emotionally abusive relationship for almost ten years, she and the children had been summarily thrown out of her apartment. This loss of her home was so that her abusive partner, father of at least two of her four children, could move in his new girlfriend and the children he had fathered with the new woman. I was assigned the role of Suzette's counselor. She was also assigned a psychiatrist, Dr. Patel,[2] who was both foreign-born and a non-native English speaker.[3] My professional assessment was that Suzette was depressed, with significant, even crippling, self-doubt, which I thought was neither unusual under the circumstances nor specifically indicative of any pathological condition. Dr. Patel also determined her to be depressed, which in his worldview indicated both pathology and the need of an ongoing medication

David Anderson Hooker

regimen. And because the research he was relying on suggests that poor people and especially black- and brown-bodied people do not conform well to self-administered medication regimens, he urged her to accept a course of injectable psychotropic medicine. In the team debriefing that took place before the medications were actually administered, I advocated against a drug regimen. I also tried to counter the pathologizing assessments that in Dr. Patel's mind were indicative of the appropriateness of pharmacotherapy. Dr. Patel argued that her inability to acquire and maintain stable housing, her inability to articulate feelings or psychological insights, her history of youthful pregnancies, her failed relationships with her immediate family, and her "choice" to endure abuse and subject her children to the same condition made her a poor candidate for psychodynamic intervention. He stated that she would be much better served by pharmacological management. I argued, admittedly with insufficient professional restraint, that the doctor's language barrier and lack of familiarity with either culture or context made him incompetent to judge or assist this woman. Further, I suggested that the fact that he was relying on a textbook-only diagnostic approach might actually make him a real and present danger to the people coming to the clinic for help. After I was admonished by my supervisor for my lack of professional decorum and restraint, we compromised and allowed Suzette to choose between injections and an orally administered regimen. She chose oral administration, which provided some space for her sense of agency.

Approximately five months later, I was delighted when Suzette returned to the clinic with a level of joy and excitement that was almost uncontainable! She told me that within the last several weeks she had found a faith community that felt to her like family; her family had long since abandoned her when her abuser used standard practices to isolate her. She said that a member of that faith community had offered her a job and arranged for an affordable apartment nearby, and because her new job was at a family-owned clothing boutique, all of her children were going to be able to start the coming school year in a new school with new safe and personal living arrangements and an entire new wardrobe. The best of all in my mind was that she had taken her medication only intermittently and for the past six to eight weeks she had felt well enough to stop taking any medicine at all. I was delighted and saw this as great progress and a hopeful development. Dr. Patel, on the other hand, determined that he had misdiagnosed her; she was not depressed, but rather her energetic expressions of enthusiasm (she cried a bit when sharing all of the news) was reflective of a manic-depressive tendency, and because she had been "nonconforming" on her drug dosing, he wanted to insist on her receiving injected medication if she was going to continue getting any services at the center. It was, after all, an adult outpatient *psychiatric* clinic. The little bits of psychosocial support she was receiving from a master's-level community/clinical psychologist would be determined to be inconsequential for her well-being.

In this and so many other instances I was asking myself: What are processes or circumstances where people can get help with problem-solving in a culturally competent manner that do not require them to accept an assertion that they have a mental defect or fatal flaw in their character? How can we account for the entire social ecology of a person and appropriately distinguish between individual, relational, systemic, and cultural impediments to full flourishing? These questions and challenges caused me to leave the practice of community psychology and pursue alternative dispute resolution (ADR)—specifically mediation. There would subsequently be the same challenges and questions, which then caused me to incorporate a restorative justice framework in my community mediation processes. Two decades later, for better or worse, the same challenges and questions have caused me to seek to push past the "classic" restorative justice frameworks to think of even more culturally transformative approaches to justice as a pillar of healthy, whole, and liberated communities.

The Search

Since I was a very young child, I have had an active commitment to creating a world in which people are not arbitrarily excluded from the benefits of society because of some aspect of their identity. As a middle and high school student, this was reflected in my advocacy for and accompaniment of children and adults, some of whom were my friends, who had been identified as having physical or emotional challenges that often caused them to be excluded from mainstream activities. Leaving the bubble of the community of my youth, which was highly integrated in terms of race and class and religion and ethnicity, I discovered that much of society had been constructed in ways that tended to create disabilities for people based on the mythical racial categories to which they were assigned and the ethnic identities they chose.

I retained a steadfast desire to help people at the individual and, more importantly to me, the community level to achieve a sense of freedom and endless possibility. As an undergraduate psychology major, there were several theoretical challenges that caused me concern in that regard. Mainly, while the history of mental health research did not include people of color (as pointed out in the title of Robert Guthrie's 1976 history of prejudice in psychology, *Even the Rat Was White*), the practice of psychology and psychiatry was often used as a means of repression. Two clear examples of the use of mental health diagnoses in the furtherance of repression are dysaesthesia aethiopica[4] and drapetomania.[5] I recognized this same application of diagnosis in the furtherance of repression, even if unwittingly, in the relationship between Suzette and Dr. Patel. Still believing in the possibilities of mental health to support the liberation and advancement of black and brown people and their communities, I became a participant in the burgeoning black psychology movement. I had the opportunity to study with and learn from some of the luminaries of the movement, such as Na'im Akbar, Robert Williams, Leahcim Semaj, Bobby Wright, Asa Hilliard, Charlyn Harper-Bolton, and Wade Nobles. While still contemplating the possibility of studying psychiatry, I first took a master's degree in minority mental health from Washington University in St. Louis and then worked briefly at an adult outpatient psychiatric clinic in St. Louis County, Missouri, where I encountered Suzette and Dr. Patel. While I worked in the outpatient psychiatric clinic as a community therapist, there were several episodes that deeply troubled me about the relationship between mental health services, modes and parameters for diagnosis, and the ways of evaluating and pathologizing the lives of mostly poor or working-class people, especially black- and brown-bodied people, who have different cultural patterns than those upon whom the diagnoses were established. Learning Suzette's story and understanding the baked-into-the-system imbalance of power in favor of the psychiatrist[6] served as immediate precursor to me finding another way to be of service.

At about that time, Bill Potapchuk and others were doing work across town at the University of Missouri–St. Louis (UMSL) in methods of "no-fault conflict resolution" and community problem-solving. Their approach made more sense to me. The constraint of individually focused psychological approaches is that until recently they did a poor job of contextualizing life circumstances. As such, behaviors that were survival-oriented and rational in resource-constrained communities were pathologized by mental health professionals, many of whom lived and were educated in resource-adequate and even resource-abundant contexts.

So, in search of a framework that allowed me to continue to advocate on behalf of people in multiple struggles, I left the professional mental health context, "seeking my fame and fortune" as a mediator.

You may say I'm a dreamer, but I'm not the only one. I hope someday you'll join us. And the world will live as one.

John Lennon

What I Found in Mediation

I was first introduced to the practice of mediation by training in what is now often described as the "classic model" or "facilitative approach" to mediation. This approach is grounded in the Fisher and Ury interest-based bargaining model[7] of negotiation articulated in *Getting to Yes*,[8] conjoined with traditional approaches to effective communication and sometimes a bit of shuttle diplomacy and the use of "reality testing" as acceptable coercion to achieve a mutually acceptable agreement. In community mediation programs and in the early days of court-appended mediation programs, the parties were given broad license to establish the issues for which they sought resolution. Especially in the early community context, mediators did not necessarily have a shared professional framing, so participants were not subjected to uniform inquiry or closely monitored societal narratives. I had a perch in the development of mediation practice while working at the National Institute for Dispute Resolution (NIDR) that allowed me to watch the development of several branches of mediation: legal practice as articulated by the American Bar Association Section on Dispute Resolution (ABA); mediation in the educational contexts as refined within the National Academy of Mediators in Education (NAME); therapeutic models advanced by the Academy of Family Mediators (AFM); and the grassroots approaches championed by Peggy Herman and the National Conference of Peacemaking and Conflict Resolution (NCPCR).

Even though the several mediation and other ADR approaches reflected a range of opinion and practice regarding the depth of issue investigation, all frameworks shared an advantage from my perspective over a strict therapeutic/clinical approach to problem-solving: They were not deficit-based. In a therapeutic space, while the person or people (in the case of family) with the problem have the opportunity to describe their life circumstances, the normative nature of assessments and the prescriptive nature of the treatment process places agency in the realm of the professional to render a problem definition and to assume a normative state of behavior. The therapist gets to define what your problem is and what you should do about it.

There were various approaches that I learned as models for conducting mediations: interest-based, facilitative, identity-based, and transformative approaches, each of which had a wave of popularity. But as the field grew, there was an experience of institutional consolidation with a concomitant professionalization. This, in my mind, ultimately had the effect of driving out the grassroots mediators, limiting the creativity and cultural diversity reflected in both practitioners and processes, and all of this was reflected most poignantly by the demise of the NCPCR. The practice was overtaken by lawyers and professional therapists who reintroduced narrow legal principles and deficit-oriented practices, and as the number of community mediation centers declined, mediation programs became mostly tethered to legal institutions or large-scale employers like the post office.

CHANGE OF VIEW

In the winter of 1992, my relationship to the field, specifically my unquestioned acceptance of the articles of faith, platitudes, and promises of the ADR movement, were jolted by the publication of UC Berkeley legal anthropologist Laura Nader's article in the *NIDR Forum* entitled "Trading Justice for Harmony."[9] Nader's critique questioned the ADR movement's putative role in establishing a more equitable national distribution of justice. Nader noticed that the rise of civil unrest in the 1960s and the resort to court relief by several social movements, including civil, women's, and consumer rights groups, coincided with a federal and corporate-sponsored effort to increase the use of ADR.

At the time that ADR and especially mediation was expanding, the suggestions/promises were that these processes saved time, expenses, court costs, *and* relationships. And while there was virtually no research to back these claims, the truths of the claims were taken almost as articles of faith. And the faith was confirmed by the number of people who came out of the processes with what were described as "mutually acceptable agreements," which was supposed to be a good thing, right?

Quoting Nader at length to give full treatment to her argument:

> The legal problems that need creative new forms of administration of justice are those between people of unequal power. While the justices of the peace . . . used their wisdom to resolve face-to-face disputes between people of relative equals; today we are faced with conflicts between dispersed citizens and large centralized structures. The parties are of grossly unequal power. Thus to focus on assistance to individuals distracts attention from economic forces, power differentials, and inequality in distribution of remedies in the US.
>
> The assumption that the change in the delivery of justice is to be achieved by adding mediators or arbitrators illustrates a blindness to the importance of social and cultural structures that produce legal problems.
>
> ADR is a clever scheme of pacification, one similar to that used by missionizing colonial powers in Africa, in the Pacific and elsewhere. The 1960's in the United States were years when many social groups felt encouraged to come forward with their agendas: civil rights, consumer rights, environmental rights, women's rights, etc. Those who thought that Americans were becoming too litigious

sought to remedy what they saw as a confrontational mode. During the same time large corporations were complaining about the costs of inter corporate litigation.[10]

In making this case, among other things, Nader references the language and tone of the remarks of Attorney General Griffin Bell at a major conference that marked a major milepost in the ADR movement. She characterized Bell's remarks as expressing "themes that hovered around efficiency and harmony, or how to rid the country of confrontation and the courts of 'garbage cases' (e.g. consumer, environmental, feminist issues)." She also noted that his remarks did not address issues about "measures that prevent wrong doing, no discussion about unequal power vis-à-vis the law, nor did the discussion of streamlining include class-action or aggregate solutions."

Nader's final assessment was this:

> ADR has been primarily geared to induce passivity, a characteristic certainly not encouraging of democracy. Disputes are symptoms of fundamental and systematic problems in our society, one of the most important being the absence of democratic control of society's resources. In sum, to consider ADR in its present form as a panacea for wrongdoing is unacceptable because it trades justice for harmony.[11]

All things are our relatives; what we do to everything, we do to ourselves. All is really One.

BLACK ELK

In times of increasing civil unrest in the United States and elsewhere around the world, and with the increasing use of nonjudicial fora to resolve matters such as the aftermaths of Hurricanes Katrina and Sandy, 9/11, the BP oil spill in the Gulf of Mexico, the Upper Big Branch Mine tragedy, and the collapse of several major financial institutions, I think that it might be valuable and timely to review Nader's critique of ADR and to apply the analysis to restorative justice.

Without taking time to relitigate this entire era, I would simply add the observation that there were practices that were attached to the harmony ideology that allowed practitioners to be "successful." We believed for the most part that conflicts were about unmet needs or conflicting interests or the desire for empowerment and recognition. The field was in many ways tethered (some of us would say "hoodwinked") by the interests-based framework in ways that overlook the structural and values propositions that produce and reproduce systemic inequities.

We built models to follow based on this ideology and the practices that ensue, which is why thirty-five years after its original publication many still teach mediation based on *Getting to Yes* and then for the past twenty-five years we have offered Folger and Baruch Bush's *Promise of Mediation*[12] as a helpful, and some would even suggest necessary, corrective without ever effectively infusing decolonizing inquiry, critical race, womanist, or queer theory into our projects. As a result, I would suggest that twenty-five years after Nader's critique was raised, her premonition was proven true: Poor and marginalized people and people of deeply unequal power have even less access to mechanisms of justice in this country, and we choke on the smoke and run blindly into the mirrors that ADR processes produce.

QUESTIONS MEDIATION DOESN'T ASK

Among the advantages that mediation has over many psychodynamic therapies is that it generally does not operate from a deficit-based inquiry. Yet there are still constraints on what seems possible to consider. A metaphor that I often used when conducting mediation training to describe the depth of inquiry in mediation was this: While law generally only considers the surface, and sometimes therapy goes to the bone, mediation inquires at the level of muscle. For instance, in much of my early training I was advised to avoid questions about a person's faith or other deeply held values: "positions and interests are negotiable and even needs can be met in multiple ways but people's religious beliefs cannot be negotiated or compromised so don't ask." These days, as a narrative mediator, those are areas and sources of meaning-making that I can effectively probe, even though many still choose to avoid them. Also, standard wisdom holds that you cannot mediate a case where there has been violence in the relationship. While I agree that there are no acceptable levels of violence and therefore the amount or type of violence cannot be negotiated or compromised, it would often be helpful to discuss the cultural and structural factors that make violence a likely or even acceptable response in the minds of the actors.

Mediators also tend to avoid the structural and cultural questions because they are not in the realm of the negotiation. The people cannot change their culture, and structural representatives (systems, governments) are most often not involved in the process, so those questions tend to be given short shrift if any attention at all. This is one of the ways in which a restorative inquiry has advantages over most traditional approaches (facilitative, transformative, identity) to mediation. Also, when a mediation is presented in a legal context and tethered to a court process, the area of inquiry is often narrowed even further to follow the contours of the legal elements of the issues before the court. In a personal injury case, for instance, when a person claims injury, the assessment of the value of the claim is based on the person's current worth and potential. If that person's potential is already limited by societal circumstances constructed because of a person's race, gender/gender conformity, or status in the labor force, then it is often the case that the mediation process affirms the inequitable assessment of value—the death or severe impairment of a poor white child from a family of professionals is valued much higher than if the same death or impairment had happened to a child of a laborer-class black, indigenous, or other person of color (BIPOC). In this way, I find that the "neutrality" of the process affirms the inequities of society. I also found that adopting a restorative justice–based inquiry framework allows a better approach to highlighting the direct and structural violences that may be contributing to the conflict.

In the world of peacebuilding and multiparty problem-solving, one of the most important developments was the movement from conflict resolution to conflict transformation. This distinction was introduced by either John Paul Lederach or Ron Kraybill (I have no intention of weighing in on that debate). One of the distinctions that Lederach wrote about that is very helpful in expanding the frame beyond typical mediation/conflict resolution inquiry was the distinction between *episode* versus *epicenter*. The episode is the instance of conflict; the epicenter is the structural and cultural conditions or institutional and societal arrangements that produced this conflict and make similar conflicts likely in the future. The episode inquiry is most appropriate in a mediation context, while inquiring about the epicenter is the proper purview of a restorative inquiry.

RESTORATIVE JUSTICE

For my purposes, a restorative inquiry framework allows the problem-solving process to go beyond the way that past breaches of laws, rules, and agreements can be addressed to focus on how to privilege relationality to both respond to the past and prepare for the future. While a traditional "justice" inquiry will focus on which laws were broken, who broke them, and what is the proper punishment, a restorative inquiry asks:

What are the harms done?

What does it take to put it right?

Who has the responsibility and who has the resources to help put it right?

What are the best processes to involve (and honor the involvement of) those most impacted and those ablest to contribute?

Before moving all the way to narrative mediation, I adopted this inquiry framework. And even this, in many programs that I have observed, falls short of the potential and promise of restorative justice.

What is now called "restorative justice" draws from a set of philosophical principles that are central to many indigenous nations and people from places that we colloquially refer to as "the Global South." What has happened in the development of the restorative justice field in the United States and Europe is that there has been an appropriation of principles and practices, such as circle, conference, and council, which has largely been applied to the reform of certain institutions, such as criminal justice and education, on behalf of communities that are often negatively impacted by the institutions' policies and practices. While the practices were bor-

If we keep telling that life is unfair but do nothing serious about it, then life will forever continue to remain unfair!

MEHMET
MURAT ILDAN

rowed and introduced with great vigor and fanfare, there was not an equal measure of energy applied to transforming the value pillars of the organizations or even doing a deep reconstruction of the entire policy platform. In schools, for instance, changing the disciplinary processes to infuse restorative practices will offer great benefit in the disciplinary spaces. However, without also examining the existing sources of harm that youth might experience through the curricular content or the architectural or aesthetics of the physical structure, reform might be possible, transformation less likely. In my estimation, the field needs to push for the adoption of restorative principles as a foundational set of philosophical and moral standards by which to organize society. It's a really hard lift and an almost impossible standard, and I have no idea how to achieve that standard, *and yet* what we know in peacebuilding is that if you take a set of practices, even principles, and export them from one context into another, something is lost. As a result, while restorative justice practices can have a mitigating impact that is valuable and laudable, they are constrained in the transformational possibilities. For instance, several program evaluations have demonstrated that while restorative discipline programs in schools reduce the overall number of in- and out-of-school suspensions, the racial disparities in the rates of suspension remain relatively unchanged. This reflects both the possibility for substantial damage mitigation within the system and significant limitations in the capacity for systemic transformation. Said differently, the episodes are well addressed, and yet the epicenter remains a viable source of concern.

INQUIRING ABOUT HARM—BEYOND IMPLICIT AND STRUCTURAL BIASES

I think the limitations to systemic transformation can best be understood in the framing of the first question in the restorative inquiry framework—the question of harm. Most articulators of restorative justice principles and practice[13] suggest that the most important principle of restorative justice is the shift away from wrongdoing and punishment to a focus on harm and relationship. If this is true, there is a subtle difference in the way the question concerning harm is posed that potentially minimizes the power of the philosophical shift. If a conference facilitator or circle steward poses the question in terms of "What harms were done in this instance?" this places the focus on the episode and locates the action with the putative actor/doer of harm. This approach also locates the source of harm in the agentic presence of an individual actor. What this construction of the question also does is allow the harms produced by the system and the violence that was possibly invoked as a reasonable response to the undergirding cultural narratives to go unchecked.

When a child breaks a rule in school and causes harm or disruption to the class or school setting, the resulting circle process will often ask the child to acknowledge how their actions caused harm to another student or teacher or how they disrupted the school processes. What is not invoked by this framing of the question are the possibilities that the system itself, in the constraining and dehumanizing physical and aesthetic conditions and practices (single-file lines to pass between classrooms, electronic surveillance, armed police presence) or the content of the curriculum as invisibilizing and ofttimes degrading with regard to certain racially, ethnically, or gender-defined identities, is also a constant source of harm inflicted upon them that they might be reactive to. In fact, the entire banking model of education, especially prevalent in urban settings, that denies the wisdom and knowledge that the students have garnered from their context, is a way of doing violence to the participants. I still find it fascinating that one of the most frequently invoked sources of disruption and "harm" is when a student is deemed by the teacher or administrator to be "defiant." The cross-racial and cross-cultural interpretation of student actions results in racially disparate rates and levels of punishment. This is a cultural value that results in disproportionate impacts on black- and brown-bodied children. Yet in the restorative process what will most often be understood as success is not the teacher or administrator recognizing their implicit and systemic biases, but rather the child learning to behave better or stifle their frustration. A similar case happens in prison. The fact that the entire penal system is organized around dehumanization and constraint of individual liberty and collective expression is not to be questioned within restorative justice programs operating inside the prison. The cumulatively traumagenic conditions that produce the cycles of victimhood and violence that exist in prisons are ignored and even denied. Rather, the containee's behavior is to be modified for more orderly operation of the system.

A different construction of the central question "What are all of the *sources of harm* present that are impacting the relationships, resources, and structures that define this episode of relational disruption?" allows a broader inquiry. In peacebuilding terminology, the process would both inquire about the *episode* and also try to discover the *epicenter* for this type of harm. Admittedly, this type of inquiry and an honest effort to engage it would require substantial time and other resource allocations and organizational vulnerabilities, investments that many systems are not yet ready to take on.

The possibility of restorative justice contributing to social transformation is very much found in the epicenter inquiry. Yet the way that many restorative justice programs are structured,[14] funded, and operating, this question is constrained. And, as such, restorative justice will need to ally with other community approaches to respond to the second central inquiry: What does it take to put it right (resolution), and in what way could it be put right that makes it less likely that it happens again between these actors or others similarly situated (transformation)?

With all of its expansion and what seems to be growing acceptance, the field of restorative justice is at an important juncture. Because there is a broad and fluid definition of what is and is not reasonably considered to be a restorative practice, there is the rising possibility that what would be reasonably described as "business as usual" in education and criminal justice could appropriate restorative language. There is also the possibility that restorative justice could overpromise. The field could effectively become an *officious interloper* in the cause of building just, equitable, and peaceful societies. Laura Nader was concerned that ADR practices and approaches did not effectively consider the existing power imbalances and the inherent inequities in the relationships. It is possible that for restorative justice, if it is practiced primarily *within or as an appendage of* the institutions that it would otherwise seek to transform, the practices will be co-opted in ways that deny the transformative possibility.

Transforming Historical Harms: The Need to Do "Dirt Work"

The primary possibility that attracted me to restorative justice as an inquiry framework (the value of the practices is secondary in my estimation) was the transformational possibility that is implied in

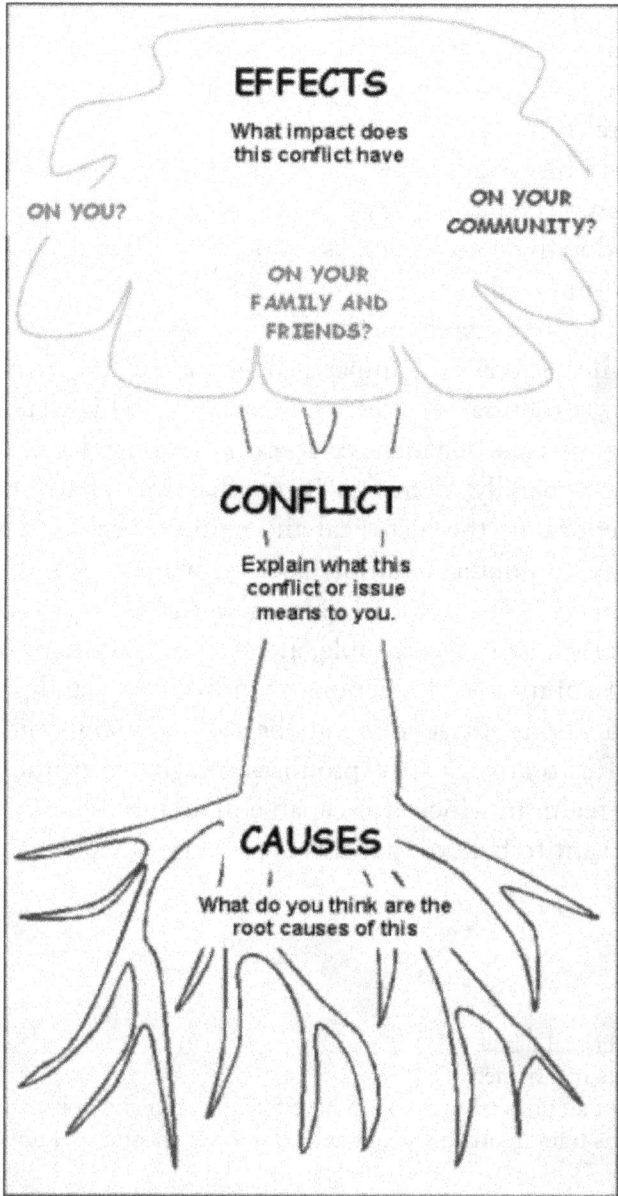

EFFECTS

What impact does this conflict have

ON YOU?

ON YOUR COMMUNITY?

ON YOUR FAMILY AND FRIENDS?

CONFLICT

Explain what this conflict or issue means to you.

CAUSES

What do you think are the root causes of this

Figure 11.1.

the focus on harms. This would allow someone who is a perpetrator now but victim in the recent past to have all aspects of their lives and context considered in conversations about pursuing a shared future. The question of harms also implies a deep dive beyond structural forms to consider identity and cultural narratives as a source of harms. The storytelling practices that play a vital role in most restorative processes leave open that we would examine people's stories and also the narratives that shape their stories and the narratives that construct the performance of their identities. Restorative justice, if it investigates and invites action at the level of structural form and discursive/narrative context, has the power to transform historical harms and pursue justice in the ways that it has been promoted as being capable.

In conducting conflict analysis, one of the more popular analysis tools is the conflict tree.

A conflict tree identifies the fruit, which are the most immediate manifestations and impacts of an issue; the trunk, representing the structural sources; and the roots, which are the deep underlying sources of violence. There is another layer altogether that is not generally identified in conflict tree analysis: the dirt. The dirt represents the historical and cultural narratives that have the capacity to nourish multiple societal inequities and violences. Narrative presence of colonial enterprise and binary thinking and hierarchical valuations of people, along with narratives of ownership, disposability, and the fictions of individuality and practices of commodification—these all lie at the root of many injustices and contexts. Restorative justice promises, maybe overpromises, that this is the realm in which it is capable of acting.

I still want to believe that this is true and possible.

It does not take many words to tell the truth.

Sitting Bull

Notes

1. Not her real name.
2. Not his real name.
3. It is not an unusual situation to have foreign-born and non-native-speaking physicians train in urban settings and treat lower-income and minority clientele.

4. From Watch the Yard: https://www.watchtheyard.com/history/drapeto mania-dysaesthesia-aethiopica/.

> According to his scientific writings, he had also found a mental illness called *dysaesthesia aethiopica* which made blacks lazy in their work. Dr. Cartwright said that a sign of this illness was a partial insensitivity of the skin and "so great a hebetude of the intellectual faculties, as to be like a person half asleep."
>
> Cartwright then went on to say that this illness is "much more prevalent among free negroes living in clusters by themselves, than among slaves on our plantations, and attacks only such slaves as live like free negroes in regard to diet, drinks, exercise, etc." according to Cartwright, "nearly all [free negroes] are more or less afflicted with it, that have not got some white person to direct and to take care of them."
>
> Once again, his cure for this "mental illness" was violent and horrible. According to Cartwright, because insensitivity of the skin was one symptom of the disease, the skin needed to be stimulated: "The best means to stimulate the skin is, first, to have the patient well washed with warm water and soap; then, to anoint it all over in oil, and to slap the oil in with a broad leather strap; then to put the patient to some hard kind of work in the sunshine."
>
> After the prescribed "course of treatment", Cartwright said the slave will "look grateful and thankful to the white man whose compulsory power . . . has restored his sensation and dispelled the mist that clouded his intellect."

5. Drapetomania is defined as an overwhelming urge to run away (from home, a bad situation, responsibility, etc.). The word was coined in 1851 by Samuel A. Cartwright as a mental illness that caused black slaves to flee captivity, but is today recognized as pseudoscience and an example of scientific racism.

6. Because public funding for mental health services was always very limited, community clinics like the one I worked in required external funding. The public and private insurance companies would pay for psychological and psychiatric assessments. However, the diagnoses and treatment regimens that could only be made by psychiatrists were the ones that achieved the highest reimbursements and the greatest margin of financial reward for the system. While people may only need help with problem-solving and some temporary measures of emotional wellness care, that is only available through private insurance.

7. An interesting aside from the editor which I thought should not be lost: Susanne Terry said,

> As someone who was trained by Bill Lincoln and started mediating in 1976, this is why *Getting to Yes* has always annoyed me in some respects. We never thought of what we were doing as interest-based bargaining. We thought of it as a process that sought to make it possible for

parties to understand each other, explore what was important, and work together to address what they said was important to them. The appearance of *GTY* began a trajectory that eventually ended up with the Fisher and Ury approach as well as the approach that I was familiar with all being called Facilitative Mediation. How it is described is foreign to me. In fact, a great deal, but not all of how Transformative Mediation is described more accurately describes my work.

8. Roger Fisher and William Ury, *Getting to Yes: Negotiating Agreement without Giving In* (New York: Penguin Books, 1981).

9. Laura Nader, "Trading Justice for Harmony," *NIDR Forum*, Winter 1992, 12–19.

10. Ibid, 12–13.

11. Ibid, 14.

12. Robert A. Baruch Bush and Joseph P. Folger, *The Promise of Mediation: The Transformative Approach to Conflict* (San Francisco: Jossey-Bass, 2005).

13. See, for example, Howard Zehr, *The Little Book of Restorative Justice* (Intercourse, PA: Good Books, 2002); and Fania Davis, *The Little Book of Race and Restorative Justice: Black Lives, Healing, and US Social Transformation* (New York: Good Books, 2019).

14. Some allegedly restorative processes are even scripted!

CHAPTER 12

Standing on Strong Shoulders

BETH ROY AND MARLON SHERMAN

Beth: "Good morning, Marlon."

Marlon: "Good morning, Beth. It's a lovely day here this morning—blue sky, birds singing."

Beth (looking up from computer to notice blue sky above the brick Public Storage building across the street): "Oh yes. Blue sky here, too."

BETH

MARLON, YOU ALWAYS REMIND ME THAT THERE IS A NATURAL world and we live in it. I find it wonderful that our friendship is laced with so many divergences and convergences. We formed consciousness in such very different worlds: you, grounded in a particular physical and ancestral landscape; me, floating out from a people scattered across the globe. I imagine you as essentially located and myself as severely dislocated.

And yet I feel so connected with you. When we've worked together—facilitating a meeting, creating an anthology—I've always been delighted by how easily we agree, as if, however we got there, we arrive at the same important nexus of values rooted in social justice. As we've begun to talk about who we are, we've

Beth Roy

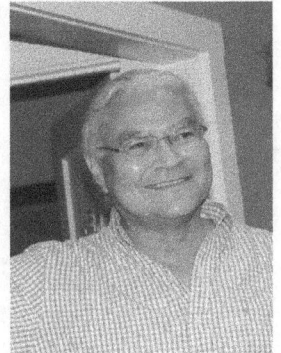

Marlon Sherman

discovered a crucial place where our histories converge: We both derive from a people that survived genocide—just barely, but here we still are—and it is their strength and spirit that have carried us this far, on their shoulders, really.

So for both of us, neutrality, quite simply, is not an option. Activism equals survival.

MARLON

That's right, Beth, our stories seem to be totally different. I'm a man raised in rural South Dakota. You are a woman raised in New York City and the Southwest. Even so, we seem to be walking the same path when it comes to dispute resolution and management.

I am Oglala Lakota, born in a log cabin just up the hill from American Horse Creek, a few miles outside the tiny community of Kyle, in the middle of the Pine Ridge Indian Reservation in South Dakota. Our little two-room house had no plumbing—we had to walk down the hill on the path through the chokecherries and dip our buckets in the spring to take water back up to the house and dump it into the milk can by the front door. Weekends, we had to make more trips up and down the hill so we could take our baths in galvanized tubs of water heated in pots on the woodstove. We had a root cellar, where we stored the crop from Mom's garden and took shelter from tornadoes in the summer. Yes, Mom and Dad were hard workers, Mom especially, because she raised eight of us in that little house.

Mom's people came from the rich bottomlands along the Missouri River, so they named themselves Plant-by-the-Water People. They were as much farmers as they were buffalo hunters, and I guess that's the reason Mom always kept a very well-tended garden in the flats down below by the creek. Dad's people, where I grew up, were the stereotypical plains buffalo hunters, so he and the older boys usually kept us well supplied with game. I spent a lot of time with Mom in the garden, but also went along on many of Dad's hunts. Most days when I wasn't helping with chores or going to school, we kids played and wandered all along the creek, sometimes hiking the miles to the reservoir near Kyle to go swimming. Eventually circumstances forced Mom and Dad to decide to leave our little house so Mom could go to college and come back to teach little kids on the reservation. Wherever we lived after that, my brother Gerald and I would always make our own paths along the creeks and rivers, into the hills and through the forested mountains, always close to the land, always finding new experiences in the lands of our ancestors. Mom had taught us how to put our fingers into the earth and help her children grow. Dad had taught us how to watch the landscape, the animals, the weather, and the seasons. Our own travels on foot taught us the rest. We knew we were Mniconjou and Oglala, of the Lakota Nation. We learned we belonged to the Earth and that She would provide for us and take care of us if we acted respectfully and with generosity toward her and all of her children.

In the old days before Americans invaded Lakota lands, child-rearing was a community project. Children belonged to the whole village. Any child who happened to be hungry could expect to be fed from any cooking fire anywhere in the village. Aunts and uncles took responsibility for teaching and disciplining (but not spanking, never hitting), while grandparents and other elders taught the children law and culture through storytelling. Older sisters and brothers protected the young ones, keeping them safe throughout the day. Mothers and fathers were where children came to receive unconditional love and comfort. Everyone loved, listened to, and mentored the children in their own particular roles. Children were seldom told what exactly to do. Rather, the lessons and morals were implied in the stories and actions of all the elders, which children listened to and watched, coming then to their own conclusions.

The US government changed all of that, with its policies of physical and cultural genocide. First, the federal government sent Christian missionaries to the reservations with the purpose of "civilizing the savages." Next, the government passed laws making it illegal, on pain of punishment, to practice their religion or spirituality. At the same time, Congress opened boarding schools far from the reservations; children were taken by force if necessary and compelled to learn English, to cut their hair, to wear "civilized" clothes, to worship as a Christian, and to live a military lifestyle, marching in formation and living in barracks.

Many people of the time—both well-meaning liberal Christians and greedy developers—believed that living on reservations and holding all their lands in common was one of the main reasons Native peoples remained "uncivilized." They felt that one of the best ways to "civilize the savages" was to convert all their tribal land to private property, giving each man 160 acres. At the same time, these people believed that if they could surround Indians with hardworking white people, the Indians would learn how they should act just by watching: monkey see, monkey do. So they began to divide up reservations lands all across the country, the Pine Ridge Reservation included. In most cases, there was far more land than there were Native families to take their small parcels, so it was easy to open up millions of "surplus" acres to homesteaders, who were more than eager to take the cheap land.

This process, allotment, had many disastrous consequences for tribes and individual Natives everywhere it was introduced, but the one that is important to this story is the way it separated families from each other. For instance, while Lakota lived in tipi villages of anywhere from a few extended families to thousands of people, depending on the time of year, the families were now forced to live on their own parcels of land, separated by distance from everyone else. This of course destroyed the traditional child-rearing process, as it was physically impossible to collectively care for the children. Mothers and fathers were now forced to perform the roles of an entire village—parents, aunts, uncles, and grandparents. Many of them were not prepared for the addition of all this extra work in addition to trying to make a living as farmers in new, harsh conditions on their insufficient lands. But also, they were not socially prepared; these new roles were not theirs. They did not believe they were the proper ones to be taking on the tasks of teachers, disciplinarians, and storytellers to their own children. As usual, the ones who suffered most from this societal degradation were the children, who had lost their teachers, protectors, elders, and mentors. This has led to huge knowledge and wisdom gaps not only in Lakota society but in all Native tribes in the United States and Canada.

Missionaries, boarding schools, the outlawing of Indianness, and allotment have all combined in Native societies to make dysfunctional people, societies, and governments. A large percentage of Native peoples are no longer able to communicate effectively or at all, either among themselves or with outsiders. Because the federal government has made decisions for tribes for so long, many have lost that ability, and are only poorly able to plan or to make rational, informed decisions. The reservation-wide government (the tribal council) on my home reservation is the best (or worst) example of this. The term of office is two years, so every two years the entire tribal council changes, as voters have become dissatisfied and angry with their elected council members' actions or inaction and look for someone new to put into office. There is little continuity and no institutional memory.

I see now that I left the reservation at age nineteen because of that history of oppression and dysfunction—it was at times a very uncomfortable place to live, and good jobs were scarce. Well, and truthfully, I wanted to have some adventures in the famous California. My move was made possible by the federal relocation program, a policy aimed at emptying the reservations and sending as many American Indians as possible to cities, where it was hoped they would assimilate into the mainstream of civilized society. Again, the federal government was trying to make Indians disappear.

I met my wife, Dale Ann, because we were both attending the same community college on the same relocation program, many miles from either of our homes. Over the years, we moved back and forth from my home reservation to her traditional territory in the redwood coastal area of northern California, with some stops in cities in between. Everything we saw over the next two decades convinced us that our home societies had been wounded from the outside and that those who had hurt us—the US government in particular and US society in general—were not willing to help us truly heal those deep wounds. They would periodically apply small bandages, but they were never enough, and in fact, they would almost as often rip those bandages off and expose the wounds anew. Dale Ann and I decided that if anything was going to happen, Native peoples would have to do it ourselves. We felt we needed to finish our college education and do something that would help us repay our ancestors for fighting to survive so that we could live. Dale Ann decided to go into museum studies so she could help bring the ancestors home from museums. I decided to go into law so I could be a courtroom warrior.

If you want peace, you don't talk to your friends. You talk to your enemies.

DESMOND TUTU

BETH

When you launched our digital conversation, Marlon, with the story of your beginnings, I felt myself rebel. Much as I am drawn to visiting *your* past, I felt an inchoate resistance to doing the same with mine. Why? I wondered. Many times, my personal origin story has begun with my birth in the "year of the Final Solution": the moment when Hitler ordered the mass extermination of Jews. My earliest emotional memories involve refugees living in our home. But having told that story often, I feel distanced from it. Our formative stories become mythologized, in the process inaccessible to the powerful emotions that once gave them meaning. No doubt I was formed by genocide in many ways. Yet in this moment a fence has appeared between me and my collective past.

Fences exclude land; they equally define the territory beyond. Our conversations are filled with signposts. You write, "We learned we belonged to the Earth . . ." I realize I do not feel I belong to the earth. I am, I realize, existentially ungrounded. The wandering Jew is more than metaphor. Like you, my people were displaced multiple times through history. Unlike yours, we turned away from the lands that turned us out. Alienation became our birthright, not connection with the earth.

So alienation is the theme that emerges most powerfully for me. From the beginning of consciousness, I felt mysteriously divorced from my family of origin. My parents were good people, kind and responsible to others. My father was the firstborn son of immigrants from Poland. My grandparents were observant Jews: kept kosher, went to synagogue even when it was not High Holy Days. Neither grandparent stood taller than five feet. That their lack of stature derived from malnutrition was suggested when my father, birthed in the new land, grew and grew and grew to over six feet tall. My grandmother set both her sons to learn musical instruments, betting they could always make a little money that way. My father was given the big trombone, his diminutive younger brother a flute. Dad played in speakeasies to fund his way through medical school. My uncle became a symphony flutist. People sometimes asked my father when he knew he wanted to be a doctor. "As soon as I could understand what my mother was saying to me," he'd reply. Those instructions must have been spoken in Yiddish when he was younger than five. I calculate that because, when he started public kindergarten, his parents were ordered by the authorities to speak nothing but English at home. They knew no English, so there was little said until Dad learned enough of the new language to teach his parents. His mother never learned to read and write. But a lack of communication tools was compensated by her fierce determination. She and Grandpa were married for ten years before their first child was born. I asked Grandma once why they waited so long. "We had to wait until we saved enough money," she said, describing to me how they both worked, she sewing in sweatshops in what's now fashionable SoHo, he as a lacquer salesman (which profession he pronounced in a way often misunderstood as "alcoholic"). "How'd you manage not to get pregnant?" I asked, imagining some folksy form of birth control. She looked up from her knitting and said in tones of steel, "Grandpa slept in the armchair!"

So my people, like yours, Marlon, lost their language. In later years, Dad remembered no Yiddish. Grandma's goal was security in the new world, but she seemed to accept as inevitable the accompanying loss of culture. My father told the story of the family's silent year with humor, never sorrow and certainly not anger. We, the next generation, might protest, but he'd merely shrug. He'd internalized the message: His generation's job was to assimilate.

Every immigrant group tends toward particular strategies for making it in the new world. Some start small businesses; others acquire real estate. Prohibited in Europe from owning land, newly arrived American Jews relied on intelligence and education to find security, often turning to professions where success required them to blend into the general population. Anti-Semitism was still rife when I was growing up. We were fully aware of what had happened to Jews in Europe, and daily events proved that prejudice lived strong at home as well: the quota my father overcame to get admitted to medical school; the debate about whether my aunt should lie about her obviously Jewish maiden name when applying for jobs; the battles we children fought with neighborhood boys at Easter when they chased us, shouting, "Christ killers!"

To assimilate was to acquire a bit of protective coloration. We could pass for white. We were genuinely affluent. In the Southwest,

even our places of worship came to look more and more like Protestant churches, choirs and all. Like many second-generation Jews, my
parents followed this path. Their world consisted of removal from
the community of the ghetto to Long Island suburbs and eventually
to Texas; acquisition of stuff; card games and cocktails with friends
on the weekends; and, in my father's case, very hard work. I grew
up, the middle of three children, in this upper-middle-class family,
fine people. We had everything we needed, and then some. From
my earliest memories I couldn't wait to get away.

Was our assimilation forced like yours, Marlon? Not obviously. But the coercive power of dominance operates in many
ways. My people warmly embraced assimilation, loved the dom-
inant culture, absorbed it hungrily. What they assimilated to,
however, repelled me: the anxious conformity, the enthusiastic
materialism. If they willingly leaped into a warm pool of dominance, I bounced off its surface.

Two other similarities I notice with your story, Marlon. I felt
trapped in our nuclear family, by the too-limited social resources
and models for adulthood. You describe so vividly what happens
when collective lives are segmented into atomized family units.
The losses to children are mirrored by losses to adults. My father
worked—night and day. My mother stayed home, making beds
day after day and cooking meals. I knew I wanted my father's life,
not my mother's.

At the same time, as in your family, the women set strong
examples of leadership. Unfortunately, some of that was manifested
in cruel judgment of others. My two sets of grandparents didn't
like each other. The more affluent and assimilated ones held the
Yiddish-speaking, observant pair in contempt.

Perhaps in part because of these family tensions, my parents
decided to leave New York in search of calmer lives when I was
ten. It was a time of migration in America, postwar and post-
Depression years when corporations were hiring again, and jobs for
white working people often required relocation to distant parts of
the country. Urban redevelopment projects resuscitated inner cities,
displacing old, established communities. Black migration north,
stimulated by wartime hiring, reached serious proportions. The US
population was on the move.

For reasons I won't detail here, my parents decided the ideal place for us was, improbably, Fort Worth. At the time, the city that called itself "Where the West Begins," but which we Yankees promptly labeled "Where Civilization Ends," sported a population of about 750,000, fewer than 5,000 of whom were Jewish. The grandparents, for once united, wept as they imagined us departing for a land of guns, cowboys, and, yes, Indians. With that drama started a major chapter in my life as an agitator.

As we entered territory legally segregated, injustice, until now difficult to identify even when keenly felt, gained a name. We went shopping for beds in a major department store—an activity endlessly boring for us kids. Entertaining ourselves by exploring, we discovered two water fountains, one on either side of the elevator doors. Once was marked "Colored," the other "White." Colored sounded a whole lot more interesting, so I headed there. As I drank, I felt my father's hands grab my waist. My steady-as-a-rock dad was shaking.

"Not there!" he exclaimed in a whisper as he pulled me away. "You have to drink from the other fountain."

As was typical of many white, middle-class children, our only direct experience of African-American people had been with a live-in maid, Fanny. She lived with us throughout the war years, until I was about five. In retrospect, I believe she must have been little older than a teenager. She was also little taller than we. We considered her a playmate, for she was a joyful soul. She handled her domestic duties as briefly as possible so she could spend most of her time with us. With the unerring intuition of dependent children, I understood that Fanny and my father did not see eye to eye. I may not have understood the class and racial hierarchy, but I knew which side I was on. I judged my father unequivocally wrong.

A truly living human being cannot remain neutral.

NADINE GORDIMER

I combined awareness about the Holocaust—I remember thinking there are people in the world who would kill me without even knowing me!—with my feelings about the struggle between Fanny and my father. How I came to think about it as being racial I don't know. But when we got to Texas, I never questioned that what we were witnessing was injustice.

So much of children's values are set through emotional, intuitive transactions like these. For me, the lines were starkly clear: Injustice must be fought, not just for "my" people (as defined by my elders, Jews) but for everyone. Perhaps because I knew I was the descendant of genocide, perhaps combined with reasons private and personal, not to stand for justice was not to survive.

Fast-forward a few years. In 1954, I started high school—a segregated high school—a few months after the Supreme Court ordered school integration. In Fort Worth, as in most places throughout the South, a legal decision meant nothing. As a thirteen-year-old, I spoke out. I joined a small interracial, interreligious group of integrationists lobbying for change. Perhaps we planted some seeds, but little more. But as resistance to desegregation hardened, I grew more and more alienated. "Wait until you go East for college," my parents reassured me. "Things will be very different there."

When I was sixteen, I did go East, entering Brandeis University as part of its tenth graduating class. But things were not different. Sit-ins and other protests of the early civil rights movement were making headlines. My northern classmates shook their heads in condemnation of those backward Southerners. But I looked around campus: Where were the students of color? There were almost none. I listened to the assumptions and life expectations of my classmates and heard unrelieved white privilege.

Let us bring equality, justice, and peace for all. Not just the politicians and the world leaders, we all need to contribute. Me. You. It is our duty.

MALALA YOUSAFZAI (2014 NOBEL PEACE PRIZE RECIPIENT)

Finding myself growing as alienated in the North as I had been in the South, I determined to leave the country. Aware that I, too, was prisoner to the limitations of my cultural mind-set, I wanted to live someplace as different from all I knew as I could find. I aimed for Burma, a place I pictured on scant information to be a model for community caring. As it developed, along the way I met and married a revolutionary from India and landed there instead.

My true education in multiculturalism had begun. When I left the United States, I entertained no doubt about my point of view, even as I knew it was limited by my experience. India taught me to see things from varied standpoints, to suspend judgment in favor of understanding, to honor cultural differences even while staying true to values of justice and equity.

MARLON

Oh, Beth, what a naïve dreamer I was! I thought law school was a way of preparing for battle. Instead, in my first day at law school, my first eight a.m. property law class, with the first lesson in the law text, I realized how wrong I had been about law as the way to change our people's situations. The lesson was about the US Supreme Court case called *Johnson v. M'Intosh*, from 1823. That case is the foundation from which all federal Indian law has been implemented in the United States. Absolutely every court opinion, every congressional statute, and every executive action having to do with tribes has come from that one opinion, which states plainly that all American Indian tribes had lost ownership of their lands when white, "civilized," Christian men laid claim to those lands. Tribes had lost their claims the instant Columbus planted the Spanish flag on an island in the hemisphere, because Indians were merely ignorant, uncivilized, non-Christian savages who had no loyalty to Jesus Christ. Almost all lawyers in the country, whether conservative, liberal, or somewhere on the outskirts, implicitly or explicitly accept that racist 1823 decision as the truth, even though it was only a justification for the genocidal colonization that characterized these two continents. I had to decide if I wanted to make a career within a legal system based on racism, genocide, fraud, and theft. Because I was so deeply opposed to the US legal system, I had an extremely difficult time finishing law school.

In the third year, I took a mediation course, but it was no help at all, as it retained most of the adversarial flavor of the rest of law school. Basically, what it taught me was to hide my bottom line and make a very high demand at the start of the mediation so my "side" would be seen as compromising as we lowered our price or expectation incrementally during the process. In other words, my starting position should be a lie.

I eventually moved into the field of alternative dispute resolution (ADR) anyway, working exclusively with tribes and Native organizations. Back among my own dysfunctional people, crossing the country, interacting with more tribal governments and societies, I found that most had assimilated to a great degree, accepting federal laws and policies along with national and regional societal norms. Yet a large number still retained their beliefs in and feelings of relationship to the Earth. Many who lived in cities far from their home reservations or territories still talked about "home" when referring to the places their parents or grandparents had lived before the relocation program, although they themselves might never have lived there.

Mediation or the various forms of dispute resolution often did not help Native peoples solve the problems, because they were trying to live in two worlds, trying to govern their lives by at least two sets of different legal and societal realities, seldom in a position of having their own realities considered as a fundamental part of the process. Underlying this was trauma, ongoing historic trauma caused by five hundred years of genocide and continuing oppression. In order to be able to work toward solutions, people needed to first find ways to heal from this trauma and find their identities so they could sit with each other like fully functioning adults. In order to heal, they would have to be educated in the reasons for the trauma and shown how to heal the wounds step by step. There could be no ADR without a little education first.

Hence, when I was asked if I would be willing to teach a few courses in Native American studies at Humboldt State University, I saw it as an opportunity to try a different pathway to my original goal of repaying the ancestors—I could help educate their children by teaching a bit about the origins of their traumas, with an eye toward helping them direct their future steps.

BETH

I wonder why I don't hark back to a lost past in the ways you do, Marlon. Perhaps what's comparable for me to your world lost is the shtetl, a grim reality from which pogroms spurred my ancestors to flee, internalizing as trauma the oppression they suffered.

I grew very angry at the Jewish community in Fort Worth. When the time came to speak up for justice, they were scared—not without reason. Hush, they told me and my family. There but for the grace of God go we. Precisely, I'd say, why we should be loud, not quiet. If not we who are also vulnerable, then who? I went to Brandeis not because it was Jewish but because Herbert Marcuse was there. But on some level, I also sought connection with other kinds of Jews, like those who would soon stand up bravely for civil rights. At the time of my coming of age, though, they were yet to appear on my Jewish horizon.

I lived in India, mostly in the rural east, for seven years. Eventually I returned to the United States. My relationship with my husband had unraveled. I had a three-year-old son. Much as I loved living in India, in a rural area as part of an extended family—the family I never had but wished for my child—it was a bit beyond my powers to live as a divorced, white, single mom in India. I moved to California, reconnecting with a dear friend from my post-college, New York days. She had joined with others to found a school of counseling called Radical Psychiatry. A large part of the work involved mediation. Begun as a self-help tool to support cooperative working relations, these experiments in solving conflict soon yielded rich lessons in understanding power. The goal of Radical Psychiatry was to reimagine individual psychology as both product and producer of social orders. Mediation evolved into something more than a highly effective way to intervene in people's painful estrangements from family, friends, neighbors, and colleagues. It was also a form of political action, because every mediation served to renegotiate divisive power relations. Once my friend convinced me to observe this work, I was a convert. Liberated by social justice grounding from the lies and manipulations you describe in law, Marlon, I dived in.

For me, therefore, working as a conflict resolver presented no contradiction to my activist sensibilities. In practice, I serve as advocate, teacher, leader, learner, guide, referee, all seamlessly integrated into effective work. Two of the core principles guiding my work are the efficacy of equality as an outcome as well as a practice within the session; and the value of idealism, holding a vision of how different options would be if we lived in a just society. This piece requires the mediator to peer beyond the hegemonic assumptions of what's possible that our various cultures impose, enabling us to express how much of conflict results from failures of justice instead of failures of individuals. No one is to blame, although everyone may act out of impulses distorted by oppression; everyone does the best they can under very much less than ideal circumstances. That mind-set counteracts blame and creates a framework for cooperative progress.

Inside of me there are two dogs. One is mean and evil and the other is good and they fight each other all the time. When asked which one wins I answer, the one I feed the most.

SITTING BULL

MARLON

While I was doing the preparatory work for my courses (I have regularly taught thirteen separate courses over the years), I realized that the conclusions at which I had arrived as a result of my personal experiences mirrored those of others around Indian country—the issues that most tribes and Native people face are a result of historic and systemic problems of settler colonial oppression, just a fancy way of saying outside forces caused our problems and now the solution will involve fixing those outside forces at the same time we try to fix ourselves. I had already known some of that, but over the years I thought deeply about the possibilities of change. It was obvious that finding a solution would not be easy.

In large part, this is because in the United States alone there are almost six hundred federally recognized tribes and nations, with another couple of hundred non–federally recognized entities. Among them there are hundreds of different languages and dialects and hundreds of completely different cultures and worldviews. In addition, different groups and individuals have assimilated to the surrounding American culture to different degrees, adhering to different religions and political views. The range of beliefs—from traditional indigenism to complete assimilation—is staggering.

Many of these indigenous groups take great pride in their self-reliance—what most of them refer to as tribal sovereignty—and prefer to solve their problems by themselves. There are many stories of their successes in working through disputes using either strictly traditional means of negotiation and settlement or a combination of tribal methods and modern alternative dispute management. After years of trial and error, many have found that what works best for their varied populations is a combination, with tacit acknowledgment that the basis for their activities is tribal traditions.

I came to realize that if I tried to play the neutral in a dispute management situation involving tribes or indigenous peoples, I would be ignoring the centuries of oppression manifest in not only the reasons for the conflict but also in the ways the disputants were acting. If I were to continue in my role, I would have to drop the veneer of neutrality and find ways of participating that more closely mirrored the roles taken by elders in their community in the past.

This might involve facilitating or at least organizing some sort of ceremony or community gathering or process. It might even involve acting as a sort of stand-in uncle, providing a scolding or at least an admonition to act in a manner that would be more pleasing to their ancestors. It might include teaching the disputants and the community how they should be acting in order to create a functioning, communicating, mostly unified body.

These ideas had been developed as a result of the research I had been doing for my coursework, so for me, as a prospective conflict management expert, they were at first merely theoretical. However, there was solid evidence from reliable sources—including peer-reviewed and published works—that many of these procedures and ideas had been tried in indigenous communities and had actually worked. And when I finally tried some of them, they actually achieved positive results.

The key to success is not in creating a set of dos and don'ts or a flowchart of alternatives that says, "If this happens, then do this . . ." Rather, it is recognizing the cultural makeup of the group with whom you are working and trying to see what their life histories might include. It's really no different from any other kind of dispute management work, or even from counseling. I simply had to use the observational and analytical skills developed in my years of study, practice, and simple life experience. And as all other facilitators do or should do, I had to keep an open mind and let the procedure flow as it needed to in the moment, according to the needs of the participants.

In my case, dealing mostly with issues of indigenous life or the racism associated with it, it helped greatly to have been formally educated in the historical underpinnings of the United States' (and other colonized countries') laws, policies, and societies, and in the genocide and oppression that has led indigenous peoples to their current state of social dysfunctions and traumas. But on the positive side, I can also see the incredible will to survive among indigenous peoples, the often unseen need to reconnect with the communities and lands their ancestors knew so well.

Therefore, in trying to bring any group closer to an understanding of everyone involved (both Native and non-Native), I do my best in the short time I usually have to explain the histories that have gone into making the current difficulties. Participants need to know how our shared histories so often affect each of us in different ways, causing our varied reactions to the many reasons for disputes. I show them that the unexpected ways we react to stressful situations may be simply a quick, unthinking, knee-jerk reflexive action that bears no resemblance to how we may feel deep down. We just need to slow our reflexes until we have had time to find our deep-down feelings.

BETH

Our convergences are greater than our divergences. Like you, I see every dispute as having histories and contexts. We in America dwell in the present, deceived into thinking we have no past and isolated from shared histories by rampant individualism. Hot conflict draws attention even further into the moment, away from all that surrounds it. My job, in part, is to restore lost vision of all that is involved, and in that context to seek wider prospects for bringing about change.

That we two conflict-folk, Marlon, come to such similar conclusions and ways of practicing from such different starting points gives me cheer. It demonstrates in action how much we do all stand on common, strong shoulders!

CHAPTER 13

Beloved Communities for All

DON EDWARDS

*We envision the creation of technologically smart, cul-
turally competent, environmentally secure, economically
just, moral, humane "beloved communities" across the
world. In support of that vision, our mission is to help
community and neighborhood residents, government
agencies and developers reach just and sustainable
agreements about land uses.*

—DON EDWARDS, 1999

BORN, BRED, AND BUTTERED TO STRUGGLE FOR JUSTICE

I WAS BORN IN THE SEAPORT CITY OF CHARLESTON, SOUTH CAR-
olina. Until I left in 1969 to attend college, during the nine-month
school year I lived in a house that family lore says my paternal
great-great-grandfather Solomon built in the early 1900s. My
paternal ancestors converged in post–Civil War Charleston, one
stream flowing up from Alabama and the other from Pineville,
South Carolina, twenty-five miles away. During my childhood, my
family lived on the first floor of what had become a huge, rambling
structure that also had two rental apartments on the second floor.
The house had a front porch on both levels that faced the street.

Don Edwards

The backyard ran behind my house and two rental houses next door. In the backyard were clotheslines, a fig tree, a big oak tree, and a toolshed. Above it was another rental apartment.

For all that, I was bred country. I learned to listen while sitting on the porch shelling beans, shucking corn, churning peach ice cream, and eavesdropping. Listening became a discipline early because children were to be seen and not heard. My sister Cornelia and I spent the three summer months in Barnwell, South Carolina (but also Ehrhardt, Bamberg, and Allendale) with my maternal grandmother, Ms. Cornelia, and my grandaunt Susannah. Ms. Cornelia had a college degree, lived on four acres that she owned, and taught school at Butler Elementary and later Butler High School, both founded by her older brother, Rev. Henry Hannibal Butler. We attended Bethlehem Baptist Church, built with wood donated by my great-grandfather Charley. As children, we went uptown to get the mail and shop. The rest of the time I spent running around "Calhoun Bottom," which was indeed on the other side of the Southern Railroad's tracks.

As to the buttering, I am a southern Negro who was raised on the teachings of both Booker T. Washington ("Cast down your bucket where you are") and W.E.B. DuBois ("The Talented Tenth"). In Charleston and Barnwell, because of landownership, I lived a life of relative privilege. And I knew that early on. When she corrected me, Ms. Cornelia's most stern admonishment went "To whom much is given, much is expected. We expect more than we have received."

On top of that "hard-shell" moral and ethical foundation, I lived the irrational and contradictory experiences "growing up Jim Crow" required. I drank from "colored" water fountains. I sat at the back of the city bus. I entered theaters by the side entrance and sat in the balcony. I changed clothes in the colored dressing "room." There is land in Charleston that I could not set foot on as a child. And as an adult, there remain a few places where I have consciously not set foot. And I probably never will.

What is essential to also know about my buttering is that Charleston is where the war that ended slavery began. It is also where Denmark Vesey planned the largest slave insurrection in US

history. Less than a decade after Emancipation, by 1872, my ancestors had made the rare journey from being owned as property to
being property owners. Despite peonage, lynching, the Depression,
and disenfranchisement, in 1952, when I was born, they still owned
their land. Today, despite massive resistance, Reaganomics, the Tea
Party, and now "45," nearly one hundred fifty years later, I am the
steward of that same land. Because of our land, I grew up certain
that I had a place in the world.

WITH LIBERTY AND JUSTICE FOR ALL

*"I pledge allegiance to the flag of the United States of America, and to the
Republic for which it stands, one nation under God, indivisible, with
liberty and justice for all."*

What happens when words are taken to heart? As did millions
of American kids who attended elementary school in the 1950s, I
said the Pledge at least five days a week. I probably started in Mrs.
Clement's first-grade class at Calvary Episcopal Day School on
Line Street. At A.B. Rhett Elementary School, the practice continued, from Mrs. Coaxum's second-grade class to Mrs. Mary Mack
Brown's fifth-grade class.

But unlike those millions of public school kids, by the time I
reached Mrs. Johnnie J. Wineglass's third-grade class, I said the
Pledge with what I now think of as a purpose. I no longer just
repeated the Pledge. I stood up with my back straight, my eyes
front, and my hand over my heart, and with a clear strong voice,
I pronounced it with fervor and seriousness. Because even by that
young age I was already living "behind the veil." Despite the unseen
but psychologically omnipresent "white people," I was already
practicing resistance. Through making that pledge I was already
claiming justice for myself, my family, and my race.

My desire for justice and my willingness to resist resulted
from being raised Negro instead of colored. By the age of reason, I
already knew that I was somebody. And being somebody of value,
I began to live the "and justice for all" deep down in my spirit. I
meant it then just as much as I mean it now.

The curious fact is, for all my life, I have always stood up and said the Pledge of Allegiance whenever the situation called for me to do so. I certainly cannot say I've always stood for the national anthem. As I think about it, pledging allegiance is one of the consistencies of my life. If I began in the first grade, the math says I've been pledging allegiance—uninterrupted—for sixty-two years.

ENVIRONMENT AND DEVELOPMENT, JUSTICE AND SUSTAINABILITY

My introduction to sustainable development came in 1988 when I participated in a panel sponsored by the London-based Panos Institute about the role of underdevelopment in the emergence of the AIDS pandemic. That experience led to my becoming the executive director of the Panos Institute-Americas. While at Panos-Americas, in 1990, I helped found the US Citizens Network for the UN Conference on Environment and Development. In June 1992, I represented the "CitNet" as a member of the US delegation to the Earth Summit in Rio.

There is nothing like a dream to create the future.

VICTOR HUGO

For me, the '90s mark when I began to reframe my childhood and young adult commitment to pursuing "freedom, justice, and equality" as one to "justice and sustainability" as defined by my role then as an international and national consultant. During that decade I organized town meetings to engage US civil society in a string of UN summits. Simultaneously, from 1993 to 1999, I undertook numerous assignments with the Citizens Network, Global Tomorrow Coalition, President's Council on Sustainable Development, Community Sustainability Resource Institute, and Meridian Institute, to name a few.

It was John Ehrmann, by then Meridian's managing partner, who had introduced me to facilitation and mediation in the late '80s while working at the Keystone Center in Colorado. It was John whom, upon my return from the Earth Summit, I had asked, "Do I have what it takes to be a facilitator?" The Rio process had led me to recognize that process designers/managers had a tangible contribution to make in the twenty-first century. And it was Meridian that provided the experience that set me on the journey I've been on ever since.

THE DOW CHEMICAL COMPANY, SHINTECH, AND THE GENESIS OF MY PRACTICE

I encountered the environmental justice movement, also in 1990, while at Panos-Americas. Panos published one of the earliest articulations of environmental justice, *We Speak for Ourselves*, edited by Dana Alston, a Panos-Americas employee. In 1991, I attended the First National People of Color Environmental Leadership Summit held in Washington, D.C. I knew many of its national leaders and local activists. So when John asked me to join a Meridian team on a project in Louisiana's "Cancer Alley," I was all in.

The Dow Chemical Company wanted Meridian to determine whether a pathway existed for Louisiana's Department of Environmental Protection (DEP) to give Shintech, Inc. a permit to build a polyvinyl chloride (PVC) plant in Plaquemine, the seat of Iberville Parish. A Greenpeace global campaign against PVC production led by my respected friend, Damu Smith, had already succeeded in lobbying the DEP to reject Shintech's first application for a permit in a poorer parish.

The goal of the Dow-Shintech project was to gain consensus and resolve conflict through a thoughtful, well-planned public involvement process *before* Shintech signed contracts and applied for any permits. This methodology was critical to forestalling litigation *after* contracts were executed and permits were in place. The Meridian team wanted to create win-win outcomes for Dow, Shintech, parish residents, and state government. Our team's charge to Dow-Shintech was to ask residents and local officials what would make a new plant more palatable. Armed with input obtained impartially from the community, Shintech might receive a more favorable reception during the public hearings required by the state.

Ultimately, the public involvement process produced a community benefits agreement that would uplift the neighboring towns and villages in measurable ways:

- Shintech moved the proposed plant farther away from nearby hamlets.
- The company put a ten-foot berm along the plant's perimeter to obscure the plant and contain any potential releases.

- Shintech committed to hire locally and to build a workforce reflective of the local community's racial diversity.
- The company partnered with Louisiana Technical College, Westside Campus, to develop a workforce development program to increase eligibility among local residents.

The Shintech project produced my eureka moment. Instead of pouring money into litigation after initiating contracts and permits, a better methodology was to reach agreement regarding benefits through alternative dispute resolution (ADR) before formal plan submission.

A New Practice—Community Development Mediation

I worked off and on in Louisiana with Meridian from 1998 to 2002. During that period I also worked with Cynthia Savo, cofounder of JSA, to translate our experiences, especially Shintech, into a plan of action. Armed with what felt to me like a sound business case, I defined community development mediation as follows:

> small and or/large group dispute resolution and/or consensus building processes which typically employ facilitation/ mediation and negotiations combined with civic engagement techniques designed to set agendas and reach consensus-based decisions pertaining to specific land parcel development/re-development, transit/transportation, or short-, mid-, long-range planning projects, that satisfy formal regulatory requirements or specified informal requirements determined by local conditions.

I set about to articulate what I thought I should do. I certainly knew what I didn't want to do. I didn't want to do any of the following:

- Community mediation
- Family mediation
- Environmental policy mediation
- Consumer mediation

And I knew that what I had in mind should be something distinct, integrative, and new. I just needed to understand the context better. So I set out to learn about development in the United States. I also aimed to determine what concepts I would incorporate into the foundation of the new organization, Justice and Sustainability Associates. Below are what I decided would be foundational themes—JSA's pillars:

- Practice social entrepreneurism.
- Build a virtual corporation.
- Have a shallow ecological footprint.
- Create vertical and horizontal integration.
- Grow strategic alliances.
- Express Kujichagulia ("self-determination").

RECREATE CIVIC CULTURE, INCREASE CIVIC INFRASTRUCTURE

In 1998, I moved back "East of the River" to Ward 8, the ward I'd first lived in when I moved to D.C. in 1986. That move proved to be exactly the right next step. At that time, Ward 8 was "the beast in the East." While all of D.C. reflected the following conditions, it was in Ward 8 that these conditions were at their worst:

- The AIDS and the crack epidemics had decimated D.C.'s neighborhoods.
- Drug trade corner "beefs" killed the guilty and the innocent indiscriminately daily.
- Corruption and criminality siphoned off already inadequate public resources.
- District government delivered public services haphazardly, if at all.
- "Black flight" had caused homeownership to plummet.
- Sinking entrepreneurship had blighted former business districts.
- All the above had resulted in a civic culture that was in tatters.

Oft hope is born when all is forlorn.

J.R.R. Tolkien

As a result, it turned out that I was in exactly the right place at the right time to test the concepts we had been considering for launching a community development mediation practice.

That's because D.C. was the hole in the regional donut. As D.C. went, so went the DMV (District of Columbia, Maryland, Virginia). But the inconvenient truth Cynthia and I realized was that Ward 8 was the hole in D.C.'s donut. And that logic was appreciated by only a few civic leaders who had a vision of what Ward 8 and D.C. could become.

I did not have a vision of what Ward 8 or all of D.C. could become at that time. But I did have an idea of what the Fairlawn, Fort Stanton, Skyland, Historic Anacostia, and Barry Farm neighborhoods could be. I knew those neighborhoods because once a year I walked door-to-door getting the signatures necessary for my church, Union Temple Baptist Church, to get a city permit to hold Unifest, a huge street festival, on the second weekend in June.

At that time, only a few civic leaders could articulate a vision of D.C. that prioritized uplifting Ward 8. That led us to consider how neighborhoods might better develop. We asked ourselves a set of logical questions: What does uplift begin with? It begins with a civic vision supported by many. What produces a civic vision shared by many? Agreements. How are agreements created? Facilitators build agreements among competing stakeholders by which everybody wins something. If done sensitively, such a methodology might also resolve legacy conflicts and establish new norms that prevent or reduce new conflicts. With close attention, time, and a few wins, we imagined a process that applied over and over would repair the tattered civic culture and begin to build new civic infrastructure from which would emerge new and better neighborhood leadership.

Soon thereafter, we realized that if we extended the logic, a bigger mission beckoned:

1. Many major US cities suffered from similar conditions as D.C., more or less.

2. Resolving legacy conflicts and preventing new ones made a solid business case—if we could identify a revenue stream, create a market, and grow it.

3. As socialists, we should aim to test our hypothesis that we could "do good" and "do well."

4. We embraced capital accumulation as a legitimate outcome of efforts to increase justice and sustainability.

5. If we could demonstrate proof of concept in D.C., perhaps community development mediation could be grown nationally and internationally.

6. We could apply a replicable methodology over and over in many geographies.

7. The methodology we envisioned could be applied at many levels: neighborhoods, cities, counties, nations, etc.

But first we needed to demonstrate that we had a methodology that we could apply over and over again in many geographies.

People who've been disrespected for no other reason than skin color, race, accent, language, etc., know when their presence is welcomed or not. As a black person, I prioritized the look and feel of a project's engagement efforts. We followed the protocol below at every meeting:

- Start the meeting at the announced time. State at the outset when the meeting will end. End the meeting when announced or ask permission to briefly run over.

- Greet and welcome people at the door. Wish them a safe return home.

- Hold the meeting in a public building—a place that belongs to the taxpayer, a safe place where they might feel at home and relaxed.

- Treat meeting participants like they are invited house guests.

- Prepare the meeting room like it is a personal den or living room.

- Create a public space for learning before, during, and after the meeting. Set up poster boards. Let people go back and forth as they wanted.

- Serve refreshments.
- Give them a way to evaluate their experiences. Ask them whether they enjoyed themselves.
- Report their words and the meeting's results back to them to demonstrate accountability.

My unchanged view is that justice begins with recognizing and respecting people's humanity. Soon enough, we had all the projects we needed with which to test our concept.

STRATEGIC NEIGHBORHOOD ACTION PLANNING INITIATIVE

In 2000, D.C.'s Office of Planning (OP) launched an ambitious neighborhood visioning program titled the Strategic Neighborhood Action Planning Initiative (SNAP). Over the course of nine months, the OP convened sessions in thirty-nine multi-neighborhood "clusters" across D.C. that incorporated the input of thousands of residents. "Visioning" was the hot idea among urban planners due to revitalization successes achieved in Chattanooga, Tennessee. I had visited Chattanooga in 1996 with the President's Council on Sustainable Development (PCSD). On that visit, I found comments by white and black residents—Southerners all—about what we call "inclusion" today, intriguing and encouraging.

That and other experiences from my PCSD days became very relevant once I began to work in D.C. Most people think of the District of Columbia only as "the Federal City." Some also recognize it as "the International City." But few nonresidents recognized the existence of "the City of Neighborhoods." SNAP introduced me to that D.C. And it was an eye-opener.

For most District residents who participated in a SNAP workshop, it was their introduction to the world of participatory citizen planning, and its tools and techniques. More importantly, it likely was their first professionally designed, executed, and documented public conversation about the future of their neighborhood. I well remember the range of expressions I saw on the faces of residents in Ward 8 and Ward 3—then D.C.'s most segregated wards—when I called the session to order. In 2000, having a black man sporting "baby locs" ask an elected Advisory Neighborhood Commissioner (ANC)—from similarly "exclusive" Upper Wisconsin Avenue and Congress Heights—to find a seat was another kind of justice (speak truth to power) in action.

D.C. COMPREHENSIVE PLAN ASSESSMENT AND REVISION

Across the United States, in most jurisdictions, land use policy (future growth corridors, future development sites, changes in use) is typically set down in what is called a master or comprehensive plan. Typically, a master plan is revised every twenty years and updated every ten years. What happens next is a revision or updating of the municipal zoning regulations to conform to the new plan. However, one meta-problem is that only a very small percentage of urban residents understand the centrality of master plans and zoning regulations well enough to use civic engagement processes to influence the future growth of their neighborhoods and communities. That lack of understanding and knowledge is compounded, with typically unjust consequences, in low-wealth, low-engagement neighborhoods.

In 2002, D.C.'s OP initiated a series of projects to completely rewrite and adopt a new comprehensive plan in calendar year 2006. The plan in force had been updated on an erratic schedule. But it had not been revised since 1983. Worse, it was an impenetrable document, understood by a handful of zoning lawyers. Most of all, it was simply outdated, irrelevant to the existing D.C. as well as the D.C. being envisioned. I was fortunate to be on the HNTB team led by Jane Dembner, D.C.'s top planning consultant, to design, facilitate, document, and evaluate what she described as a "bullet-proof" information, engagement, and consensus-building program that would achieve adoption on schedule. Key to delivering that outcome would be the land use policy recommendations made by a twenty-seven-member citizen task force appointed by the mayor and each of the thirteen city council members. I was responsible for delivering as many consensus recommendations possible.

I facilitated a monthly meeting of the task force for a little over two years. For me, every meeting could have been a disaster because the appointees represented diverse, entrenched, and articulate policy interests. Each meeting tested my process management skills. The key turning point was the meeting where I distributed the summary notes from the two previous meetings. My summary accurately captured task force agreements about key changes in zoning designations. But more importantly, as promised, my summary captured all views expressed on every item—even those that were contradictory. By honoring the disagreements, I demonstrated my impartiality to all the members. I garnered credibility by delivering on my promise of impartiality.

11TH STREET BRIDGES REPLACEMENT

You don't have to make any more U turns, no more illegal turns, no more going the wrong way going to downtown Washington, DC . . . you don't have to come through our neighborhood. And we will be happy about that.
—ANTHONY MUHAMMAD, WARD 8 ADVISORY
NEIGHBORHOOD COMMISSIONER, 2013

In 2009, when the District's Department of Transportation (DDOT) acted to replace two bridges built in the 1960s with three new bridges that would separate local and freeway traffic, I jumped at the opportunity offered again by HNTB. For decades the old bridges had forced motorists to use neighborhood streets to connect to and from both freeways. The new 11th Street Bridges would provide critically needed infrastructure, relieve local streets of interstate traffic, and connect pedestrian and multimodal traffic on both sides of the Anacostia River. The DDOT even made cuts for the eventual use of streetcars. My charge was to design and facilitate an engagement process that would attract and engage the culturally and geographically divergent populations on either side of the Anacostia River. Further, I needed to build consensus through education at the neighborhood and District level.

In truth, I had additional motivations. It is widely recognized by city dwellers of a certain generation that the National Interstate and Defense Highways Act of 1956 destroyed more central-city neighborhoods during the '60s than all the riots of that period put together. To implement a more just approach, I designed and facilitated the 11th Street Bridges Community Communications Committee (11CCC). This multi-stakeholder body included representatives from the relevant neighborhoods with diverse backgrounds and competing visions for the project. The 11CCC met quarterly over a four-year period to discuss the latest progress and changes. The committee provided a platform to resolve conflicts and tension between neighborhoods whose residents assumed that they had different interests. At the conclusion of the project, the DDOT adopted the CCC model for its large infrastructure projects to increase buy-in for its mega-million-dollar public transportation and infrastructure projects.

Prior to this project, one of the rationales regularly pronounced as fact was that "too much participation" led to residents thinking they were "in charge." As if. Instead, that project convinced all its participants that fifteen to nineteen people—whites from Capitol Hill and blacks from Historic Anacostia—could meet quarterly for four years with the key material results being that D.C.'s largest infrastructure project ($360 million) came in below budget and ahead of schedule.

The things you do for yourself are gone when you are gone, but the things you do for others remain as your legacy.

KALU NDUKWE KALU

NATIONAL MUSEUM OF AFRICAN AMERICAN HISTORY AND CULTURE

I have a photograph that shows me and my teenaged daughter, Asha, standing on the parcel where the National Museum of African American History and Culture (NMAAHC) now stands. I wanted Asha to be able to look back one day and see bare land before it becomes—something more. I also hoped that she'd look back and feel pride about what her daddy did for a living. When President and Mrs. Obama, President and Mrs. George W. Bush, Congressman John Lewis, and other notables opened the NMAAHC, I felt that I had left my fingerprints on something that would absolutely please my ancestors and my descendants.

From the standpoint of increasing justice and sustainability in the District of Columbia, I would say that the museum project had more at stake than any other project to which I'd contributed up to that point. With its placement at the foot of the George

Washington Monument and within the viewshed of the White House, the building of the NMAAHC on the National Mall was a project of tremendous and controversial importance.

The project stands out as one of the most technically and politically complex I've done in my career. To begin with, the construction design aimed to dig down very close to the water table underneath the National Mall. Not many people know that the Mall is the result of "fill" dumped into Tiber Creek to create "America's Front Porch" in the first place. Then there was the subtle resistance within Congress to siting a museum honoring black history and culture on the last "one-hundred-percent parcel" on the Mall. (A one-hundred-percent parcel is the best parcel from a site selection standpoint, having close to all of the site selection attributes.) So it was with some trepidation that I brought to bear my experience executing the stakeholder component of an environmental impact statement as well as a Section 106 process. To resolve the political and environmental complexities of the project, I provided much-needed consensus-building in the Section 106 process to allow the title transfer process to successfully move forward. But more importantly, I demonstrated that an African-American professional could do his job with equanimity and impartiality. The people (mostly white and federal) among whom I helped build consensus had real "juice," and they didn't have to accept "win-win" outcomes. But I believe I helped make the project less conflictual simply by vigorously and rigorously demonstrating "best practice" ADR principles and practices.

GEORGETOWN UNIVERSITY VISION 2037

> *I am deeply grateful to all those who came together through our Georgetown Community Partnership (GCP)— established in 2012 to facilitate consensus-based decision making among University and MedStar Georgetown University Hospital administrators, faculty, staff, students, and leaders in our Washington, D.C. community—to create this collaborative plan.*
> —JOHN J. DEGIOIA, PRESIDENT, GEORGETOWN UNIVERSITY, DECEMBER 5, 2016

This is the project that I have been leading for the past nine years. It's now in its third phase. Along the way there have been some memorable moments. A pair of meetings that I remember most vividly took place in March 2012 in the offices of the Citizens Association of Georgetown (CAG), one of, if not the, most influential neighborhood associations in D.C. Sometimes, for a mediator, the purpose of a meeting is just to get agreement to hold a second meeting. At the first meeting, I met alone with most of the leaders of the three neighborhood civic associations (West Georgetown, Burleith, and Foxhall Village) and their ANC representatives. On behalf of GU, I brought a request from its COO, Chris Augostini, to allow three senior administrators to present a "Vision for Georgetown 2037" to the communities. It had taken two years, but with my help, internal consensus had emerged among Georgetown's operational and academic leadership to articulate a set of development principles that would guide the university's growth for the next twenty-five years. Rather than continuing to defend GU against what they considered scurrilous attacks by the leaders of the neighborhood associations, the administration agreed to develop and articulate a vision that they would pursue collaboratively and transparently in partnership with the people at the table. The community representatives were surprised by GU's request and my statements attesting to GU's seriousness. Hearing GU "blink," those leaders could have collectively rebuffed GU's offer. Instead, they accepted.

The second meeting took place in the same venue a week later. All the community leaders attended. Georgetown University was represented by its COO, vice president for student affairs, and vice president for public affairs. I was there alone. Augostini led GU's presentation. As I watched the faces and body language of the community leaders, I knew that the corner had been turned when Ron Lewis, chair of ANC 2E and the community's overall leader, thanked GU for the breadth of their vision and the courage to invite their adversaries to help them achieve it.

Today, Georgetown University enjoys a highly positive local standing in D.C.'s neighborhoods, from its fence line to the farthest reaches East of the River. Further, the GCP has proceeded from success to success. In seven years, all decisions have been made by consensus. Not a single vote has ever been taken.

What should young people do with their lives today? Many things, obviously. But the most daring thing is to create stable communities in which the terrible disease of loneliness can be cured.

KURT VONNEGUT

FORWARDS EVER; BACKWARDS NEVER

Is advocacy incompatible with being a third-party neutral? Absolutely not. I became a facilitator and mediator precisely because in my professional life, by designing excellent agenda-setting and decision-making processes, I could create the conditions out of which more just and sustainable decisions were most likely to emerge. Now I have seen the results in many jurisdictions that emerge when people develop a shared vision for their neighborhood and larger community. I am certain that my "best and highest use" is to make sure they can resolve their conflicts and reach smart development decisions. Further, I am convinced that just as humans need bread and water, homeowners, business owners, government planners, and real estate developers need impartial process designers and managers. I have deep trust that the vast majority of human beings desire coordination, cooperation, collaboration, consideration, and consensus. I also have abiding faith that the arc of the moral universe does bend toward justice. And though I will not live to see it, I am certain that white supremacy, patriarchy, militarism, materialism, and atheism will lose their global hegemony. I'm reminded of the hundred-year period between Emancipation and the passage of the Voting Rights Act.

I believe that developing a professional career as a process designer and manager is a highly suitable vehicle for persons of conscience who are also looking to own a home, send kids to college, and be self-determining. There will always be conflict about land uses because there is no more land being made! So, I invite every reader to do as I did—help neighborhood residents create and sustain beloved communities.

In the Beloved Community, poverty, hunger and homelessness will not be tolerated because international standards of human decency will not allow it. Racism and all forms of discrimination, bigotry and prejudice will be replaced by an all-inclusive spirit of sisterhood and brotherhood.

—THE KING PHILOSOPHY,
WWW.THEKINGCENTER.ORG

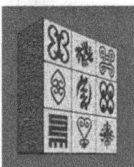

JSA logo

CHAPTER 14

When the Steel Shutter Melts

*The Power of Acknowledgment
within a Relational Justice Process*

GEOFFREY CORRY

Preventing the poison of the past seeping into the present and the future.

—ANN CADWALLADER[1]

The effects of harm (broadly defined) and the experience of injustice carried by a particular generation can, if not addressed or resolved, be passed on to the next generation to produce a range of social and psychological pathologies, such as self-harm, suicide, anti-social behavior, anomie and inter-personal violence.

—IRISH PEACE CENTRES[2]

Hate is just as injurious to the hater as it is to the hated. . . . Hate is too great a burden to bear.

—MARTIN LUTHER KING JR.[3]

We owe a debt to the victims. . . . By remembering and telling, we prevent forgetfulness from killing the victims twice.

—PAUL RICOEUR[4]

> *You cannot move on without acknowledgement of what happened.*
>
> —JOHN WINSLADE[5]

> *Forgiveness is the only way to reverse the irreversible flow of History.*
>
> —HANNAH ARENDT[6]

Geoffrey Corry

IN ALL, 3,532 PEOPLE DIED DURING THIRTY YEARS OF INTERCOMMUNAL violence in Northern Ireland. In an area only one hundred thirty miles wide, the political violence affected almost all families either through the direct trauma of having a loved one killed or indirectly through the loss of a member of their extended family. It is estimated that one third of survivors have spoken of serious suicidal thoughts. Behind those statistics and events, there is an enormous amount of unprocessed hurt and pain across the different Catholic nationalist and Protestant unionist communities.

It is now fifty years since the Troubles broke out in Northern Ireland, and it was not until thirty years later, in 1994, that the hidden political peace process—growing step by step under the surface—achieved a major breakthrough in the putting down of arms by both the republicans and the loyalists. That allowed negotiations to begin, with the wonderful outcome of the Belfast Good Friday Agreement (1998), accomplished in the very last hours of Holy Week after four days of nonstop high-level proximity meetings.

I lived through those years and was privileged to have played a second-track role in the unfolding peace process as a dialogue facilitator at the Glencree Centre for Reconciliation.[7] As a southerner and Methodist from the Protestant community, I have found myself in the middle as an insider mediator helping each side to understand the religious/political fears and grievances of the other. After Bloody Friday in Belfast in 1972—the bloodiest year of the conflict—a small number of people like myself in the ecumenical and peace movement formed the Glencree Centre up in the hills outside Dublin.

Looking back from a distance, I can see that the start of my own process journey was in 1974 when I was moved by the documentary film *Steel Shutter*, shown as part of Peace Week in Dublin. The film featured two facilitators, Carl Rogers and Pat Rice, sitting in a circle with a selected group of nine Catholic and Protestant participants in a Pittsburgh TV studio telling each other the shock of what happened to them on the streets of Belfast during July and August 1972. On the second day, one of the participants made a statement about the essence of survival in Belfast that provided the title of the film: "You have a steel shutter that comes down in your mind . . . inside your head . . . the real person's on the other side of it." This triggered another participant, a schoolteacher, to reflect on his own painful experiences and to talk about the same thing: how he pulls down that emotional "steel shutter" between his functioning self and the seething feelings within. Otherwise he would go berserk. In a quiet, soft voice, he speaks of this inner trauma as a wild beast: "Yeah, I know myself. I am quite aware of this kind of thing and it scares me to know that it is there . . . because it is violent and emotional and daft. . . . I take long walks and let this thing inside of me talk. It isn't quite the same as human feelings—it isn't quite the same as having a beast inside you—some sort of animal feelings, you know."[8]

If Carl Ransom Rogers (1902–1987) could facilitate interpersonal encounters in a nondirective style like that to melt emotional obstacles, I said to myself at the time, "Why could I, who believes in the power of group work, not do something similar?" It looked so simple to do! Yet it took many years for that germ of a process idea to take shape and for me to have the courage and the skills to sit calmly in the hot seat. This is my favorite quote from Rogers: "To my mind, empathy is in itself a healing agent . . . because it brings even the most frightened client into the human race. If a person is understood, he or she belongs." Rogers was hugely influenced by Martin Buber's notion of the "I-Thou relationship," in which your inner spirit reaches out to touch the inner spirit of the other. It echoes the Ubuntu spirit of South Africa demonstrated by Nelson Mandela and Desmond Tutu.

What I have learned in recent years in the post-violence phase of our peace process is that victims who have experienced horrendous violence have had to create that emotional wall of the steel shutter in order to survive and keep the past in check. The good news is that Israeli social psychologist Dan Bar-On has shown us how to work with the undiscussable and the indescribable through

*In the depth of winter,
I finally learned that
within me there lay an
invincible summer.*

ALBERT CAMUS

a storytelling process.[9] The process principle involved is that when a person feels *respected, heard, understood, and acknowledged*, in effect, the steel shutter melts. Those four outcomes need to be seen as four sequential layers of a listening and storytelling process. It took me some time to identify and learn how to achieve each of those layers of skills that ultimately leads to the humanizing moment of acknowledgment. Crucial to the breakthrough of being acknowledged is a deeper third layer in which a bilateral understanding between disputants develops when, as a facilitator, you elicit the bit that one side does not yet believe or feel the other side understands or appreciates about their concerns.

FOUR RESPONSES TO THE PAST VIOLENCE

Even though we have the Good Friday Agreement, unfortunately, no agreed-upon healing and truth recovery process was put in place by the Irish and British governments in the aftermath of the accord. There was political resistance to it at the time. Minds were focused on achieving the decommissioning of weapons in order to get the power-sharing government up and running. Unlike in South Africa, people were not ready for a Truth and Reconciliation Commission (TRC). Over the years, despite the efforts of political leaders, officials, lawyers, nongovernmental organization (NGO) leaders, and third parties to arrive at some overall political agreement to address the issues of the past, the Stormont House proposals[10] have not been implemented.

A good quarter of people don't want to go there to revisit the dark days of conflict, as we discovered in Glencree listening circles: "Haven't we suffered enough; why do we need to go back over those terrible events?" Their need is to draw a line under the pain of the past, to move on and try "to get our lives back to some semblance of normality." By facing into the future, they hope that political violence of that kind will never ever return. Nevertheless, there are some in Quadrant 1 in figure 14.1 who remain silent about the past: "Whatever you say, say nothing." Socially, opening up that can of worms could make matters worse and retraumatize people. Let the stories remain untold.

Remembering

Forgetting

2. Moving on but not forgetting

TIPPING POINT

JUSTICE ANCHOR POINT

MORAL ANCHOR POINT

3. I am not moving on until the person is brought to account

1. I have moved on and put the past behind me

4. I don't want to move on

PAST   PRESENT   FUTURE

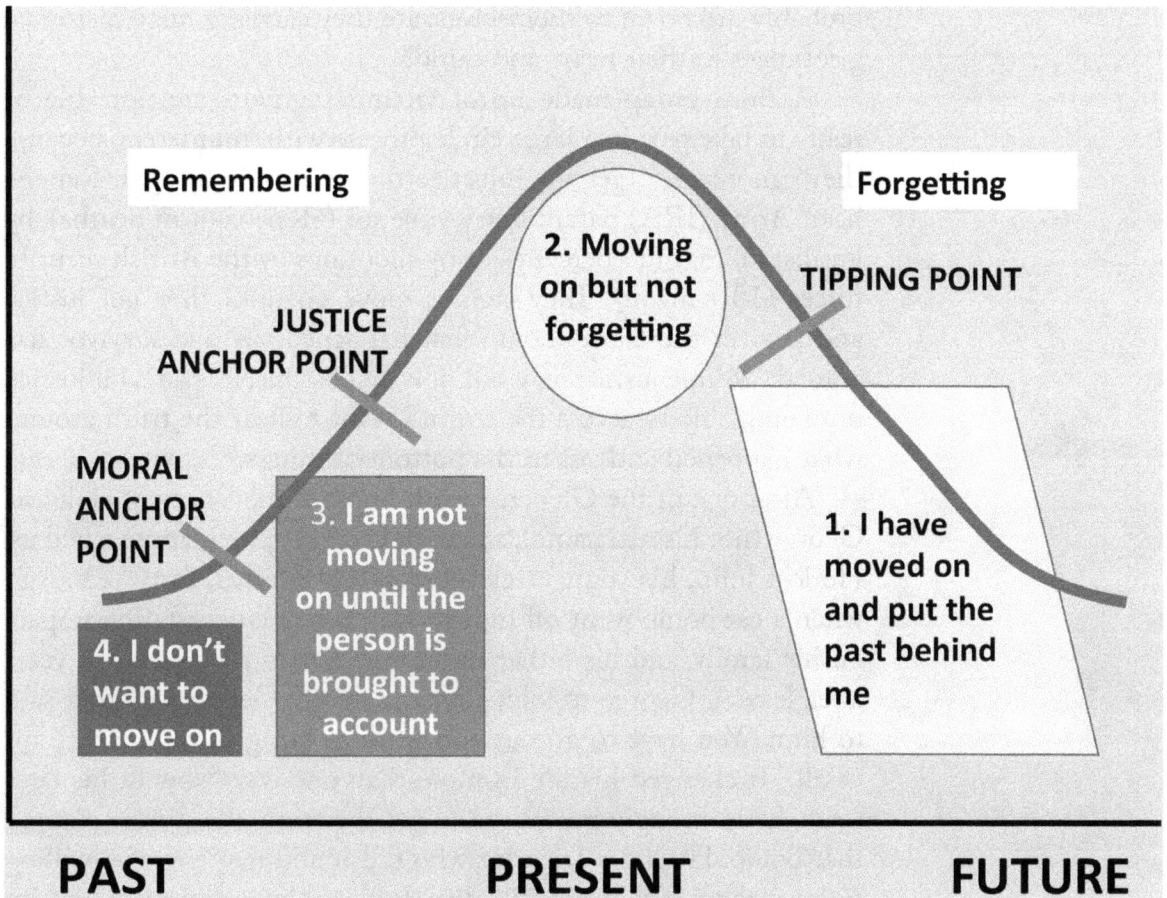

Figure 14.1.   Critical mass bell curve diagram showing the tension between forgetting and remembering

A second group want to remember the loss of their loved ones in an appropriate way by having a beloved picture of them nearby: "My mother still remembers that day of the bomb when my father was killed; she looked up at his photo every night since then." In the large circle dialogue process facilitated by the Glencree Centre, one victim/survivor said to former combatants: "I have worked through it myself and just about able to move on. But what do I tell my grandchildren about why you took up the gun to kill?" There is a family and collective responsibility being spoken about here that goes beyond a personal decision to move on: "I want answers to my questions. You did that shooting and I need to understand why." Hidden in this gentle open question to a former combatant is the need to explore why they chose to use violence for a political objective. Did they take up the gun to secure their national identity? Or, probably unknown to themselves, are they carrying huge historical grievances in their heart and mind?

A third group made up of victims/survivors are not able or ready to take part in a large circle process with "murderers" because they can never forget the injustice that was done by Irish Republican Army (IRA) paramilitary violence (58 percent of deaths), by loyalist killings (29 percent), or by shootings by the British security forces (10 percent). They cannot move on until they get justice and recover the truth about what happened. As one survivor has argued: "While justice may not now be possible, it is a real injustice not being able to access the truth. I want to hear the truth around what happened and get to the bottom of things."

After one of the Glencree workshops on the legacy of violence, George (not his real name), a man in his mid-sixties, approached us. He lost John, his younger eleven-year-old brother, forty years ago when a car bomb went off in his town. It had a devastating impact on his family, and his father never got over it; he died three years later, leaving George to look after the family. George's mother said to him: "You have to go out and work to bring in the income for us all." It changed his life in more than one way. Now in his later years, he is strongly motivated to get the truth about who planted that bomb. He has a fair idea who did it and may even be willing to meet them if they are still alive. It would be horrendous for him to go through those pearly gates of heaven supervised by St. Peter, to meet up with his wee brother John on the other side and have to tell him that the person who planted that fatal car bomb has not been found or brought to justice. He owes him that he tried his best. George is emphatic that everyone must learn from the mistakes of the past and hopes to God the violence will never happen again.

For our fourth group, there can be no lasting peace without legal justice: "I don't want to be reconciled to the IRA." Taking human life is unforgivable and beyond the moral circle. For them, the peace process has been turned into an appeasement of those who persist in their mind-set. It leaves them with no alternative but to never forget and never forgive unless repentance is genuinely offered. They need a harder form of justice that goes all the way to prosecution and punishment: "You cannot tell me to move on. I cannot forget what happened to me and my family. For the sake of the future, I want those who perpetrated the deed to be brought to Justice and be prosecuted. I know they may only get two years in prison but they must serve time in prison." Those who find it most difficult to move on are Protestant unionist victims of IRA republican violence of the 1970s and '80s who live on isolated farms in the remote borderlands of hilly country and green laneways. The events they describe with deep emotion are as fresh now—decades later—as when the individual circumstances of violence, bereavement, and loss were first initiated. Psychology has named this zone as "time collapse," where the horror of the violent moment is preserved and ever-present as if it happened just forty minutes ago.

WORKING WITH THOSE WHO CANNOT FORGET

By placing these four groupings into a bell curve diagram, we get a picture of how the two human needs of *remembering loss + getting justice* and *forgetting + moving on* are poles apart in a post-violence society. They don't talk to each other. Those groupings on the left-hand side of the curve remain emotionally and morally anchored in the wounds of the past. Without a healing process that links truth recovery and accountability with repentance, the residual anger cannot be released. Does that mean they have become trapped in an endless time zone with memories of their loved one unless some form of justice can be achieved? At the same time, there is a sense in which victims may not want to let go of their victimhood, as it would shatter their sense of identity because it gives them security and meaning.

The challenge for peace process facilitators like myself is to reach out to groups of victims/survivors in a post-violence situation where no legacy architecture exists and offer a more interactive and intercommunal path to address their emotional wounds. There is an urgency about this task because those who lived during this era are getting older, losing their memory, and beginning to doubt whether legal justice and factual/forensic truth are now deliverable. They find themselves in a situation where they feel abandoned. The goal of achieving a peace *with* justice may not now be fulfilled. But that begs the question: What kind of justice are we talking about?

There is a saying in Tibetan, "Tragedy should be utilized as a source of strength." No matter what sort of difficulties, how painful experience is, if we lose our hope, that's our real disaster.

14TH DALAI LAMA

What we know from other conflict situations—and indeed from our own civil war history in Ireland a century ago—is that if the untold stories of past horrific or unjust events remain silent, not heard, and unprocessed by wider collective society, especially the families impacted directly by them, then they continue to ferment under the surface. It does not go away. The cycle of bitterness erupts in the third or fourth generations of families to get at the truth, or more dangerously, it goes the other way and gets recycled through the virus of violence being reborn in young fighters. That is what happened in our Irish past. Civil society must not allow the two governments to kick the can down the road for a number of additional years just because powerful interests will not disclose the truth. We need to do all we can to heal the open wounds and transform the past now. This is the gap that relational justice attempts to fill.

THE SEARCH FOR MEANING OUT OF THE SUFFERING

In reading Viktor Frankl's very moving account of surviving his Auschwitz experience,[11] I discovered that making meaning out of suffering is central to the healing process for victims/survivors. In supporting each party to explore and name the predicament and suffering of a single personal situation, Frankl challenges us to unfold its potential meaning. It is a human achievement to turn it into a mutual learning experience so as to ensure it will never happen again. Meaning gained and owned gives you the inner strength not to seek punishment of the offender but to engage them on what happened in the incident and what led them to do what they did. Out of such a personal growth experience may come the possibility of forgiveness through accountability to undo the deeds of the past.

The more I have gotten involved in working with victims, the more I have realized the importance of hearing the story and validating the emotional impact of the event on them. Because they feel abandoned, victims have a huge need to be accepted in an emotionally safe space and for their subjective experience to be validated and acknowledged at their pace: "You felt afraid at that point and did not know what to do." You may well ask: "Is not *validation* the same as *acknowledgment*?" Maybe they are the same interactive elements of empathy, but I find it helpful to make them separate process steps because validation is a step along the way before acknowledgment.

I first came across the validation process designed by Interaction Associates when I had my formative mediation experience in San Francisco in 1986. I had the privilege of spending two weeks with Ray Schonholtz of Community Boards, who was pioneering a neighborhood justice system delivered by trained volunteer mediators. Before you went anywhere near problem-solving or the negotiation bit, you worked first with processing the emotional content of the dispute and helped disputants understand each other, particularly how the conflict was impacting them. This piece of empathy work was called "validation"—to attach value to the expressed emotion in the telling of the personal story. Through reflective listening, you support the disputants in understanding their conflict experience and validate their efforts in working together.

For me, it connected to our cultural experience in Ireland of building relationships through hearing the story. By supporting each disputant in the presence of the other, not just to talk about a conflict incident but to acknowledge how they felt about it, it prepared the way for them to understand each other's experience.

DESIGNING A BOTTOM-UP APPROACH

The unique contribution of the Glencree Centre in Ireland has been to organize private confidential workshops from the bottom up since the 1994 cease-fires. In the first of our projects, I acted as dialogue facilitator for more than fifty residential political dialogue workshops with political activists at the second-track level from the main political parties in Ireland and Britain.[12] It contributed to building new relationships between younger politicians who went on to strengthen and deepen the political peace process. The full story of what flowed from the workshops has yet to be told. It gave me considerable experience in adapting the problem-solving workshops devised by Herb Kelman[13] in the Israeli/Palestinian situation but shifting the process into circle work and interactive dialogue.

Building on the contacts generated, Glencree launched a victims/survivors project called LIVE (Let's Involve the Victims'

Stop wishing and be the good that needs to happen to this world.

ABHIJIT NASKAR

Experience)[14] after the Good Friday Agreement. We used a peer storytelling process to support victims in starting their journey out of victimhood. Their pain had been kept private for far too long. We all learned a huge amount about working with trauma in an informal process. It attracted survivors from Northern Ireland mainly on the nationalist side and from British cities where car bombs had caused horrific damage. We did not stop there but went on to design a parallel series of separate workshops with former combatants recently released from prison as part of the Agreement.[15] As the work progressed, participants from each of these projects then requested opportunities to meet up with each other.

THE GLENCREE HUMANIZING PROCESS IN THE LARGE CIRCLE

Unfortunately, the Glencree Centre had to close down for financial reasons in 2009, and the rhythm of the work was broken. This allowed us to regroup and figure out how we could put relationships back at the heart of the post-violence phase of the peace process. That is when we stumbled on the need to reach out to the Protestant unionist victims of IRA violence, whom we had found difficult to engage in the LIVE project ten years earlier. It became more possible because support groups had sprung up for families of former Royal Ulster Constabulary police officers and Ulster Defence Regiment army men who had borne the brunt of IRA gunmen in the forgotten rural areas.

We managed to get the Centre reopened in 2014 and initiated the Glencree residential large circle process, combining interactive dialogue with relational justice principles. Unionist victims of IRA violence from the border areas meet with a representative group of southerners from the Republic of Ireland who have held senior positions of responsibility in the police, security forces, and Justice Department. One participant at a workshop was a former government minister who spoke of the difficult time when the Irish state was under threat from the IRA.

The dynamic of the large circle is that victim families from a community from one side of the border can tell their story of suffering to people on the other side who have held significant power in the past and still have influence. The southerners are perceived by northern unionists as having been part of a system that turned a blind eye to militant republicanism. Out of these encounters can come acknowledgment, apology, and renewed dignity. It is essentially a relational encounter, and so there is no expectation of any document as an outcome.

It is also a victim-led process. To codesign the large circle workshop, the Glencree facilitation team traveled up across the border to build a trusting work relationship with the victims' agency. Hearing their concerns and discovering where they want to go with the event is essential. There is usually a second preparatory meeting to ensure we got it right so there are no surprises at the event. Each circle workshop is designed as a closed event for invited participants only, most of whom stay overnight at the Centre.

The conference room at Glencree Centre, which is an old British military barracks, is rectangular in shape, so it is not possible to have a perfect circle. Yet the space is sufficient for everyone to see and hear each other without microphones, making it an intimate atmosphere for storytelling (fig. 14.2).

Figure 14.2.   The conference room at Glencree Centre

The large circle process starts with the ground rules followed by a sequential "go-round," which allows each of the thirty to forty participants to introduce themselves uninterrupted and tell where they are from. This is a first step in bonding the whole group and building collective emotional support for the next stage, when a number of personal stories are told by those willing to talk about the violence their family experienced. It is not easy for a victim to suddenly be at the center of the circle's attention and to talk about a previous traumatic incident. Yet somehow the emotional moment becomes ripe for the story to surface and for the teller to decide what to share and what has meaning. Indeed, telling their family story for the first time outside their own communal group is a huge step forward in their healing journey from silence to truth-telling. Victims telling it for the third or fourth time become more self-confident, having recovered much more of the detail from their memory and through owning the story. It becomes a "speak-out" when offered, often with a tinge of anger, in a group setting.

A widow read out a list of thirteen people killed in the 1970s and '80s whom she still remembers fondly to this day and will never forget. "I want to think about the people I knew who were murdered—because the people who were murdered by the IRA all had families who were left behind." Among them were a postman, a missionary, and a delivery man, all of whom went to school in the village and shopped there. For one of those killings, she was the first on the scene and the first to have to tell a relative what happened. "My husband was a policeman and he was murdered with an undercar bomb. Another person was shot in their own shop and it was a beautiful day. Another was shot outside his back door."

Later in the workshop, a southerner acknowledged the story: "It grieves me in my heart to know that any Irishman killed one of your relatives in the interest of any Irish cause and it will continue to be a blot on our Irish character." Another southerner was moved to say: "It is a great service what you are doing [as a group] and you are the real heroes and heroines at the genuine frontline of the conflict."

Such acknowledgments of the pain and suffering in the large group by significant officeholders from the other community can become a moment of healing of emotional wounds carried for many years. The survivor and their fellow group members can look back on and feel proud of their contributions. Participation restores both self- and collective dignity. It also makes it safe for others to speak about heartfelt moments. These are the humanizing moments that are the stuff of relational justice. While the lead facilitator can attempt to offer an acknowledgment, it is better coming from another member of the circle or someone linked to the facilitation team. Because there is no legal immunity available, it is not possible for specific incidents of truth recovery to be pursued in the circle, but this can happen discreetly outside it. We still await action by the two governments to put in place a legacy architecture to allow truth recovery exchanges between victims and former combatants on what happened in specific past incidents.

Out of the dialogue come other opportunities, such as an apology. At a workshop with senior church people brought together from all the churches, we heard the experience of victims who believed that some clergy did not stand up to the gunmen during the Troubles. A churchman made this clear statement: "Please hear an apology: I am so sorry for how people have been harmed by the church and for the tokenism given to victims. I may not have understood."

The fourth part of the circle event is an interactive dialogue session on the issues agreed by the preparatory meetings or raised directly in the room by participants. This allows for a free-flowing exchange of viewpoints across the circle that go a long way toward understanding the complexity of the security and counterinsurgency strategies on both sides of the border. Topics like extradition, lack of communication between the respective security forces, and the role of the media during the Troubles get discussed. Each side is able to construct a more complex image of the "other" than the one conveyed through their respective media.

The circle ends with a final go-round for participants to share new insights and understandings gained from the experience of talking together. Each person speaks only once, and we don't go back into discussion mode. Here is the insight of a southerner: "I am grateful for what I heard and it increased my understanding. I lived in a place of peace and did not have to put up with what you had to experience. We want to support you in whatever way we can."

One of the most important things you can do on this earth is to let people know they are not alone.

Shannon L. Alder

Participants stay together in the large circle, not breaking down into small groups, for the duration of the workshop to hear everyone's story. Some worry that not everyone can participate. There are of course some victims who are not yet ready to tell their story but get courage from being part of the experience for whenever the next time comes. Kurt Lewin (1890–1947), pioneer of group dynamics, reminds us that silent group members participate emotionally in the group through observation—by observing the actions and reactions of others both subjectively and objectively. He demonstrated that change comes about in the owning of the issues that surface in the interactive dialogue whether participants speak or not.

We know that people connect with each other after the workshops to continue the conversations and that southern victims of violence have traveled north to tell their stories at other events. Over the years, we have learned the value of running not just one-off meetings but a series of workshops. They have a ripple effect as relationships are forged.

IT IS A GIFT, NOT AN EXERCISE

In summary, relational justice gets fulfilled when the dignity of individuals and groups is respected in profound interactive and qualitative ways in a circle process through moments of validation, acknowledgment, apology, and the recovering of self-worth. The last words go to a unionist participant: "It is my first time down here. I had other things to do today but I was convinced to come. Now I realize I was right to come here. . . . While some of the discussion was fairly raw, there was nothing held back. We engaged each other. I learned some of the security difficulties across the border that I didn't appreciate. It is a gift, not an exercise. We can't stop here."

NOTES

1. Anne Cadwallader, *Lethal Allies: British Collusion in Ireland* (Cork, Ireland: Mercier Press, 2013), 17.

2. Irish Peace Centres, *Intergenerational Aspects of the Conflict in Northern Ireland* (Belfast: Irish Peace Centres, 2010), 78.

3. From King's speech in 1967 on the burden of hate, based on Hebrews 12:14–17.

4. Paul Ricoeur, *Figuring the Sacred: Religion, Narrative, Imagination* (Minneapolis: Fortress Press, 1995), 290.

5. Quote by John Winslade in a workshop on narrative mediation at the annual conference of the Mediators Institute of Ireland, 2013.

6. Not a specific quote but a synopsis of her work on forgiveness in Hannah Arendt, *The Human Condition* (Chicago: University of Chicago Press, 1958), 236–243.

7. For the background leading up to the 1994 cease-fires, see Geoffrey Corry and Pat Hynes, "Creating Political Oxygen to Break the Cycle of Violence 1981–1994: Lessons from the Northern Ireland Peace Process," *Journal of Mediation & Applied Conflict Analysis* 2(2), 2015, 259–275, http://mural.maynoothuniversity.ie/6251/7/GC-Creating-2015.pdf.

8. The film *Steel Shutter* (56 minutes, 1973) was directed by Tom Skinner and produced by Bill McGaw with Fr. Shaun Curran, SJ. For Carl Rogers's own reflections on the encounter weekend, see his book *On Personal Power: Inner Strength and Its Revolutionary Impact* (New York: Delacorte Press, 1977), 129–133.

9. Dan Bar-On, *The Indescribable and the Undiscussable: Reconstructing Human Discourse after Trauma* (Budapest: Central European University Press, 1999), 127.

10. Northern Ireland Office, Stormont House Agreement, 2014, paragraphs 21–55, https://www.gov.uk/government/uploads/system/uploads/attachment_data/file/390672/Stormont_House_Agreement.pdf. Other background documents can be found under Legacy Resources on the website healingthrough remembering.org.

11. Viktor E. Frankl, *Man's Search for Meaning: An Introduction to Logotherapy* (Boston: Beacon Press, 1959).

12. Geoffrey Corry, "Political Dialogue Workshops: Deepening the Peace Process in Northern Ireland," *Conflict Resolution Quarterly* 30(1), October 2012, 53–80.

13. Herbert C. Kelman, "Experiences from 30 Years of Action Research on the Israeli-Palestinian Conflict," in *Zeitgeschichtliche Hintergründe aktueller Konflikte VII: Zürcher Beiträge zur Sicherheitspolitik und Konfliktforschung*, edited by K.P. Spillmann and A. Wenger, 54, 1999, 173–197, https://scholar.harvard.edu/files/hckelman/files/Experiences_from_30_years.pdf.

14. Jacinta De Paor was the coordinator of the "LIVE: Let's Involve the Victims' Experience" project at Glencree Centre from 1999–2008. See her chapter in Eamon Rafter (ed.), *Deepening Reconciliation: Reflections on Glencree Peacebuilding* (Dublin: Glencree Centre for Peace and Reconciliation, 2014), 115–129.

15. After working with the TRC, Wilhelm Verwoerd came from South Africa and coordinated the former combatants project (2002–2008). See his chapter "Working with Former Combatants and the Sustainable Peace Network," in Rafter (ed.), 131–149.

CHAPTER 15

When Mediators Sue

JULIE MACFARLANE AND BERNIE MAYER

SETTING THE SCENE: JULIE

HIGH IN A TOWER BLOCK IN CENTRAL LONDON, EIGHT PEOPLE SIT around a meeting table in a bland boardroom. The mood is tense. A discussion of possible settlement outcomes in a historic sex abuse case involving an Anglican Church minister is about to begin.

I am the plaintiff in this case; I have been waiting two years for this first face-to-face meeting. I am here with my husband, Bernie Mayer; my oldest daughter, Sibyl Macfarlane; and my lawyer, David Greenwood. Sitting at the table with us are the lawyers representing the Ecclesiastical Insurance Company, the insurer for the Anglican Church; a representative of the insurance company; and a deaconess of the Anglican Church.

The meeting begins, as I had previously insisted, with my prepared opening statement. I describe what had happened to me as a teenager in the 1970s, when I was pursued by an Anglican minister for almost a year and forced into sexual activity. As I speak, the insurer's representatives and the church deaconess look down at their yellow legal pads. Having the victim take control of the meeting is not what they had been expecting, but over the course of two meetings in central London, that is what will transpire. The outcome will be a significant first step in changing the way in which the Anglican Church in England deals with victims of sexual abuse.

Julie Macfarlane

Bernie Mayer

This is our story; Julie as the primary actor, survivor, and plaintiff, and Bernie as my husband and advocate, who was my strategy partner and emotional support person throughout.

How did we get here?

My Abuse

I grew up in Chichester, a small town in the United Kingdom where there was little to occupy teens. My friends and I were excited to read about Billy Graham's evangelical movement, and when an evangelical group formed in town, we joined up. Before long we were singing and praising the Lord and I had an entirely new social circle. I covered my bike and my school desk with "Jesus Loves You" stickers and, much to the exasperation of my parents, who were not religious at all, became absorbed with Bible study and trying to bring more people into our group to "accept Jesus."

After a year or so, the group began to disintegrate, and I looked for a church to join. Some of my friends came with me; some had dropped out by this stage. I, however, was earnest and committed and decided to become a congregant at the St. Pancras Anglican Church. Shortly after I joined, a new minister arrived, Meirion Griffiths. He was in his thirties and had an evangelical bent. I joined the church youth group, and Rev. Griffiths often came to our meetings. He seemed pretty cool.

Fast-forward another year, and I was starting to lose interest in my new "hobby." Or putting it another way, I was beginning to have doubts about my faith. I did what seemed the logical thing. I asked Rev. Griffiths if I could meet with him to discuss this. I thought he could provide me with spiritual guidance. I had no one else to ask.

As his young children played in the room next door, I met with the minister in his study. That day was the first of a series of sexual assaults over the next year. The minister forced me to give him what I (much later) understood to be oral sex, telling me to get down on my knees in front of him in the study. He said that that this was what God wanted, and it would help me resolve my doubts. He then harassed and stalked me in my hometown until I left to go to university, almost twelve months later. He showed up regularly at my home, offering to take me out for driving lessons. No matter how many excuses I came up with, my mother always insisted that I go with him. ("So kind of the minister!") He would expose himself to me and masturbate or force me to give him oral sex in the car, in remote country lanes, on isolated beaches, even in hayfields. He would lie in wait for me as I walked home from my Saturday job as a dishwasher in a restaurant—the most direct route home went through a dark alleyway—and, grabbing me, would rub himself on me over my clothing. I escaped, with inordinate relief, to attend university on the other side of the country in 1976.

My Complaint

It took me many, many years to tell anyone about what had happened to me in any detail, and even longer to resolve that I had to do something about it. I knew that the minister was still out there somewhere, and likely doing the same things he did to me to someone else. I finally accepted that I had to step forward and tell my story.

As a young mother now with two children, I located him in the Diocese of Perth, Australia. I brought a complaint against him using the internal diocesan process. I was lucky to find such a process in place at this time (this was 1999), and it worked well. After I finally brought myself to write out a statement and submit it to a committee comprising both church insiders and outside specialists, things moved quickly. The church asked for Rev. Griffiths' response to my statement. The committee indicated that they were not impressed with his response and informed me that there would be a full canon law "hearing."

A few weeks later, Griffiths resigned. I received a letter from the Archbishop of Perth, stating that Griffiths would not be employed again by the Anglican Church. "I am very grateful to you for being prepared to make your complaint known in the way that you did. I hope now that you will be able to live with some peace of mind." I felt jubilant. He would no longer be able to harm other young people—or so I thought.

My Lawsuit

It wasn't until 2013 that, on a trip home to the United Kingdom, I discovered that my experience was only one of multiple allegations of sex abuse by a number of Anglican clergy, some of whom had by this time been criminally convicted, and all of whom had worked for the Diocese of Chichester. There had even been a formal inquiry—by Dame Elizabeth Butler-Sloss[1]—into the activities of some Anglican ministers in the diocese (not Griffiths), and what the church hierarchy had known at the time. At this point in the unfolding story of the extent of sexual abuse within the Anglican Church, there was a widespread sense that Chichester had exhibited a high level of tolerance of sexual abuse among members of the clergy. Increasingly it appears that this was not unique to Chichester.

So it wasn't just me. The story had so many other people in it. And the story was much bigger than me, bigger than I could ever have foreseen.

I went online and almost immediately found a website, Stop Child Abuse,[2] which David Greenwood and other lawyers and survivors had started to raise awareness of their call for a public inquiry into sex abuse and its cover-up by the Anglican Church in England and Wales (a call that would eventually be successful[3]). I wrote to David that evening, and he replied almost immediately. This was the beginning of a professional and personal relationship that continues today. From the start, David made it clear that his preferred strategy was to bring as many lawsuits as possible against the church. He believed that this was the most effective way to make the church accountable to the victims of clerical sex abuse. He did not believe that the church would "do the right thing" for moral reasons, and instead would have to be fought through the courts.

When I first heard David's pitch for a lawsuit, I was strongly opposed to the idea. As a law professor, and as a frequently appointed mediator in civil disputes, I was painfully aware of the risks and potential traumas of litigation. My hope was to be useful by speaking publicly about my own abuse and the steps I took in Perth years earlier to have Griffiths removed from the ministry.

Justice will not be served until those who are unaffected are as outraged as those who are.

BENJAMIN FRANKLIN

But I was also familiar, as a longtime advocate and activist for issues including abortion rights, children's rights, and my more recent work to counter Islamophobia, that the courts had a useful symbolic and strategic role to play in both raising public consciousness and forcing "the other side" to take a rights complaint seriously. Gradually I began to see that what David was proposing was an important part of a complete strategy to bring about change, and that as a law professor with a successful complaint already behind me, I could be a highly credible plaintiff. At this point, my family also began to encourage me to consider a lawsuit and offered their full support.

My decision-making process was also affected by my discovery that Griffiths was in fact still operating in a position of religious authority. Some Googling quickly turned up the fact that after leaving the Anglican Church he had joined the Uniting Church in Perth, which now listed him on their website as a pastor. The realization that he still had the same access to young women, in the same position of authority, made it clear that I was not done with this yet.

Of course, I hoped that the church would settle with us as quickly as possible. Even before issuing proceedings for sexual assault against the church, I had proposed that we talk about a settlement that could be publicly announced. I was to discover that any type of effort to settle was not in the ballpark for the Anglican Church, and that they responded to each and every lawsuit in a ferociously adversarial manner. Having spent so much of my academic career researching and writing about the adversarial nature of litigation, I really should not have been surprised by this—but as a novice plaintiff, I am embarrassed to admit that I was shocked. I had heard the public apologies the church frequently offered in the media for the long history of sexual abuse by their clergy, and now I was trying to square this with the refusal of the litigators representing them to even consider settlement, especially in a case where the church had already accepted that the minister had abused me.

I was even more shocked (and traumatized) when I received the statement of defense, which argued consent, stating that I had

We are not to simply bandage the wounds of victims beneath the wheels of injustice, we are to drive a spoke into the wheel itself.

DIETRICH
BONHOEFFER

"welcomed" the sexual activity. Really, as a sixteen-year-old girl with no sexual experience seeking religious and spiritual advice from her minister, I consented to giving him regular fellatio? Of course, the adversarial instinct of many lawyers is to act as "hired guns" no matter what the facts—and no matter what the moral implications. Receiving the defense argument was the tipping point for me. First I was crushed. Then I was galvanized. I was going to make these people talk to me.

The reason we were sitting in that London boardroom in January 2016, two years after the lawsuit had begun, was that in the hours after I received the church's defense I had written an explosive article for the *Church Times*, the world newspaper of the Anglican Church. Despite three injunction threats,[4] my article had been published in the *Church Times* the previous December.[5] It had laid out the hypocrisy and contradiction between the church's public expressions of regret and their extraordinarily defensive and adversarial strategy, and pointed out that as the client they should and could be controlling the approach taken by their (wholly owned) insurer, Ecclesiastical Insurance Group (EIG). The article caused a firestorm. I heard from dozens of other victims of clerical sexual abuse. Suddenly the church wanted to talk.

THE POLITICAL BECOMES PERSONAL: BERNIE

Sitting in a London café with Julie, Sibyl, and David Greenwood (whom I had just met for the first time), I anticipated the negotiation, which was to begin at a nearby law office in about twenty minutes, with eagerness and trepidation. Since beginning the lawsuit, we had traveled a long road, and we were finally approaching the denouement, we hoped. How would this play out when we were finally face-to-face with the church and its insurer, who had been approaching this as a hardball, money-focused negotiation? And what was my role?

Clearly, my most important obligation was to support Julie and help her to evaluate her options. But I also brought thirty-five years of experience as an advocate and conflict intervener to the table. I could imagine that being both an asset and a hindrance to my primary role. This experience was bringing into sharp focus the complex interplay of profoundly different but very connected aspects of my identity.

I came to conflict resolution, particularly mediation, from a background as an activist and a social worker. While studying for my social work degree from 1968 to 1970, I participated in intense debates about whether social workers, by focusing on how to help individuals cope with profound problems that were rooted in an oppressive system, were in fact enabling the continuation of that system. For me, this was an early iteration of a lifelong quest to work on structural or systemic issues while helping individuals, families, or groups deal with the stresses they face in their day-to-day lives.

Finding a path to work for social change at the same time as fulfilling my professional responsibilities, starting a family and rearing children, while offering an important and creative challenge, was often difficult. And as the 1970s moved toward the '80s, the political climate was becoming less conducive to progressive social movements.

But this was also the time when mediation and conflict resolution first appeared in my life. My work in conflict began with my participation in popular protests against the Rocky Flats Nuclear Weapons Plant, located near my then home in Colorado. My specific contribution to these actions was as a trainer in nonviolence and peacekeeping. This led naturally to an interest in conflict resolution.[6]

Working to help people and communities resolve their own conflicts seemed a natural integration of a professional role and a commitment to social change. My colleagues and I believed that our work was contributing to the development of what we thought of as "deep democracy," or to use more current terms, "deliberative democracy" and "civic engagement." But the longer I practiced as a mediator, the more I realized that our focus on intervening as neutrals, while assisting individual disputants and contributing to the development of a new culture of decision-making, also recreated the age-old dilemma of systems change versus systems maintenance.

With Julie's decision (which I encouraged and supported) to confront the Anglican Church over her historical sexual abuse, what had been primarily a professional and social struggle became intensely personal. I naturally took on the role of supporter in her efforts over the ensuing years to hold the Anglican Church (and others) accountable. I did this as her life partner, but my years of work in conflict did not suddenly become irrelevant. The dilemma of social change versus personal healing was everywhere in this case. While Julie's decision to become part of the movement of sexual abuse survivors stemmed from her desire to effect social change, it was inevitable that this effort would have many personal ramifications as well.

From the outset, it was clear to both of us that the biggest challenge would be to move the church and its wholly owned insurance subsidiary (Ecclesiastical Insurance Group[7]) out of their standard operating procedures in such situations—which was to deny, delay, throw roadblocks, intimidate, and then maybe offer a minimal financial settlement (usually tied to a nondisclosure provision), without dealing with the fundamental structural and moral problems that enabled this kind of abuse to occur. We wanted to use this opportunity to make a difference to the policies that revictimized those who took the daunting step of reporting the abuse they received from church officials. We also wanted to confront the practice of what has come to be referred to as "passing the trash,"[8] i.e., allowing a sexual predator to relocate by concealing the circumstances of his departure.[9]

It's hard to fight when the fight ain't fair.
TAYLOR SWIFT

To do this, there were three subsidiary challenges—framing the issue in systemic terms, finding an effective way to marshal power (after the disempowering experience of sexual abuse), and exercising that power in a way that was consistent with our goals and our values. All of this took a great deal of discipline and determination, particularly on Julie's part, and imposed a significant emotional cost, particularly on Julie, but on me as well. The response of the church to the abuse Julie suffered under its auspices infuriated me and evoked a desire for revenge, but I knew that was not a helpful basis on which to move forward. Julie's clarity of strategic vision and her emotional strength helped me keep my eyes on the prize of system change, and I believe our emotional energy in the end helped us achieve our goals. We were fortunate to be aided throughout this process by the wise counsel of David Greenwood, who represented Julie throughout.

DEVELOPING A NEGOTIATION STRATEGY

Bernie

We faced three core strategic challenges in pursuing this lawsuit, none of which could be said to be "typical." The first was to clearly convey our willingness to reach a principled agreement, but without focusing on agreement itself as our end goal. We had to hold fast to our understanding that resolution was a strategic decision to be made at the right time but that it was not our essential purpose. The second was to connect Julie's personal experience to the systemic problems within the church. For example, we knew that the church frequently retraumatized complainants by (among other strategies) hostile expert examinations, the use of consent defenses, and excluding survivors from their church congregations.[10] The third challenge was how to use the power we had in a constructive and sustainable way—in service of a mutually beneficial outcome if possible, but with a willingness to resort to less collaborative alternatives if necessary.

As conflict professionals, we often talk about the importance of taking an integrative approach to the use of power. We were offering the church a way to work with us rather than against us, but we were ready to use public shaming to apply pressure to both them and their insurer in order to make it clear that it was in their interest to deal with us in a principled way. This tension between our preference to use "power with"[11] along with our willingness to use some coercive power to entice them to work with us was necessary to set this negotiation in motion. It also required a constant look inward to make sure that we were acting in an intentional and not reactive way. For both of us, this called on all our experience as both conflict practitioners and activists.

Julie

My experience of the litigation and claims process made it clear to me what I wanted in a settlement. The process that claimants were forced through with its multiple retraumatizing, discouraging, and unnecessary elements had to change. I explained, first to David

As my sufferings mounted I soon realized that there were two ways in which I could respond to my situation—either to react with bitterness or seek to transform the suffering into a creative force. I decided to follow the latter course.

MARTIN LUTHER
KING JR.

and then to Ecclesiastical, that I would be seeking an agreed new claims process for survivors of clerical sexual abuse.

Monetary compensation had never been my goal. In terms of a damages amount, all I felt that I truly needed was enough to pay David (who was operating on a contingency basis) for his work on my case. I had always been far more motivated by the need to hold the church accountable and to strike back against the abusive process in which claimants were obliged to participate: being attacked with the customary defense that victims had "consented" to their own abuse; waiting months and even years for any serious settlement discussions; and being asked to sign "gag" clauses in the event of any settlement that would pressure them to conceal the terms of the settlement (important information for other survivors in setting fair levels of compensation). When I made it clear to David at the outset that I had no intention of being constrained in any way by confidentiality, he roared with laughter and said he had figured that out and that was his practice as well.

We developed an agenda for the first meeting that would address the question of a new claims process as the heart of my settlement with the church. My goal for this meeting was to arrive at a settlement that would be subject to an agreement on a new claims process.

I was teaching dispute resolution in the winter term of 2016, and so informed my class that I would have to reschedule class one week in January in order to attend the first settlement meeting in London. Once I realized I would need to provide them with an explanation for my absence so early in the term, it seemed too good a teaching and learning opportunity to miss. I took the plunge and told the class of thirty upper-year law students that as a plaintiff in a historic sexual abuse case against the Anglican Church I needed to attend a settlement negotiation in January. A silence settled on the room. Slowly a young man raised his hand and said: "Excuse me, Professor, how did you come to be the mediator in this case in England?" "I'm not the mediator, I'm the plaintiff," I replied. Now I had their attention.

I told the class that I would like to involve them in planning my settlement process. I was very clear that anyone who found this upsetting or triggering was not obliged in any way to be part of these discussions, and I would be clear in advance when they would take place. The first step was to help construct an agenda for the first meeting and find a way to convey my commitment to a systemic settlement.

We provided Ecclesiastical with the detailed agenda prior to the meeting. They were clearly baffled. But I knew that I needed to take hold of the narrative to move them from their business-as-usual approach.

SYSTEMIC ENDS IN NEGOTIATION: BERNIE

> *Whoever saves a single life is considered to have saved the whole world.*[12]

Asserting that we were about systemic change seemed easy, even though this was about settling an individual suit. But how would we make this a concrete, actionable proposition that might make a genuine difference on a systemic level?

We knew that many disputants face this challenge. Both of us have worked as mediators with parties who have been clear that their goals were system change—for example, how workplaces respond to reports of sexual harassment or bullying or how hospitals respond to complaints about malpractice. What plaintiffs so often want is an acknowledgment of the pain and damage caused and a commitment to take action to ensure that others do not encounter the same problem, thereby giving some positive meaning to their own suffering. However, even the most well-intentioned settlement efforts usually devolve quickly into a negotiation over dollars and cents.[13]

Julie and I had already experienced this dynamic in the medical system in what in hindsight seems like a rehearsal for the church negotiations. In 2010, Julie received a severe and very painful chemical burn while being treated for cancer. This was a result of what were, in retrospect, obvious mistakes on the part of nursing staff in the hospital where she was receiving chemotherapy. We were not interested in taking legal action, but we did want an acknowledgment of what happened and a commitment to change the procedures that led to it.

However, we were sorely tempted to sue when in response to the concerns we raised with the hospital's "patient advocate" we were initially told, "All procedures were correctly followed." My response to that (by phone) was, "In that case, the procedures are clearly inadequate" (actually, I used more colorful language). Unintentionally but perhaps inevitably, I moved into conflict trainer mode, explaining to the patient advocate that her challenge in our case was not to make a determination about who was right or wrong, but to set up a forum for us to communicate with those in the hospital who could take meaningful responsibility and who could initiate the necessary procedural changes.

This meeting took place several weeks later. Two powerful people in the hospital hierarchy (the medical director and the nursing director) expressed sincere regret and came prepared with a plan for changing their procedures, creating better safeguards, and providing more information to patients about chemical "spills" and their aftereffects. We were satisfied.

While these two negotiations are obviously very different, some of the dynamics are similar. The challenge in both was to use our experience to precipitate systemic change. In both circumstances, we needed to come prepared with concrete suggestions about change; to be clear that we really meant it when we said that systemic change was at the heart of our concerns; and to convey, without hostility or threats, that we would be willing to resort to a more adversarial approach if necessary but offer to work together in good faith in order to find a constructive way forward.

There were also important differences in how these two negotiations played out. One was the role of apology, which was important to us in the case of the hospital—Julie was continuing treatment at this facility, and reestablishing trust was important. We were totally uninterested in an apology from the church, which we felt was unlikely to be authentic or meaningful given their long history of cover-up and denial (see below for a description of how this actually played out). Furthermore, despite the disappointing beginning, we did not feel revictimized by the hospital process, whereas the church's legal strategy significantly added to the trauma Julie experienced at their hands. And of course, as horrible as the chemical burn Julie suffered was, it did not compare to the trauma of church-abetted sexual abuse.

In both situations, we had to find a strategy to use our experience to foment a system reorganization. In systems terminology, we had to find a way to "nucleate" change, or to insert a "negative attractor" into the system, to disrupt self-reinforcing patterns of behavior.[14] And in both situations, we had to encourage a cooperative stance by expressing a positive vision while at the same time indicating a willingness to compete if needed. This integration of cooperation and competition is at the heart of most constructive conflict processes.

CRITICAL MOMENTS IN OUR NEGOTIATIONS

After the publication of the *Church Times* article in December 2015, we had two face-to-face negotiations with the insurer (Ecclesiastical) and the church. The first was a settlement meeting where we thrashed out the basis of a legal settlement conditional on the development and implementation of a new claims process. The second meeting was to negotiate the substance of that new process. In each case, representatives of Ecclesiastical and the church were present, along with outside litigators acting for them. We will present our discussion of these two negotiations around "critical moments" and what they tell us about the tension between advocacy and resolution.

THE FIRST SETTLEMENT MEETING

The Opening Statement

Julie
When I discussed planning for this first settlement meeting with my class, we had just finished an overview of negotiation and mediation, beginning with opening statements and agenda-setting. We discussed how important these were for setting a tone, and had practiced constructing and presenting them.

When I asked my students to help plan the agenda for the upcoming settlement meeting, one of them immediately inquired, "Professor, have you planned what you are going to say in your opening statement?" Gulp, how embarrassing—I hadn't thought about this yet. "Great idea!" I responded. "You can help me think about what I might say in an opening statement."

Over the next ten days I worked on writing an opening. I wanted it to convey something about me—who I was and what I did. I wanted to focus right away on systems change and picked three process issues to introduce in this statement (which I wanted to be no longer than ten to twelve minutes). These were the default use of a consent defense; the standard use of a limitations argument; and the common contention that there was no or extremely limited impact from the abuse.

The most personal part of my opening was about the defense's use of a consent argument against me. From my statement:

> We all understand that this is a standard strategy by the defence in a sex assault case. For example, in your statement of defence it was claimed that the forced fellatio I was subjected to as a 16 and 17 year old over a period of almost a year was "not unwelcome." The psychiatric report is filled with innuendo about my "consent." So was the examination.
>
> Let's roleplay this. I am on my knees before the minister, to whom I have gone for spiritual counseling. He unzips his pants and tells me that God wants me to suck his penis (I have never seen a penis before). I am told that this is how I will resolve my spiritual crisis—this is a "test" of my faith that I must pass. So let's script this—how exactly do we think that the "consent" conversation would have played out here between the person I regarded as my spiritual mentor and myself at 16, with zero sexual experience and a strong commitment to my faith? Or on the multiple other occasions when a similar assault took place?
>
> We are all, I hope, far too sophisticated and sensible to even entertain such a ludicrous notion. But I am most interested in ensuring that others who come after me do not have to endure this offensive and immoral treatment.

I stopped reading from my statement and glanced around the room. Everyone other than Bernie, Sibyl, and David—who were all smiling encouragingly at me—was looking down at their yellow legal notepads.

Bernie

The effect of Julie's opening statement was stunning. Her frank, heartbreaking, but very calm and even slightly humorous discussion of the consent fallacy could not be dismissed. The emotional impact on her of what happened was undeniable, but her presentation also made it impossible to dismiss what she was saying as an overwrought expression of emotional distress. The dialogue could no longer be about just the extent of the church's liability. Instead, the focus around this table would be on how the church should respond to what happened to Julie and to so many others. Power in negotiations requires the use of emotion, but finding a way to bring emotion to the table in a way that draws people into one's story rather than allowing them to distance and discount it is always challenging. The most powerful change agents are masters at this.

The (Non) Apology

The pathetic inadequacy of the typical response of the church to victims of sexual abuse was driven home by one of the most pro forma and insincere apologies I have ever seen. Representing the church establishment was a deaconess from the Diocese of Chichester. At a clearly planned and scripted moment following Julie's opening statement, the representative of Ecclesiastical turned to the deaconess and cued her to make a statement. She looked up, leaned forward, and for the only time that day spoke up to say "how very, very sorry the church is for what happened." She then returned to her disengaged and disinterested posture and stayed that way for the rest of the meeting. What this was supposed to accomplish is beyond me, but what it did do was underscore the lack of any genuine commitment on the part of the church to deal with the systemic problems that led to Julie's experience, or to truly understand the impact that this had had on her and other survivors.

"The Monetary Settlement Will Take Twenty Minutes"

In Julie's opening statement, she emphasized that settling on the quantum of damages would not be difficult.

> I am distressed by the hostile and offensive manner in which the compensatory components of my claim—the quantum—is being contended and minimized.
>
> Nevertheless—and it is important that you hear this— settling quantum with me is by far the easiest part of this case. . . .
>
> My financial settlement must include fair compensation for my solicitor, and it should cover my past and future expenses for therapy, and the expenses incurred in this and any further meetings.
>
> But further than that—this is not going to be difficult. I would be willing to bet that we can resolve this in an hour. But any such interim agreement shall only become final once I am satisfied with movement on the systemic issues, the issues of process that I want to focus on today.

Once we began to negotiate over money, Julie revised her estimate of resolving this in one hour down to twenty minutes. And that was exactly how it played out.

We didn't think the church was being particularly generous, but we did not make a real effort to challenge their offer, which would cover David's costs and fee as well as Julie's therapy and expenses. Here I had to consciously clamp down on my desire for revenge. Perhaps if we had pushed the issue, threatened to walk away, or left without an agreement, we might have eventually received a little more, and this might have been emotionally satisfying to me, but that was neither our purpose nor a reflection of our values. We also knew that Ecclesiastical and the church representatives would have to sell our settlement to their superiors, and we wanted them to focus on the systems change proposal, not the quantum of damages.

The rapidity with which we got through this part of the negotiation, as we predicted, clearly surprised the church and Ecclesiastical representatives. Despite our efforts to flag in advance the importance of a systemic outcome, the negotiation over money is what they had clearly spent most of their time preparing for. This may have thrown them off-balance, perhaps to our advantage, but more importantly, it underscored that we really meant what we said about the goals of this meeting.

THE SECOND SETTLEMENT MEETING: NEGOTIATING A NEW CLAIMS PROCESS

Julie

I returned from my trip to the United Kingdom in January with a conditional agreement and a plan for a second meeting to revise the current Ecclesiastical claims process and change the default litigation strategy used by their lawyers. David, Bernie, and I did a great deal of advance work on the April meeting agenda, with input from my dispute resolution class (the perfect vehicle for teaching them about dispute systems design). For example, we wanted a commitment to provide church-funded access to therapy for all claimants regardless of the stage of their claim or arguments over "proof." Some of our proposals—for example, over the timing of settlement discussions and the use of joint experts for psychological examinations—we knew would be difficult to pin down definitively because of the way that lawsuits are managed, and inevitably resulted in statements of intentions rather than firm commitments, but we wanted these statements to be as strong as possible. On some issues we proposed actual wording. For example, we argued that "the disconnect between the reality of rape and sexual abuse and the way it is dealt with by the legal system is most noticeable in the context of sexual abuse of power stemming from professional and institutional relationships. Where there is a relationship of power, consent has to be seen completely differently." This was ultimately reflected in the new claims protocol.

Power in the Room

I decided to ask my first cousin, Elizabeth Macfarlane, to accompany me to this meeting. Elizabeth is a minister of the Anglican Church (chaplain of St John's College, Oxford) and a leading proponent of women's and LGBTQ rights inside the church. I thought that bringing my indomitable cousin, who had long been a thorn in the side of the Anglican Church establishment, had an ironic twist to it. We notified the participants in advance that she would attend. Watching the face of the representative of the church commissioner when Elizabeth and I walked into the room together was a moment that stands out for me.

The question of who had power in the room that day was a fascinating study in misplaced assumptions and unexpected dynamics. While she had no formal decision-making power and said almost nothing, Elizabeth clearly had representational power, and as she sat beside me when I spoke, her every expression, sigh, and gesture were watched carefully. The "chair" of the meeting was a senior lawyer hired to represent Ecclesiastical at the upcoming Independent Inquiry into Child Sexual Abuse (IICSA), which had a statutory mandate to investigate the response of the Anglican Church (and other institutions) to sexual abuse allegations. He introduced himself, presenting his qualifications at length. His initial approach was to adopt a very directive tone that implied that I could make suggestions, thank you, and they would listen politely.

I explained—firmly—that I was there not to be listened to politely but to work directly on a draft revised claims protocol, and that this was the purpose of the meeting. He got the message and said less after that. I had also imagined that the representative of the church commissioner, effectively the church's in-house counsel, would play a larger role, but it quickly became clear that they had little real power in the ensuing discussions. It was left to David; Ecclesiastical's in-house counsel, whom we had worked with at the first meeting; and me to do most of work in crafting the elements of the new process.

The Shadow of the Future

The negotiation was undoubtedly affected by the beginning of hearings at IICSA, the largest public inquiry ever launched in England and Wales, which had commenced just a month before. The inquiry was attracting a great deal of media attention. I have no doubt that this focused both Ecclesiastical and the church on making some improvements to the claims process that they could then show off to the inquiry. In other words, change was coming one way or another, and this discussion—as I was not shy about pointing out—gave them a perfect opportunity to demonstrate their good faith and willingness to move forward from a grim past of suppressing sex abuse complaints. Moreover, I had just been appointed a "core participant" at the inquiry, which meant that I would be testifying there myself.

"We Got 80 Percent"

Ecclesiastical and the church agreed to a revised claims protocol crystallized in ten new "Guiding Principles." After the meeting, these were posted, along with a plain-language version that I drafted, on the website of MACSAS, a survivor's group. I also wrote a piece for the *Church Times*.

The Guiding Principles are, in effect, a "Bill of Rights" for survivors bringing forward legal claims where the insurer is Ecclesiastical. They are a significant step forward in humanizing the brutal legal process.

The commitments made in the Guiding Principles can be read in full on the EIG website. In summary, they commit to the following:

- Treating claimants with "sensitivity, empathy, and integrity" and "an overriding principle of fairness." The church is advised by its insurer to respond "constructively" to claimants from the outset.

- Claimants will have immediate access to counseling. The insurer recognizes that "offering to pay for some counselling or treatment [is not] . . . an admission of legal liability."

- No exclusion from pastoral care for claimants who are still part of a church community.

- The defense of the statute of limitations (the defense that an action is time-barred) will be used "very sparingly" and only in exceptional circumstances and will require a special internal vetting procedure.

- A "consent" defense will never be used where the victim was under the age of sixteen. For those aged sixteen and over, the Principles recognize "the power imbalance that is often presented in such cases" where consent cannot truly be given. The use of a "consent" defense should now be exceptional.

- Ecclesiastical will always consider using a single, jointly agreed expert.

- Once liability is accepted, an offer to settle will be made and a joint settlement meeting (JSM) offered. A JSM may also take place before formal legal action is begun.

- Unless the claimant requests confidentiality, he or she will not be asked to maintain confidentiality about the settlement.

After the meeting ended late in the afternoon, David and I reflected on how far we had managed to move Ecclesiastical and the church. Still slightly amazed at how successful the negotiations had been, we agreed that in the end we had achieved about 80 percent of what we had been hoping for.

There is still plenty of work to be done, for example, changing the way that complainants are responded to when they first disclose to someone inside the church. It is also important to ensure that survivors receive a fair and reasonable amount of compensation, and there is nothing in the Guiding Principles that directly affects the hardball approach many litigators continue to take, as other survivors will attest. In addition, it is critical that the Guiding Principles are properly monitored and that survivors are familiar with their "rights" here. And this agreement in its entirety only applies to the United Kingdom. There is still a world of work to be done to institute similar principles throughout the Anglican institution worldwide. But on that April day in 2016, with the inquiry ongoing (as it is to date), 80 percent felt like a good start.

Final Thoughts: Julie and Bernie

Social change does not follow a linear path. We felt fortunate, even privileged, to be a small part in a larger effort here. We did our part, but we entered a stage that had been set by the efforts and suffering of so many others. The slowly emerging revelations and growing outrage about the shocking level of abuse that occurred within the Catholic Church, the Anglican Church, and so many other social institutions have accelerated and intensified in recent years, making it much harder to isolate and ignore our demands. This has been reflected throughout our culture (e.g., *Spotlight* won the Best Picture Oscar, the #MeToo movement became a major phenomenon, and "Silence Breakers"—those who spoke out against sexual abuse—were named *Time* magazine's "Persons of the Year" in 2017). But collective action and popular culture tend to follow the courageous actions of many individuals.

We all have a responsibility to do our best to ensure that redress processes for victims and survivors take place in as safe and supportive an environment as possible. Do conflict specialists have something particular to offer? Without taking away from the important fact that everyone has something they can offer to empowering victims of abuse, our experience suggests that conflict specialists may have a perspective that is useful here—although not in the way we might expect. We did not need a mediator or other neutral. But we did need advice, coaching, strategizing, rehearsing, debriefing, emotional support, and ongoing reinforcement. We received this from friends, family, colleagues, and others, but of course we also provided it to each other. Our experience in the nuanced uses of power, effective framing of issues, and multidimensional communication strategies were critical to our efforts. By the second meeting, this negotiation had morphed into a dispute system design process, and that was probably the most critical conflict experience we brought to the table. But in the end, determination, courage, and the audacity to speak truth to power were the irreducible requirements to go forward. No professional discipline has a monopoly on this.

NOTES

1. Diocese of Chichester, The Church of England, "Historic Cases Review of Roy Cotton and Colin Pritchard," 2017, 39, https://cofechichestersafeguarding.contentfiles.net/media/documents/document/2017/05/EBS_Report__Addendum1202282.pdf.

2. David Greenwood, "Stop Church Child Abuse," stopchurchchildabuse .co.uk/. (Stop Church Child Abuse was originally founded by a group of survivors and their lawyers to call for a public inquiry into cover-ups of abuse in the Anglican Church.)

3. The Independent Inquiry into Child Sexual Abuse (IICSA) was established by the UK government in 2014 and opened in 2015. It had a rocky beginning, with three chairs resigning before the business of the inquiry was taken forward by the current chair, Professor Alex Jay. The inquiry has a wide remit, investigating historical suppression of complaints of abuse inside not only the Anglican Church but also the Catholic Church and eleven other institutions. See https://www.iicsa.org.uk/about-us.

4. In a sign of the firestorm to come, the article faced three injunction threats—from the Diocese of Chichester, the Chichester police, and the Crown Prosecution Service—but the editor of the *Church Times*, Paul Handley, and the deputy editor, Rachel Boulding, were remarkable and impressive in their determination to publish.

5. Julie Macfarlane, "An Abuse Survivor's Tale," *Church Times*, December 11, 2015, https://www.churchtimes.co.uk/articles/2015/11-december/com ment/opinion/Church-litigation-means-my-ordeal-continues.

6. I was introduced to both nonviolence training and mediation by Christopher Moore. Together with Mary Margaret Golten and Susan Wildau, we became the founding partners of CDR Associates, a partnership that lasted for thirty years.

7. Ecclesiastical has been the subject of numerous media articles in recent years exposing what survivors have long argued—that it is in effect owned and operated by its major client, the Anglican Church, who sit on its board and receive a share of its profits. See, for example, Martin Bashir and Callum May, "Church of England 'Withdrew Emotional Support for Abused,'" *BBC News,* July 21, 2017, https://www.bbc.com/news/uk-40668079; and Keith Porteous Wood, "Church of England's Links with Insurer Undermines Justice for Survivors of Clergy Abuse,*" National Secular Society,* July 26, 2017, https://www .secularism.org.uk/opinion/2017/07/church-of-englands-links-with-insurer -undermines-justice-for-survivors-of-clergy-abuse.

8. See, for example, Billie-Jo Grant et al., "Passing the Trash: Absence of State Laws Allows for Continued Sexual Abuse of K–12 Students by School Employees,*" Journal of Child Sexual Abuse* 28(1), 2019, 84–103; and Sandy K. Wurtele, "Preventing the Sexual Exploitation of Minors in Youth-Serving Organizations," *Children and Youth Services Review* 34(12), December 2012, 2442–2453.

9. Case law is developing on this issue in relation to public schools in the United States proscribing such practices. See, for example, *Doe-3 v. McLean County Unit District No. 5 Board of Directors*, 973 NE (2d) 880 (Ill 2012); and *Davis v. The Board of County Commissions of Dona Ana County*, 19, 176 (NM Ct App 1999).

10. Many survivors were told that they "could not" attend church if they were bringing forward a complaint, thus losing an important community to them.

11. For excellent and early descriptions of "power with" contrasted with "power over," see Genevieve A. Chornenki, "Mediating Commercial Disputes: Exchanging 'Power Over' for 'Power With,'" in *Rethinking Disputes: The Mediation Alternative*, edited by Julie Macfarlane (London: Cavendish Publishing, 1997), 159–168; and Bernard Mayer, "The Dynamics of Power in Mediation and Negotiation," *Mediation Quarterly* 16, Summer 1987, 75–86.

12. From multiple sources in the Quran, Old Testament, and Talmud—for a description of this phrase's genesis, see https://mosaicmagazine.com/observa tion/history-ideas/2016/10/the-origins-of-the-precept-whoever-saves-a-life -saves-the-world/.

13. For an especially striking example of this phenomenon in practice, see Julie Macfarlane and Ellen Zweibel, "Systemic Change and Private Closure in Human Rights Mediation: An Evaluation of the Mediation Program at the Canadian Human Rights Tribunal," May 2001, showing that many human rights complainants began with systemic goals but ultimately settled for individual redress.

14. For a discussion of complex adaptive systems and conflict, see Peter T. Coleman et al., "Intractable Conflict as an Attractor: A Dynamical Systems Approach to Conflict Escalation and Intractability," *American Behavioral Scientist* 50(11), July 2007, 1454–1475.

Bibliography

Abbott, Alison. "The Mental-Health Crisis among Migrants." *Nature* (October 10, 2016). At: https://www.nature.com/news/the-mental-health-crisis -among-migrants-1.20767.

Alexander, Jeffrey. *Trauma: A Social Theory*. Malden, MA: Polity Press, 2012.

Arao, Brian, and Kristi Clemens. "From Safe Spaces to Brave Spaces: A New Way to Frame Dialogue around Diversity and Social Justice." In *The Art of Effective Facilitation: Reflections from Social Justice Educators*. Ed. Lisa M. Landreman, 135–150. Sterling, VA: Stylus, 2013.

Arendt, Hannah. *The Human Condition*. Chicago: University of Chicago Press, 1958.

Bandaragoda, C., et al. "Lower Nooksack Water Budget (LNWB)." Hydro-Share under Creative Commons License (2019). At: http://www.hydro share.org/resource/d15b9934f34e4c57913b3cb53966d5c7.

Bar-On, Dan. *The Indescribable and the Undiscussable: Reconstructing Human Discourse after Trauma*. Budapest, Central European University Press, 1999.

Baruch Bush, Robert A., and Joseph P. Folger. *The Promise of Mediation: The Transformative Approach to Conflict*. San Francisco: Jossey-Bass, 2005.

Bashir, Martin, and Callum May. "Church of England 'Withdrew Emotional Support for Abused.'" BBC News (July 21, 2017). At: https://www.bbc .com/news/uk-40668079.

Beer, Stafford. *Brain of the Firm*. 2nd ed. New York: Herder and Herder, 1981.

Berghof Foundation. "Multipartiality." At: https://www.berghof-foundation .org/en/featured-topics/multipartiality/.

Brofenbrenner, Urie. "Toward an Experimental Ecology of Human Development." *American Psychologist*. Vol. 32(7) (July 1977): 513–531.

Brown, Brené. "The Power of Vulnerability." TED Talk (July 8, 2019). At: https://www.ted.com/talks/brene_brown_on_vulnerability.

Cadwallader, Anne. *Lethal Allies: British Collusion in Ireland*. Cork, Ireland: Mercier Press, 2013.

Carpenter, Susan, and W.J. Kennedy. *Managing Public Disputes: A Practical Guide for Government, Business, and Citizen Groups*. New York: John Wiley & Sons, 2001.

Chornenki, Genevieve A. "Mediating Commercial Disputes: Exchanging 'Power Over' for 'Power With.'" In *Rethinking Disputes: The Mediation Alternative*. Ed. Julie Macfarlane. London: Cavendish Publishing, 1997.

Cobb, Sara, and Janet Rifkin. "Practice and Paradox: Deconstructing Neutrality in Mediation." *Law & Social Inquiry*. Vol. 16(1) (Winter 1991): 35–62.

Coleman, Peter T., et al. "Intractable Conflict as an Attractor: A Dynamical Systems Approach to Conflict Escalation and Intractability." *American Behavioral Scientist*. Vol. 50(11) (July 2007): 1454–1475.

Coogler, O.J. *Structured Mediation in Divorce Settlement: A Handbook for Marital Mediators*. Lanham, MD: Lexington Books, 1978.

Corry, Geoffrey. "Political Dialogue Workshops: Deepening the Peace Process in Northern Ireland." *Conflict Resolution Quarterly*. Vol. 30(1) (October 2012): 53–80.

Corry, Geoffrey, and Pat Hynes. "Creating Political Oxygen to Break the Cycle of Violence 1981–1994: Lessons from the Northern Ireland Peace Process." *Journal of Mediation & Applied Conflict Analysis*. Vol. 2(2) (2015): 259–275. At: http://mural.maynoothuniversity.ie/6251/7/GC-Creating -2015.pdf.

Darling-Hammond, Linda. "Reframing the School Reform Agenda: Developing Capacity for School Transformation." *Phi Delta Kappan*. Vol. 74(10) (June 1993): 752–761.

Davis, Fania. *The Little Book of Race and Restorative Justice: Black Lives, Healing, and US Social Transformation*. New York: Good Books, 2019.

Davis v. The Board of County Commissions of Dona Ana County. 19, 176 (NM Ct App 1999).

De Paor, Jacinta. "LIVE: Let's Involve the Victim's Experience." In *Deepening Reconciliation: Reflections on Glencree Peacebuilding*. Ed. Eamon Rafter, 115–129. Dublin: Glencree Centre for Peace and Reconciliation, 2014.

Dewey, John. "Democracy and Educational Administration." In *John Dewey: The Later Works 1925–1953*, Vol. 11: 1935–1937. Ed. Jo Ann Boydston, 217–225. Carbondale: Southern Illinois University Press, 1987.

Diamond, Louise, and Ambassador John McDonald. *Multi-Track Diplomacy: A Systems Approach to Peace*. New York: Kumarian Press, 1996.

Diocese of Chichester, The Church of England. "Historic Cases Review of Roy Cotton and Colin Pritchard" (2017). At: https://cofechichestersafeguarding .contentfiles.net/media/documents/document/2017/05/EBS_Report__ Addendum1202282.pdf.

Doe-3 v. McLean County Unit District No. 5 Board of Directors. 973 NE (2d) 880 (Ill 2012).

Dukes, E. Franklin. *Resolving Public Conflict: Transforming Community and Governance*. Manchester, UK: Manchester University Press, 1996.

Dukes, E. Franklin. "Righting Unrightable Wrongs." *ACResolutions*. Vol. 7(4) (2008).

Dukes, Frank. "From Enemies, to Higher Ground, to Allies: The Unlikely Partnership between the Tobacco Farm and Public Health Communities." In *Participatory Governance: Planning, Conflict Mediation and Public*

Decision-Making in Civil Society. Ed. W. Robert Lovan, Michael Murray, and Ron Shaffer. Farnham, UK: Ashgate Press, 2004.

Dukes, Frank. "Public Conflict Resolution: A Transformative Approach." *Negotiation Journal.* Vol. 9(1) (January 1993): 45–57.

Dumas, Mary. *Toolz for Tough Conversations Instructors' Manual.* Everson: Dumas & Associates, Inc., 2018.

Falkenburger, Elsa, Olivia Arena, and Jessica Wolin. *Trauma-Informed Community Building and Engagement.* Washington: Urban Institute, April 2018.

Fieldstone, Linda, Sue Bronson, and Hon. Michelle Morley. "Association for Conflict Resolutions Guidelines for Eldercaring Coordination." *Family Court Review.* Vol. 53(4) (October 2015): 542–561.

Fisher, Roger, and William Ury. *Getting to Yes: Negotiating Agreement without Giving In.* New York: Penguin Books, 1981.

Frank, Arthur W. *Letting Stories Breathe: A Socio-narratology.* Chicago: University of Chicago Press, 2010.

Frankl, Viktor E. *Man's Search for Meaning: An Introduction to Logotherapy.* Boston: Beacon Press, 1959.

Freire, Paulo. *Pedagogy of the Oppressed.* 2nd ed. New York: Continuum, 2003.

Gardner, Howard. *Frames of Mind: The Theory of Multiple Intelligences.* New York: Basic Books, 2011.

Grant, Billie-Jo, et al. "Passing the Trash: Absence of State Laws Allows for Continued Sexual Abuse of K–12 Students by School Employees." *Journal of Child Sexual Abuse.* Vol. 28(1) (2019): 84–103.

Greenwood, David. "Stop Church Child Abuse." At: stopchurchchildabuse .co.uk.

Guthrie, Robert V. *Even the Rat Was White: A Historical View of Psychology.* New York: Harper & Row, 1976.

Halverson, Jeffry R., H.L. Goodall Jr., and Steven R. Corman. *Master Narratives of Islamist Extremism.* New York: Palgrave Macmillan, 2011.

Hirsch, Susan F., and E. Franklin Dukes. *Mountaintop Mining in Appalachia: Understanding Stakeholders and Change in Environmental Conflict.* Athens: Ohio University Press, 2014.

Hooker, David Anderson. "Legacy and Aftermath: The Mechanisms of Power in the Multigenerational Transmission of Trauma." In *Understanding Power: An Imperative for Human Services.* Ed. Elaine Pinderhughes, Vanessa Jackson, and Patricia A. Romney, 23–47. New York: National Association of Social Workers, 2017.

Hooker, David Anderson, and Amy Potter Czajkowski. *Transforming Historical Harms.* Harrisonburg, PA: Eastern Mennonite University, 2012.

Idriss, Shamil. "Why Should I Seek Common Ground with My Fellow Americans?" Medium (November 7, 2018). At: https://medium.com/ @SFCG_/why-should-i-seek-common-ground-with-my-fellow -americans-d1430fd6dfa5.

Irish Peace Centres. *Intergenerational Aspects of the Conflict in Northern Ireland.* Belfast: Irish Peace Centres, 2010.

Jung, C.G. *Memories, Dreams, Reflections.* New York: Vintage, 1989.

Kelman, Herbert C. "Experiences from 30 Years of Action Research on the Israeli-Palestinian Conflict." In *Zeitgeschichtliche Hintergründe aktueller Konflikte VII: Zürcher Beiträge zur Sicherheitspolitik und Konfliktforschung.* Ed. K.P. Spillmann and A. Wenger, 173–197. 54, 1999. At: https://scholar.harvard.edu/files/hckelman/files/Experiences_from_30_years.pdf.

Kenney, Jeffery T., and Ebrahim Moosa (ed.). *Islam in the Modern World.* New York: Routledge, 2014.

Kreisberg, Seth. *Transforming Power: Domination, Empowerment and Education.* Albany: State University of New York Press, 1992.

Lang, Michael. *The Guide to Reflective Practice in Conflict Resolution.* Lanham, MD: Rowman & Littlefield, 2019.

Lather, Patti. "Research as Praxis." *Harvard Educational Review.* Vol. 56(3) (September 1986): 257–278.

Laue, James, and Gerald R Cormick. "The Ethics of Intervention in Community Disputes." In *The Ethics of Social Intervention.* Eds. Gordon Bermant, Herbert C. Kelman, and Donald P. Warwick, 205–232. New York: Halsted Press, 1978.

Lederach, John Paul. *The Little Book of Conflict Transformation.* Intercourse, PA: Good Books, 2001.

Macfarlane, Julie. "An Abuse Survivor's Tale." *Church Times* (December 11, 2015). At: https://www.churchtimes.co.uk/articles/2015/11-december/comment/opinion/Church-litigation-means-my-ordeal-continues.

Macfarlane, Julie, and Ellen Zweibel. "Systemic Change and Private Closure in Human Rights Mediation: An Evaluation of the Mediation Program at the Canadian Human Rights Tribunal" (May 2001).

Maté, Gabor. *In the Realm of Hungry Ghosts: Close Encounters with Addiction.* Berkeley, CA: North Atlantic Books, 2008.

Mayer, Bernard S. *Beyond Neutrality: Confronting the Crisis in Conflict Resolution.* San Francisco: Jossey-Bass Publishing, 2004.

Mayer, Bernard. *The Conflict Paradox: Seven Dilemmas at the Core of Disputes.* San Francisco: Jossey-Bass Publishing, 2015.

Mayer, Bernard. "The Dynamics of Power in Mediation and Negotiation." *Mediation Quarterly.* Vol. 16 (Summer 1987): 75–86.

Mezirow, Jack. *Fostering Critical Reflection in Adulthood: A Guide to Transformative and Emancipatory Learning.* San Francisco: Jossey-Bass, 1990.

Nader, Laura. "Trading Justice for Harmony." *NIDR Forum* (Winter 1992): 12–19.

The Nation: Web Desk. "10 Things You Need to Know about Pakistan's Blasphemy Law" (October 14, 2016). At: https://nation.com.pk/14-Oct-2016/10-things-you-need-to-know-about-pakistan-s-blasphemy-law.

Niamatullah, Abu Eesa. "The Best of the Best." At: https://sunnahonline.com/library/purification-of-the-soul/194-best-of-the-best-the.

Northern Ireland Office. Stormont House Agreement (2014). At: https://www.gov.uk/government/uploads/system/uploads/attachment_data/file/390672/Stormont_House_Agreement.pdf.

Pakistan Agricultural Research Council. "Quotes of Quaid-e-Azam." At: http://www.parc.gov.pk/index.php/en/quotes-of-quaid-e-azam.

Piscolish, Marina, et al. "Righting Un-rightable Wrongs: Finding the Courage of Our Convictions." Presented at the annual meeting for the Association for Conflict Resolution, Denver, Colorado (June 12, 2005).

Ricoeur, Paul. *Figuring the Sacred: Religion, Narrative, Imagination*. Minneapolis: Fortress Press, 1995.

Rogers, Carl. *On Personal Power: Inner Strength and Its Revolutionary Impact*. New York: Delacorte Press, 1977.

Society of Professionals in Dispute Resolution (SPDR). "Guidelines for Using Collaborative Agreement-Seeking Processes." White paper (1997).

Solomon, Robert, and Fernando Flores. *Building Trust in Business, Politics, Relationships, and Life*. New York: Oxford University Press, 2001.

The Steel Shutter. Film directed by Tom Skinner and produced by Bill McGraw. Project Media-N presentation of The Center for Studies of the Person, La Jolla, California, 1973.

Turk, A.M., and J. Ungerleider. "Experiential Activities in Mediation-Based Training: Cyprus, 1997–2013." *Conflict Resolution Quarterly*. Vol. 34(3): 281–300.

Tutu, Desmond. "Truth and Reconciliation." *Greater Good Magazine* (September 1, 2004).

Van der Kolk, Bessel. *The Body Keeps the Score: Brain, Mind, and Body in the Healing of Trauma*. New York: Viking, 2014.

Van der Kolk, Bessel A. *Post-Traumatic Stress Disorder: Psychological and Biological Sequelae*. Washington: American Psychiatric Association Publishing, 1984.

Verwoerd, Wilhelm. "Working with Former Combatants and the Sustainable Peace Network." In *Deepening Reconciliation: Reflections on Glencree Peacebuilding*. Ed. Eamon Rafter, 131–149. Dublin: Glencree Centre for Peace and Reconciliation, 2014.

Vivian, Pat, and Shana Hormann. *Organizational Trauma and Healing*. North Charleston, SC: CreateSpace, 2013.

Watch the Yard. "In 1851 a Scientist 'Discovered' a Disease That Caused Slaves to Run Away, This Was the Prescribed Cure . . ." At: https://www.watch theyard.com/history/drapetomania-dysaesthesia-aethiopica/.

Wheatley, Margaret J. *Who Do We Choose to Be? Facing Reality, Claiming Leadership, Restoring Sanity*. Oakland, CA: Berrett-Koehler, 2017.

Winter, Helen. "Sharing What Divides Us." Harvard Negotiation & Mediation Clinical Program (March 27, 2019). At: http://hnmcp.law.harvard .edu/hnmcp/blog/sharing-what-divides-us/.

Wood, Keith Porteous. "Church of England's Links with Insurer Undermines Justice for Survivors of Clergy Abuse." National Secular Society (July 26, 2017). At: https://www.secularism.org.uk/opinion/2017/07/church-of -englands-links-with-insurer-undermines-justice-for-survivors-of-clergy -abuse.

Wurtele, Sandy K. "Preventing the Sexual Exploitation of Minors in Youth-Serving Organizations." *Children and Youth Services Review*. Vol. 34(12) (December 2012): 2442–2453.

Zehr, Howard. *The Little Book of Restorative Justice*. Intercourse, PA: Good Books, 2019.

Index

About the Contributors

Gastón Aín coordinates dispute resolution at the Inter-American Development Bank's compliance review office. Previously he was the United Nations Development Programme's Latin American and Caribbean regional advisor for conflict prevention and political advisor to the Organization of American States. He has facilitated dispute resolution processes and peacebuilding initiatives in various countries including Haiti, Colombia, Ecuador, Guatemala, El Salvador, Rwanda, and Congo-DRC. Gastón holds a master's in international affairs from Universidad Autónoma de Madrid and a master's in public policy from Universidad de Alcalá de Henares, Spain.

Rachel Barbour served as vice chair and chair of the Executive Committee of Trailblazers PAC, a national, nonpartisan organization dedicated to transparency and clean government, from 2017 to 2019. She has worked for a range of international and domestic conflict resolution organizations, and more recently on political campaigns, doing messaging, media, and opposition research. She holds an M.S. in conflict analysis and resolution from George Mason University and a B.A. from Mount Holyoke College.

Erricka Bridgeford trains mediators, teaches conflict resolution skills, co-organizes a movement that rallies Baltimore City to avoid violence during three-day weekends, and performs rituals for every person who is murdered in Baltimore. Her life has been impacted by murder since she was twelve years old, and she has been working for more than twenty years to ensure that murder does not have the last say. Erricka is director of training at Community Mediation Maryland and cofounder of Baltimore Ceasefire 365.

Sue Bronson, M.S., L.C.S.W., has been a mediator and trainer in Milwaukee, Wisconsin, since 1983, mediating family, elder, and workplace disputes, and teaches mediation at the University of Wisconsin–Milwaukee School of Continuing Education. As cochair of the ACR Eldercaring Coordination Initiative, Sue is focusing on the needs of older adults, teaching experienced mediators and other qualified professionals the process and skills for working with high-conflict families.

Geoffrey Corry is a mediator and trainer in Ireland with more than thirty years' experience. He started the first community mediation scheme in 1991 and was a family mediator for the state-run Family Mediation Service (1992–2015). He is a former chairperson of the Mediators Institute Ireland and the Glencree Centre for Reconciliation. He facilitated more than fifty political dialogue workshops at Glencree and currently teaches the Peacemaking modules in the master's programme at the Edward M. Kennedy Institute, Maynooth University.

E. Franklin Dukes, Ph.D., is a mediator and facilitator with the Institute for Engagement & Negotiation (IEN) at the University of Virginia. He founded University and Community Action for Racial Equity (UCARE), leads IEN's Transforming Community Spaces project, and was a member of Charlottesville's Commission on Race, Memorials and Public Spaces. He has written a number of books including *Mountaintop Mining in Appalachia* (with Susan Hirsch) and *Reaching for Higher Ground: Creating Powerful, Purposeful, Principled Groups and Communities* (with John Stephens and Marina Piscolish).

Mary Dumas is an independent dispute resolution professional in private practice for more than thirty years. Mary helps universities, public agencies, tribes, interjurisdictional bodies, research institutes, nonprofit organizations, and businesses translate technical information and regulatory mandates into effective processes, accessible resource materials, actionable information, and strategic plans. Mary is known for bringing best practices in trauma-informed approaches to multiparty mediation, change management, and interest-based problem-solving with organizations and communities.

Mencer Donahue "Don" Edwards is the founder, CEO, and a principal of Justice and Sustainability Associates, a for-profit alternative dispute resolution consulting firm in Washington, D.C. He is considered one of the deftest facilitator-mediators and civic engagement designers working today in the field of community development and land use by international, federal, regional, state, and local planning, transportation, parks, and economic development agencies; corporations; universities; foundations; and community-based organizations.

Linda Fieldstone, M.Ed., is cochair of the ACR Eldercaring Coordination Initiative. She is past president of the Association of Family and Conciliation Courts and was instrumental in the development of parenting coordination. After serving as supervisor of Family Court Services with the Miami-Dade court for twenty-six years, she now provides conflict resolution options for families of all ages before, during, and after court actions.

David Anderson Hooker, Ph.D., J.D., M.Div., is associate professor of the practice of conflict transformation and peacebuilding at the University of Notre Dame's Kroc Institute. His research and practice focus on the role of generational and cultural trauma and narrative in identity construction in post-conflict contexts. He is the author of *The Little Book of Transformative Community Conferencing* (Skyhorse, 2016) and coauthor (with Amy Potter Czajkowski) of *Transforming Historical Harms* (Eastern Mennonite University, 2012).

Dr. Julie Macfarlane is professor of law and Distinguished University Professor at the University of Windsor. Her books include *The New Lawyer: How Clients Are Transforming the Practice of Law* (2nd ed., UBC Press, 2017) and *Islamic Divorce in North America:*

Choosing a Shari'a Path in a Secular Society (Oxford University Press, 2012). She is currently the director of the National Self-Represented Litigants Research Project (www.representingyour selfcanada.com). Her next book is *From Personal Grief to Public Advocacy: Confronting Sexual Violence* for Between the Lines Press.

Bernie Mayer, Ph.D., is a professor of conflict studies, Program on Negotiation and Conflict Resolution, Creighton University, and a founding partner of CDR Associates. Bernie has worked with families, communities, nongovernmental organizations (NGOs), unions, and governmental agencies throughout North America and internationally for more than thirty-five years. Bernie's most recent book is *The Conflict Paradox: Seven Dilemmas at the Core of Disputes*. Earlier books include *The Dynamics of Conflict, Beyond Neutrality*, and *Staying with Conflict*.

Lucy Moore is a facilitator, mediator, and trainer, specializing in complex natural resource and public policy conflicts. Based in New Mexico, she works regionally and nationally, often on issues that include a cross-cultural component. With a strong background in Indian country, much of her work includes tribal issues and parties. Lucy is an active mentor for those in the field needing a helping hand. She is author of *Common Ground on Hostile Turf: Stories from an Environmental Mediator*.

Marina Piscolish, Ph.D., is founder of Mapping Change, LLC, a full-service conflict and collaboration consultancy serving sectors from education to environment and diverse clients from single agencies to cross-sector collaborations. Marina works across the continental US, Hawaii, and the Pacific, delivering creative, culturally responsive, and socially responsible services that address place, power, and client capacity of constructive confrontation. She coauthored *Reaching for Higher Ground: Creating Powerful, Purposeful, Principled Groups and Communities* (2009).

Julian Portilla is associate professor at Champlain College, where he also directs the Center for Mediation and Dialogue. In addition to teaching, he designs and facilitates complex, multi-stakeholder

consensus-building processes on such issues as fisheries management, national park management plans, climate change legislation, and others. He works mostly in Mexico and the United
States. Julian holds a master's degree in conflict analysis and
resolution from George Mason University and a bachelor's degree
from Vassar College.

Beth Roy, Ph.D., mediates organizations and communities confronting challenges to diversity. She teaches workshops on ways
to talk and listen across differing identities. Her published works
include *Some Trouble with Cows: Making Sense of Social Conflict*
and *41 Shots . . . and Counting: What Amado Diallo Teaches Us about
Policing, Race, and Justice*. She is a cofounder of the Practitioners
Research and Scholarship Institute and coedited the anthology
Re-centering Culture and Knowledge in Conflict Resolution Practice.

Vishal Shamsi is a litigation lawyer at Hafeez Pirzada Law Associates and a mediator at the National Centre for Dispute Resolution in Karachi, Pakistan. Over the course of the past few years she
has trained more than one hundred fifty individuals in the art of
mediation, including senior civil judges, police officers, chartered
accountants, ombudsmen, and lawyers from all over Pakistan. She
is also a lecturer of law at a local institute and on the panel of arbitrators of the Pakistan Stock Exchange.

Marlon Sherman is Oglala Lakota, born in a log cabin outside
Kyle, South Dakota, and raised there on the Pine Ridge Reservation. After a harrowing brush with a law career, he worked in
the areas of peacemaking, mediation, facilitation, leadership, and
multicultural issues for tribes and tribal organizations. He teaches
in the Native American Studies Department at Humboldt State
University and consults privately.

Susanne Terry, M.S., is a conflict engagement practitioner based
in northern Vermont. She works as a mediator, reflective practice
coach, trainer, parent coordinator, and organizational consultant.
She is the case supervisor for the Vermont Superior Court Parent
Coordination Program and was the creator and director of the

Woodbury College Mediation Program. She and Michael Lang are coeditors of the Rowman & Littlefield reflective practice series.

Helen Winter is an intercultural mediator and founder of R3SO-LUTE, an NGO empowering refugees and Berlin locals with conflict resolution skills. Winter completed her law studies at the University of Heidelberg and holds an LL.M. in dispute resolution from Pepperdine's Straus Institute. She has worked as a mediator at the L.A. Superior Court and associate for On Deck Mediation. Her prior work experience includes supporting the systemic causes of conflict unit within the United Nations. She is currently also pursuing her Ph.D. in Alternative Dispute Resolution at the European University Viadrina.